Before you start reading!

Scan this QR Code for a special and personal message from Peter.

Peter Sage

THE INSIDE TRACK

The Ultimate Guide To Conquering Adversity

www.influencepublishing.com

Published by Influence Publishing, July, 2018

Second Edition Printed January 2021

ISBN: 978-1-9996694-3-0 (Softcover)

ISBN 978-1-9996694-6-1 (Hardcover Limited Edition)

ISBN 978-1-9996694-9-2 (eBook)

Editor: Wesley Thomas

Typeset: Greg Salisbury

Book Cover Design: Quantum Ventures

Authors' Disclaimer:

Today's world is a very litigious one which, in layman's terms, means that we like to sue each other, blame each other and pass the buck of responsibility to anyone who is conveniently nearby. However, as this book aims to underscore, the art of taking responsibility for everything that happens to us in life is one of the cornerstones to personal empowerment. As such, the space usually reserved for the disclaimer is being used to make an additional and, I believe, more important point.

You've seen the words many times: 'The following material is not intended as a substitute for the advice of a medical professional or mental health care practitioner...' - or words to that effect. The all-purpose liability firebreak that sadly is becoming all too common.

Disclaimers are a legal necessity, but they are also a cop-out. Used correctly, the information in this book can be devastatingly effective in providing a framework for how to think in ways that prevent the effects of negative thinking. However, this is no shortcut for the reader taking personal responsibility for their own lives. Therefore, I have an important recommendation to make: If you really need to sit behind the cushion of a disclaimer when it comes to taking charge of your own thinking, then please put this book away now and send it back unread for a full refund.

I hope you don't - because what lies in the pages ahead has the potential to dramatically improve your life.

Peter Sage

DEDICATION

To the tens of thousands of people who supported me on the journey and held a space for me. Your letters, energy and love were always a source of strength.

Praise for The Inside Track

"The Inside Track letters are some of the best and most compelling writing I have ever read. And I have read and studied everything!"
Mark Anastasi, New York Times Bestselling Author of 'The Laptop Millionaire'

"I couldn't put this down. It is one of the BEST books I have read in the last 10 years! Very open, real, raw, authentic, honest and inspirational. An unbelievable contribution."
Gerry McKinney, Master Trainer for Anthony Robbins

"This book is utterly life changing and has made a huge impact on my self-esteem and success. Whether you're having a tough time with money, relationships or other people, Peter shows you exactly how quickly turn it around and live a spectacular life!"
Karen Loke, Three-time Emmy award winner

"Think of the most inspiring person you know. They are now probably the second most inspiring person."
Dave Asprey CEO Bulletproof.com

"A great demonstration of applying the power of positive living...that life is not so much about what happens to you as it is about how you choose to deal with what happens to you... that where you are and where you are going is not as significant as what you make of the journey between the two."
Tom Campbell, Founding scientist at the Monroe Institute, NASA nuclear physicist, leading expert on consciousness research and author of the sensational My Big TOE Trilogy

"To begin with I thought he has to be making it up. Then I read the letters from the Prison Governors, staff and inmates and thought – wow, this is actually real!"
Jimmy Naraine – Worldwide Bestselling Udemy Instructor

"I've been a serious student of personal development for over two decades and a member of some of the most expensive and highest-level coaching programs in the world. The lessons I got from this book are life changing. It is THE best practical, step-by-step guide to overcoming your own limiting beliefs and challenges I've ever seen. Peter doesn't just talk the talk, he walks the walk."
Ryan Phillips, Three-time WKA World Martial Arts Champion

"This book is full of amazing insights that we can all use to live at the highest version of the highest vision of ourselves. Peter never fails to deliver."
Tim Han, Founder of Success Insider

"This is your get out of jail card for any adversity you are experiencing in your life. I literally sat on the edge of my seat as I read Peter's book because I realized through writing his incredible adventure behind bars, he had given me the exact tools I needed to overcome my own challenges. This is a must read for anyone who wants to CRUSH an obstacle in their life!"
Kathy McDevitt, Two-time Emmy Award Winner

"Humble, warm and witty. Compulsively readable."
Shaun Atwood, Speaker, Activist and Best-Selling Author of 'Hard Time'

"WOW! Peter's story is authentic and mind-shifting! A must read for any entrepreneur about the journey of life and contribution."
James Blackwell, CEO Ronald James Group

"Peter acts as a secret agent of change, being able to positively influence a prison system that is rotten. Imagine someone delivering a class in a war zone and teaching us how to face and overcome any adversity in life!"

António Santos, EMF 4 Graduate

"This book blew me away and had such a positive impact that I've recommended it to my loved ones. Having studied psychology, spirituality and human potential for over twenty years, it's been a long time since I've came across a book with so much depth and wisdom, together with powerful tools that will last you a lifetime. What Peter went through, in the process of writing this book, is nothing short of profound. I'm grateful that he has captured his experiences within these pages and my hope is that you too can pass this book along to people you care about and give them the gift that it has given to me."

AJ Mihrzad, Best Selling Author of Mind Body Solution, and Founder of OnlineSupercoach.com

"If anyone ever wonders if Peter walks his talk – this answers any doubts"

Dr. Klaus Schustereder, Switzerland. Founder of The Physis Foundation, Switzerland

"Because of what I've been through, many people look to me for inspiration and how to deal with adversity. But Peter Sage is who I look to when I need to up my own mindset. Many self-help gurus talk a good game. But wouldn't you love to see how their techniques work for them when true adversity hits? Peter Sage is the real deal, and his new book is full of lessons on how to master your emotions in the most difficult of circumstances."

Ted Ryce, High Performance Health Coach and Host of Legendary Life Podcast

CONTENTS

FOREWORD
by Dov Baron

There are many versions of a prison; there is the concrete and high-wire fence version, and there is a far more insidious kind that keeps us stuck in patterns of limitation. With time served, those imprisoned in the concrete and high-wire fence version will be released, but very few escape the latter. However, if we can free ourselves from the insidious kind, we can remain free, even in a concrete and high-wire fence prison.

It is said that change is the only constant. We are repeatedly reminded of this when something comes along that completely alters our lives. Often, this can be seen as a nuisance at best or a catastrophe at worst, shattering the plans and expectations we had fully invested in. After more than thirty years of being an international speaker and strategist, guiding individuals and teams in how to be fully empowered and purpose driven, I've learned that the most joyous, most successful and fulfilled people aren't the ones frantically trying to control the outside world. As many have found out too late, stress is simply the price of admission to that unwinnable game.

Instead, life seems to favour those who adapt and roll with the punches, those who take on the inevitable challenges, rather than avoid them. The problem is, this is not a skill we are likely to receive from traditional education (at any level). To fully step into our greatness requires not just a different skill set, but a very different mindset.

A MASTER IS ALWAYS A STUDENT

It was over a decade ago when I first met Peter Sage as an attendee at one of my events. I had no idea who he was or the experience he had. Many great teachers are also avid students; Peter is no exception. I remember him sitting near the front and taking copious notes. He's a very unique individual with an incredible energy about him. Peter's style and wisdom are not for everyone; some people can be put off or, more often, feel threatened by his overwhelming positivity and seemingly insatiable zest for life. But like him or not, once you meet him, you will not forget the impact of being in his presence. I was immediately drawn to Peter because, not only did we resonate with the same level of thinking, he was and is committed to serving others in a variety of ways.

After he attended my live event, he and I would meet at his spectacular five-million-dollar penthouse he had just built for himself in Vancouver, where he would share with me his wisdom on how I could reach more people with the message I wanted to share with the world. We became fast friends and I remember speaking to him some years later when he was living in Dubai. Things were not going so well and he had just lost his beautiful Vancouver home. It didn't seem to faze him one bit. He cheerfully cast it off, saying, "Oh well, if life were simple, it wouldn't be as fun!"

Some while after, I learned that he was in prison in England, even though he hadn't committed a crime, and for something nobody really understood. Like a lot of folks, I was shocked, although, not hugely surprised. The shock came from the fact I was, and still am, certain that Peter is both an honest and honourable man. However, oftentimes those with the mover and shaker energy cross the boundaries of institutional authority, either inadvertently or deliberately. What's far more telling is what they do with it. Depending on the level of ego involved, such individuals either crumble or grow wings and rise to the challenge. They become either a warning or an example. Knowing Peter, I expected him to grow wings and rise to the occasion, and as you are about to find out, he did far more than that.

Peter's commitment to serve didn't end when he was imprisoned. Actually quite to the contrary. Some time had passed and I remember reading the first few letters he sent out and I was amazed. What he was sharing would have made a best-seller on the fiction list. Except this was real!

Each beautifully intimate and deeply vulnerable letter also contained a wealth of how-to knowledge, wisdom and tradecraft forged from his three decades in high-level personal growth... and presented in a way that people can use in their everyday lives.

What you are about to discover in these pages, made me both laugh and weep. Personally, it brought up emotions of anger (at a clearly broken system) but also hope and inspiration at what is possible with the right attitude and skills. That alone makes this book a hell of a gripping read.

Through Peter's dedicated commitment to serving on the inside, we, the readers, get access to how his mind works and see the truly inspiring difference he was able to make. I was also honoured to be the first person to interview Peter when he was released for my Podcast, Full Monty Leadership. It's a must watch!

To sum up, when reading the Inside Track, I am reminded of the great coach, John Wooden, who famously stated, "Things turn out best for those who make the best of the way things turn out." Peter is a living example of that and the book you are now reading offers a beautiful guide and tool box for how you too can face adversity with a smile, learn, grow and be ready for whatever life brings next.

This book is designed to assist you, the reader, to break out of the most fortified prison any of us have ever been in...the mind!

Dov Baron
Impact Strategist. Inc.com Top 100 Leadership Speaker, Top 30 Global Leadership Guru.
Bestselling Author of: Fiercely Loyal. How high performing companies develop and retain top talent.
www.FullMontyLeadership.com Host and Executive Producer of Dov Baron's Leadership and Loyalty Podcast, the Global #1 Podcast for Fortune 500 Listeners

"The most fortified prison that exists is one that has no locks, where you believe the jailer is your best friend!"
Dov Baron

INTRODUCTION

In January 2017, Peter Sage was held in contempt of court for a civil matter and ended up serving several months in Pentonville, widely recognised as one of the worst and most dangerous prisons in the UK. Needless to say, it was totally unexpected and had a massive impact on all aspects of his life. This resulted in the collapse of what was just starting to become a flourishing business helping thousands of people, the cancellation of his wedding, gloating ridicule in the press and more.

In one of his popular Ted Talks entitled 'Stop Waiting for Life to Happen', he shares precisely why the extraordinary challenges of September 11th, 2001 made it one of the most incredible and life-changing days he's ever lived. In a similar way, The Inside Track takes the reader on Peter's remarkable journey of being the only non-criminal in Britain's toughest jail and why it turned into one of his most challenging yet inspiring adventures to date. Would he be able to apply and practice what he teaches in order to survive, even thrive, in one of the harshest environments he had ever faced? Would his background and tools work amongst serial killers, armed robbers, drug dealers and organised crime gangs? More importantly, would he be able to make a lasting and positive difference, not only to people whom society had written off, but to a system whose dysfunction and failings are kept hidden far from the public eye?

The Inside Track is not a normal book, nor a work of fiction. It is the collection of Peter's eleven private updates, written every two weeks as he went through the experience. Initially, these were shared in real-time with members of his popular coaching groups; *'The Elite Mentorship Forum'* (EMF) and his *'Masters Circle'*. They offered a first-hand account of exactly what he was doing and how, inviting and enabling them to apply the same insights and techniques to challenges in their own lives, with stunning effect. It is these updates and this invitation that Peter now shares with you. Along with the solemn wish that through all the lessons, stories, violence, heartache and magic moments, you too can find the tools and inspiration to live a happier and more fulfilling life.

Volume 1: The Adventure Begins (Week 2)

This first letter covers Peter's arrival and assessment of jail. He quickly spots two areas that he can focus on adding value to and creates a plan for improving a system that is in crisis. He has three cellmates in the first week, each with their own issues which he breaks down and helps to solve. He also lays out the tools he is using to cope with the mental and emotional challenges and presents them in a syllabus that's teachable to the readers. We are introduced to a powerful tool that maps out different levels of 'conscious awareness' and which provides a strong context for a lot of his work. The letter finishes with a powerful exercise designed to show you how to neutralise negative emotions and explains why Peter is genuinely grateful to be there.

My dear and amazing family, students and friends

I'm writing to you from the inside of Pentonville, one of the toughest and most violent prisons in the UK. It is quite literally the perfect setting for what I have planned. Sorry it's taken a few days to get this to you. I've spent a week settling in and getting things in place. Before we start, let me assure you that everything is amazing with me. I've never felt better, and the river is winding perfectly. There's so much I want to share!

Finding myself in this prison was so unexpected and happened against so many odds, that I feel it could only have been engineered at a higher level of intelligence and from a place I trust completely.

It's not difficult to figure out; my mission has been clear and publicly stated for a long time: to help raise the global consciousness of humanity in a way that can make a lasting difference. That has to especially include those who are at the bottom of the ladder when it comes to society. Well, I guess I should be careful what I wish for! Seriously, I'm often blown away by how the outer world arranges itself in alignment with what we ask for (both good and bad!). Though in this case, I have to tip my cap in utmost respect. I mean, what possible way could Life manage to smuggle me into jail without ever being accused of a crime and bring me out afterwards, still without having a criminal record? Total genius. I feel like Sylvester Stallone in Escape Plan, though rather than test prison security, I'm here to be a *secret agent of positive change*. It also offers a once in a lifetime opportunity for me to give you a window into my world as this journey unfolds. To give you a live demonstration of a real test or what I call a 'graduation event'.

What are graduation events? They are scenarios and bends in the river of Life that appear throughout our journey and mostly come wrapped in an outer layer of adversity. They serve several functions but the two most predominant ones are key. The first is to present us with an opportunity to grow. To learn something we need to learn, or to hear a message we've been ignoring. The second function is to test if we can demonstrate something rather than just know it. That's because there is a world of difference between intellectually understanding something and having it actually show up as who you are, particularly under stress. Graduation events are designed to test this and also to remind us of the number one rule of personal development. The inescapable law that separates those who talk from those who do. And that, my friends, is this:

Theory does not cover the price of admission to the higher levels of growth or conscious awareness.

I'll say that again. *Theory does not cover the price of admission to the higher levels of growth or conscious awareness.* I suggest you tattoo that phrase on the inside of your eyelids for whenever the next bend in your river shows up.

This for me is no doubt a graduation event that encompasses the above. Together with many lessons I am sure I still need to learn and that will present themselves as I go through this journey. Therefore, I have a special invitation for all of you to join me and walk alongside as I share the experience and see what turns up. I'll also aim to dissect and breakdown the tools I'm using to adjust, adapt and get through this. My hope is that this will prove to be just as useful in various aspects of your own life, as I am sure it will be to me. And of course, by learning through the examples and the work I'm doing in here, you will also get to see how real it is.

So, let's begin. I'll start with an overview of my first week and then we'll get into some key learnings and insights…

Walking down the stairs after court to the holding cells was when I first noticed how low the energy was around me. No real surprise there. But being and feeling cheerful, I decided to see if I could make all the staff smile. It didn't take long. Although these people were used to angry and complaining criminals, underneath they were just begging for permission to lighten up. It's a great reminder of how we judge people on their attitude. The challenge is we then usually reflect back the very same attitude towards them, reinforcing the negative mood, but blaming *them* for it. A good phrase to remember here is that if you bring neutrality to something, you neutralize it. If you bring energy to something, you energize it. Basic stuff, but costly if we forget.

Next, I was then told my barrister was in the next room waiting for me. I walked in ready to say "Wow, they didn't give you a sentence too did they?" when instead I saw Fayez, my CEO, sitting in the room having tricked his way in as my legal rep. I nearly laughed out loud. He'd taken a business card from my barrister in court and used it as ID. What a legend! I assured him I was fine and he didn't need to worry, although I was concerned for my fiancée, Thea. Seeing her in tears as the judge sent me down was harder than hearing the sentence. After we'd had a good chat, there was a tap at the door. It was time to be taken to Pentonville, a 200-year-old Victorian prison with the renowned reputation of being one of the toughest in Britain.

A funny thing happened on the way. I stared out the window, still chuckling to myself about Fayez, when a street we were passing caught my eye. It was desolate. Run down with broken bottles, trash and homeless people's belongings. In that moment, I was reminded of an interview between Oprah and Dr David Hawkins, the author of one of my favourite books - *Power vs. Force* - where he recalled a similar scene. But instead of seeing disarray, he was struck by the raw beauty and perfection of what IS. It's on YouTube - a twenty-minute radio interview I'd encourage you to listen to. But in that moment, boom - I really felt it too. Not just intellectually but somewhere much deeper. It was a significant reminder that *an event is always just an event* and that first, everything just *is*. Only then do we label it. And, of course, it is our labels, not the event itself, that controls and determines the meaning. This is a foundational awareness and one all my coaching clients and forum students are guided to own. You'll also see why I give a throwback to this later on.

On arrival at the prison reception area, I was checked in, and as I was getting changed into my prison clothes, the officer asked: "Are you a copper?" According to him, I was too calm and casual to be a prisoner. I smiled but assured him I wasn't. Not the best label to be going inside with. I was then escorted to a waiting room where I watched a few dozen or so inmates get checked in over a three-hour period. By this point, I was already developing a strong sense of why I was here and how I could make a difference. It didn't take long before opportunities began to present themselves.

One thing I'm grateful for from the background I had as a Trainer for Tony Robbins for so many years is the fact we were trained to have a high standard of sensory acuity. Such as closely observing and analysing physical data, like language patterns, breathing rhythms, body language, pupil dilation, group dynamics, micro movements, unconscious 'tells' and more. On top of this is non-physical data which includes individual level of consciousness, top driving needs, spiral dynamics, meta-programs, energetic signature and the like.

The point being, there is an enormous amount of useful information that's available to us but is often completely missed. This is because we are either not looking, not trained to spot it or, more commonly, too busy focusing on our own egocentric agenda. Or worse, judging people against our own beliefs and model of how we see the world. Looking around the room with open eyes, it was easy to see where people were at. There were those who were new, those who were repeat or serial offenders, and those who defined their identity through being in the system.

One such man was Jamie. In his early thirties and already on his fifth time inside, Jamie was a self-proclaimed high-risk offender. This means he was happy to use violence to keep him in isolation because he "preferred not to share a cell". Like many in the waiting room, he held himself out to be a tough guy. He had a shaved head, black goatee and had been transferred that day from another jail. He was also loud and opinionated, as if he was challenging people to disagree. I listened and relaxed on my seat, observing the scene. It didn't take long for me to find some leverage and pick an opening. He was telling another prisoner how bad the food was. He said he liked cooking and could do a better job and that his dream one day was to own his own café or deli. He also mentioned his son and how upset he was (meaning angry) that the system had kept him from his kid that Christmas. I waited until he took a breath and casually asked: "How old is your boy?"

It broke his pattern and he looked over at me, saw I was sincere, and smiled (his first I'd seen). He then told me about his three-year-old son; how he missed him, how it was the one thing he hated about his life inside and how he felt he was letting him down. I concentrated on listening, as people can sense when they are genuinely being heard, but also kept my peripheral attention alert to the rest of the room. After he finished, I came back with: "Well, imagine how proud he'd be of his dad after you got out of here and started that deli. You'd teach him that, despite what anyone else says or thinks, you can always bounce

5

back stronger from any challenge". He thought for a minute and once again saw that I meant it. His face beamed and he said:

"Wow, you think so?"

I said: "Sure, why not? Many people do it. It only takes a strong decision, and you look like the kind of guy who can stick with strong decisions". From that moment on, Jamie and I became friends and he helped guide me in some of the ins and outs of first time insiders. We also trained together a few times in the exercise yard, where I continued watering the seeds of his dream.

By now it was getting late and I still needed to be seen by the prison doctor for the standard check-up before being given a bed for the night. I finally saw him at about 10pm. He was a great guy but after ten minutes he looked at me and said,

"Do you mind if I ask you something?"

I replied, "Sure."

"Are you undercover?"

I laughed, telling him no and he said in his whole career he'd never seen anyone so relaxed and happy on their first day in prison. I smiled, sharing some of my thoughts as to why I was here and how I was hoping to make a difference. Luckily, he didn't prescribe me any crazy pills, which I took to be a good sign.

At 11pm I got called out of the waiting room with another man called Ali. An Asian guy from Bangladesh who looked as if his world had caved in. We were to be cellmates. We were taken to A-wing and shown our cell. I couldn't believe it - it was like they had given me my very own meditation room, complete with a bed and a toilet. We put on our bed sheets and Ali and I got chatting.

It soon became apparent why he was so depressed. He'd been in court that day to be given a trial date for a minor assault charge. He was expecting to go home and prepare for whenever the trial would be. He'd even left his car outside in a one-hour parking zone. But instead of being given a trial date and then sent away, the judge placed him on remand. It was unexpected. He had no previous history and, while this in itself may not have been too bad, the problem was that Ali had spent most of his life savings on his wedding, which was to take place the next day. Talk about a kicker.

I spent three days with Ali in our cosy room before I was transferred to D-Wing (non-smoking) and without taking your time up with all the details, his parting comment made my *magic moments* list when he said: "I came here thinking my life had fallen apart. Now I'm convinced I came to prison just to meet you." (Oh yes, I've started a prison *magic moments* list and I am up to 15 as I'm writing this). It was so touching and genuine that I nearly cried. But that wouldn't have been great in here, so I didn't. We also made a deal. I've invited him to my next event and he's invited me to his wedding.

By day four I had begun to get a feel for the place. It also became apparent there were two main areas I believed I could really make a difference with.

The primary focus would definitely be first-time inmates. The shock of going from living a normal life at home to coming here must be hard for the vast majority of people. Especially if they have no mental and emotional tools to fall back on. Apart from my commitment to the mission, I feel fortunate to have the kind of tool-set and skills to deal with this as easily as I have. It is these tools, along with how I apply them, that I want to share on this journey with you. In addition to giving you an account of what is happening in here, I am going to break down and delineate these tools and distinctions so you can see exactly how they work, what they are, and how you can use them in your own lives. For students of my work and those who have graduated from one of my programs, this should turn out to be a mixture of good revision, a deep-dive into the material that I teach, or even a classic case study.

Returning to where I can add value, for first time prisoners, such as Ali, the deer-in-the-headlights effect is nothing short of traumatic.

To the prison's credit, there are some support systems in place, such as the Samaritans and a few trained inmates called 'Listeners'. However, my experience coming through the system is that they are not utilised enough and none of the people I've spoken to here have ever used them. Nor did they even understand how to do so. It's fertile ground for reinventing their mental journey but first one has to understand it. This is not hard to figure out. Neither is it surprising, yet it could so easily be addressed.

From what I've seen so far, first-timers tend to cycle through the following emotions: shock, denial, despondency, depression, despair, anger (at the system, the judge, themselves, the world, etc.) This is followed by prolonged periods of thinking, 'what if' and 'if only' scenarios. This is a massively destructive cycle. Even if someone had a remote chance of facing their circumstance positively, thinking like that will lead them down a path of low-level conformity at best, or mental self-destruction at worst. Neither of which is a laughing matter.

There are many ways to address this. The first and obvious choice would be to provide or facilitate the awareness of an alternative choice of how to think. Combined with an elementary skill set on managing their own state. One thing is for sure and that is; if they are left with just an auto-pilot reaction to this environment, it will suck most people into a vortex of negativity. From there it's an easy path into apathy (which puts many here on anti-depressants) or fear, which leads to even poorer choices on how to cope with their new environment. It's no wonder that drug use in here is so rife and I'm not just talking about the prescription drugs, which are as common as M&M's. For example, the government's own figures show that 20% of those in Pentonville are on antipsychotic medication. Many more are on antidepressants. And that's just the legal ones. The illegal drugs are even more rampant. In just my first week I've seen people on crack, heroin and a new synthetic drug I've never heard of called

Spice. In fact, it's so normal, many smoke it openly. It also makes any interactions I have unpredictable, and any interventions I plan on doing, potentially dangerous.

Prisoners who face their situation head-on and try to deal with it in an empowering way are few and far between. Though, having said that, I've now had many interactions with people this last week and I'm absolutely convinced that the majority of people *are* open to being helped. I'll address the existing and serial inmates in a moment, but for the new guys (like Ali), helping them shift into a new corridor of thought early on is a situation that is just *begging* to be addressed. And, having given it some thought, there are some quick wins in how I could achieve this.

The easiest way would be as part of their induction and I'd approach this in two ways. The first would be a story that enrols them via third party. I'm toying with various titles but am thinking along the lines of *Mud or Stars?* taken from the old adage, *"Two men sat behind prison bars, one saw mud, the other saw stars"*. It would be a short story that would follow the journey of a new inmate from arrival at the prison and their journey through their sentence. It would be written to engage and effectively show the difference in their circumstances as a result of the mental choices they make. I see this as a leaflet or booklet given to them on arrival, though it could also be given by the doctor during their initial medical. If I don't manage to influence that then I'll work with the existing charities here as at least they have distribution.

The good news is that not only have I been helping several inmates as part of my research, but I've also been asked to write an article for the prison magazine and so this will serve as an initial draft. It's been a busy week. I'll keep you updated on the progress, though this should be an easy way to make a big difference to the newbies. And if some of the reactions I've had so far to some 'stealth interventions' are anything to go by, then this whole adventure has been worth it already and I'm just warming up.

One example was Dell, my second cellmate. A 59-year-old Jamaican who is serving three years for cannabis related offences. Turns out he was quite a spiritual man and a deep thinker, and our first conversation also made my *magic moments* list. He was feeling down, negative and depressed when I first moved into his cell on Monday evening. His basic problem was resistance. I worked with him on how to reach acceptance (one of the tools I'll share with you later in this Volume) and his transformation has been profound and beautiful to watch. He was moved to another cell the next day and now always comes and finds me during our forty-minute social time to chat and tell me how his whole experience in here has changed since we met. However, the most touching part was about his son. During our first night's chat he told me that his son Romario was a champion amateur boxer. But there was a problem. Young Romario had been virtually unbeatable as a youngster but had suddenly developed jitters on the adult circuit. Plus, if he lost in the ring, he would get angry at himself and then depressed, and sometimes not even speak for several days. Not only that, but he was now losing interest in boxing and had backed off from his training.

Dell really wanted to help his son, but he couldn't. Firstly, because he was in here and secondly, because he didn't know what to tell him on the phone. It was another reason why he was so down and was resisting being in here (note - this is a good example of how negativity will escalate, also known as 'stacking', if not kept in check). I shared my thoughts with Dell on what was going on with Romario. It was a classic blend of being driven by GOOP (Good Opinion of Other People) combined with his projections of what he felt others, especially his parents, expected. In addition, he'd tied winning in the ring to his self-worth, which, conversely, would then link losing to the fear of not being good enough. This would not just be triggered if he lost but, more destructively, even at the *thought* of losing. This future-pacing of negative 'what-if' scenarios would then cause him to feel disempowered in advance. Both his heart and mind would align in fear which would create pressure and require more energy to deal with. Energy that would not then be available to him in the ring. This whole mental demon would then become a self-fulfilling prophecy.

I gave Dell a few key points to make and also advised him as to how to steer his son's thinking in order to link his self-worth to his performance, not a score card. At the same time, this would need to be reinforced through parental support, not judgement. I also suggested a couple of my YouTube videos his son could watch. A few days later Dell came into my cell beaming! He'd spoken to his son that day and had just found out he'd started training again. I told Dell he was an amazing Dad and that he'd just proved that no matter what happens, there is always a way. That was magic moment number 15.

My next and current cellmate is a different kettle of fish. His name is Mark and he is a 42-year-old father of five, serving ten months for assault. It's his first time inside and he's probably one of the most negative people I've ever met. In fact, he makes Eeyore from Winnie the Pooh look happy. Not surprisingly, he is also a news addict and a serial daytime TV / soap watcher. Plus, he's depressed about his weight and massively upset that in the five weeks he's been inside, his wife hasn't visited or written and he's been moved from two cells already as no one could get along with him.

He's a tall guy with a large frame. Over six foot and with a body he admits has been built on late night kebabs and many pints of Guinness. Needless to say, Mark has had quite a shift in his thinking. Our cell is now strictly a news and Jeremy Kyle / Jerry Springer free zone. He's inspired to pursue a new health goal and we are training twice a day in the cell together and he's now pushing *me*! We have a rule that bans all negative talk and I wrote him a letter for him to copy and send to his wife. I'll let you know if she responds. As I said, underneath, almost everyone wants to live a more positive life. They've either never been shown how or, commonly, they have become too addicted to the secondary gain that comes with the average victim mode. More on that later. However, many people who are 'default negative' are so because they have conformed to a negative peer group or environment. This brings me to my next point; existing and repeat offenders.

For prisoners like Jamie and the countless other 'Jamie's' in the system, conformity is king. In fact, the overwhelming force of negativity that ebbs and flows through prison life is so prevalent, that it's tested me several times. If I'm off my game (sleeping awake) or if my energy is low, it's easy to start being tugged at by the undercurrent of low frequency thoughts. It's as if the candle of hope I am trying to shine is forever subject to a fickle wind that wallows through the corridors like a bad draught. What I know for sure is that, unless the right insulation is applied, the 'deterrent' of jail is nothing more than a euphemism for 'see you back inside again soon'.

To help existing offenders, I see two quick wins. The first is as obvious as it is available and that is an educational / edutainment channel on the cell TV's. Something that helps program the mind to a more positive direction with a mix of interviews from inspirational people. This could be video podcasts or stories of hope mixed with lessons in personal development. Something like the LondonReal.tv channel or a powerful Podcast such as Joe Rogan or Tim Ferris would be an excellent example. Anything as an alternative to the standard mind-fudge of mainstream TV. There's a reason I call television 'the electronic income reducer!'

Next would be education in class. The prison offers a variety of standard classes, which while definitely useful in the context of basic employment, do little to change the thinking habits of those studying. I'll explore this further once I've had more chance to observe, as it sits at the core of why I believe prisoners reoffend. In short, teaching them skills does not suddenly change criminal behaviour or tendencies. This flawed thinking is based on the belief that people commit crime because they do not have enough education to get a job. While this may be true for a tiny percentage, it misses the point that without changing the thinking patterns and beliefs that lead to crime, education will just make them smarter criminals.

Therefore, a basic class on 'Life skills' that would act as a personal development foundation course could really help them make a shift. Of course, a section in the library would be useful too but the challenge is that few are encouraged to read *and* getting to visit the library requires a drawn-out application process which can take weeks. I'm still waiting.

With regard to classes or work-related skills, every inmate takes a maths and English test and is assessed as to where they can go or what they can apply for. My spelling aside, it may not come as a shock that instead of being placed within three to five days of taking the test (which I've heard is usual), I got a note pushed under my door within three hours telling me that I would start in the business class the next morning. I've had two lessons so far (the third is today). The main teacher is called Jose and as you would expect, he is really trying to help make a difference. He and I are getting on great. I've already been asked to be the classroom assistant and I'm helping some of the guys with their business plans in my spare time. Not that I'm getting much 'spare time'. My point is that I could easily design a course here for educating the inmates in a different way. Something which I intend to start work on this week and then present an outline to the staff and Governor. Stay tuned.

So, these are the two main areas I've been focusing on:

1. The new prisoner journey.
2. The serial offenders who see being here as normal and even part of their identity.

Now let's shift gears.

Tools & Techniques For Staying Positive

At the beginning of this letter, I promised to share with you the tools and techniques I've been using here to stay on track. As part of the invitation to join me on this journey, I'd like to outline them so you can see them for yourself. Then, each time that I write, I will drill down on certain techniques, allowing you to see how I'm using them in here and in the context of this exciting detour I'm taking. More importantly, you will get to see how you can apply these to your own life or, just as I've done with others such as Dell, use these skills and insights to help those around you who are literally prisoners of their own thoughts, problems and self-imposed limitations.

Here's an initial list. I'll work through a couple of them with you now and then the others as we progress. This is so that:

You actually have time to digest, reflect, apply and practice what you learn without being overwhelmed. Remember, the common route of emotional paralysis is that being in overwhelm leads to confusion, which then leads to inaction. In other words, people learn or read so much, they do nothing. Or worse, they buy courses and books with the best intentions but never follow through. This often leads to an ever-increasing pile of expensive and unopened learning called 'data for later'.

That's why I am going to deliver the learning I want to share with you now, bit by bit. I'm also going to split it into two levels. Standard and advanced.

In the standard section I'm going to cover the following:

1. Building A Solid Psychological Foundation
2. The Power of Acceptance vs the Force of Resistance
3. Contrast Frames
4. Gratitude / Emotional Transformation

5. Supportive and Go-To Affirmations, including the ones I'm using in here
6. Sex Energy Transmutation
7. Ethnocentric Purpose
8. Passive Meditation

In the advanced section I am going to cover:

1. Collapsing Powerful Egregores
2. Energy Projection and Logarithmic Counterbalance (as per Dr. Hawkins 'Map Of Consciousness')
3. Active Meditation (which includes hacking the Virtual Reality model and using Quantum Alignment to sidestep the materialism based rule-set)

In addition, I'll aim to break down and explain more about the various patterns of behaviour and thinking (both constructive and destructive) that run so many of us at an unconscious level. Finally, if I get the chance (which I am hoping I will) I'll also describe any serious interventions that I do, so again, you can see how I use the various tools and techniques in what are likely to be more extreme circumstances than you'll need to encounter on the outside. In short, if I think I can share or teach you something that can help you in your own life on the outside, I'll try to include it.
OK, let's start with Number 1:

Building A Solid Psychological Foundation

Having a rock-solid psychological foundation may seem an obvious first step to surviving the turmoil of being in here, but what are the key components that go into it?

First, one has to start with looking at what I call our 'Governing Beliefs'. These are the beliefs that form the blueprint of many other beliefs. They act as an overarching umbrella that many other beliefs fall under, are influenced by, or follow. I'll share some examples of mine so you get the idea.

One of my primary governing beliefs links to Einstein's famous statement where he said the most important question a person could ever answer in their lifetime, was whether or not they lived in a friendly or hostile universe. Straight away, you can see the implications of these two possible answers and the drastically different lives they would result in. Seeing the world and everything in it as potentially threatening or even just indifferent to you, sets up a relationship to it that is based in fear and self-protection. Seeing the world around you as purposely designed for your well-being, growth and enjoyment, sets up a different relationship to how your day *and life* unfolds.

I'm sure there's no surprise as to which side of that equation I subscribe to. You may have even heard me refer to myself as an 'Inverse Paranoid'. This basically means I'm convinced that the entire universe is involved in a secret conspiracy to make me happy and successful.

This isn't just positive thinking. When you take into account the benevolent nature of what quantum mechanics calls 'The Field', the bio feedback you get when you are in harmony vs disharmony and the fact that every spiritual teacher taught Love over Fear as their core message, you realise it's not really that much of a 'secret', let alone a conspiracy but rather a statement of subjective reality for those who choose to believe.

My second governing belief centres on what kind of life I want to live. To answer this, I invite you to look at life through the metaphor of a movie. It is an indisputable fact that you, me and everyone else on the planet, are each the central star in the movie called 'Our Life'. In fact, we are the only one to appear in every scene. What this means is that everyone else, by definition, is either a supporting cast or a film extra *in your movie*. This then begs the simple question, "What kind of movie do you want to make?"

Let me give you a clue as to my answer by asking you a different question. Would you pay good money to watch a bad movie? Most likely not! My point being, is that when I walk out of a cinema at the end, I want to feel "Wow. Now THAT was a Movie!" And, ladies and gentlemen, what makes a great movie? Everything! Drama, romance, tragedy, intrigue, comedy, unpredictability and a feel-good factor at the end. Too many people are trying desperately to act their way through life by avoiding challenging scenes, rather than realise that it is the dark squares on the chess board that force us to grow into more of our potential. In other words, if I really want to live the best movie, why would I only want to act in the scenes that were easy?

To look at it another way, if I wanted to win the academy award, or even just get better as an actor, why would I not want to challenge myself? Think of classics such as Dustin Hoffman in *Rain Man* or Bob Hoskins in *Who Framed Roger Rabbit?* Ground-breaking roles, not only for film but also for the actors themselves who were taken way past their comfort zone. Being in Pentonville, not only do I get to test my 'acting skills', I also get to add depth to the script. Intrigue and drama? You bet! Unpredictability? Absolutely. Romance? A scary thought. A feel-good factor at the end? Who knows? Time will tell. My role is simply to concentrate on being the best actor I can be while I'm busy filming the prison scene of my incredible movie.

Another way of looking at this, is that I want to try as many dishes as I can in the buffet of life. As long as I'm not intentionally hurting anyone, that is. I also know in advance that I'm going to like some dishes more than others and some, I'm just never going to try again. But that's not the point. At least I get to try! The safe, bland dish for the rest of my gastronomic life is just not for me and would make for a very safe yet boring movie that no one would watch.

Being here has, in just under two weeks, been an amazing experience and one I am honestly and thoroughly enjoying. An experience that even a month ago I thought I would never get to have. Now I get to see things I've only ever seen in movies AND I get to help people at the same time! Why would I complain instead of celebrate?

These are just two governing beliefs. Let me share one more and then we'll move on. Enter the classic Good Opinion of Other People, aka GOOP. I will openly say that in my twenties, GOOP ruled my life at a level where most of the decisions I made, both consciously and unconsciously, were filtered through and influenced by what I thought other people were thinking. Luckily, I've grown out of that. Mainly by realising that we are only the star of our movie in our own eyes but never in theirs. Instead, when it comes to other people, we are simply film extras on their set. In other words, and please listen carefully; most people don't care enough about you to even bother to judge you! Why? Because they are too busy being worried about what *they* think *you* are thinking of *them*. Welcome to reality. And the sooner we learn that, the more mental and emotional freedom we have.

I can honestly say, that if I hadn't escaped the destructive clutches of GOOP, my journey here would have been much harder as I'd be thinking things like, "Oh no, what will everyone think?" I'd be focused on and worried about certain consequences of what may or may not happen to my reputation, along with the judgements and projections of others. As I said, I am grateful to have escaped the strong gravitational pull this pattern of thinking has. I'm also aware that it still traps the vast majority of people, keeping them hostage on planet Misery. But, let's look for a moment at a topical example. Currently, half of the entire United States hates its own elected leader. At the time of writing, Donald Trump is completing his first 100 days in office and never has a country been more polarized in its support or hate. However, the fact that President Trump is so immune to GOOP is the very reason that he's starring as the most powerful man in the world in his own movie. Note - I don't offer this as an endorsement of whatever his values or policies may be. As many of you know, two things I give zero energy to are the media and politics. That aside, he does offer a powerful lesson in living by his own creed and rules, independent of criticism and the need to pander to the good opinion of other people. For that alone, you've gotta hand it to the guy!

Hopefully, with just these three mental corner stones; the universe is inherently friendly, I'm here to create an amazing movie (not a boring one) and being free of the need of the good opinion of others, you can start to see the role a strong psychology plays. Especially in avoiding, or even being immune to, many of the negative influences of the prevailing energy and thought patterns of people in here. If we add to that a conviction that everything happens for a reason and that it serves my best interests, then you can appreciate why I chose this as number one.

Acceptance vs Resistance

This next tool is an absolutely critical part of the whole process of emotional maturity and if used properly, is one of the fastest ways out of anguish and into mental freedom. When I think of the amount of energy that's wasted in resisting things that have already happened, I feel tremendous compassion for those who are so naively blinded to the futility of their own thoughts. One thing I immediately implemented as soon as I arrived was zero-tolerance to any 'what if' or 'if only' mental self-talk. These cancerous thoughts operate at, and perpetuate, grief, guilt, suffering, resentment and false hope. They also usually lead to increased frustration as the mind and body are powerless to go back and change anything.

In my experience, the first step to dealing with *any* adverse condition or circumstance is to fully accept what has already happened. When you do this, two things occur. First, you stop wasting and giving away energy pointlessly. Second, you can use the energy you save and apply it to making better decisions within the moment right now, especially as it relates to what it was you were resisting. Acceptance is also the first step in transitioning out of the mode that I call 'By-Me' and into the more elegant state of 'Through-Me'.

By-Me is where we do not accept the world as it is but instead try to change it by force to fit the mental pictures of what we want. The battle cry goes something like, "If Life doesn't give me what I want then it will happen by me!" It has its basis in resistance and is exhausting. By contrast, Through-Me is where Life is more effortless and things tend to fall into place on their own. It has its basis in acceptance and being in the flow. In short, Through-Me recognises the uselessness of trying to control the current of the river of life and instead concentrates its energy on better positioning itself IN the river. People resist everything from bills to weather - pointless! It's far better to accept 'what is' and then act appropriately by taking the next best move that relates to the situation.

Now, if you want to step up your game with a more advanced version of this technique, try this. Accept whatever has happened *as if you had chosen it deliberately* at some level. This shifts the thinking from complaining about being given a bad deal to recognizing it's a gift that's simply been wrapped in a thin layer of paper disguised as a problem to stop people from stealing your gift! The magic in this is that it also allows you to do something that Steve Jobs said could not be done and that is to join the dots going forward.

Further Understanding Levels of Consciousness

Before going further, I must touch on one thing and that is what I mean when I use the word 'consciousness'. This is one of the most misunderstood terms in science today. It's an easy rabbit hole to get lost in, with biology on one side of the fence and esotericism on the other. However, what I am about to share offers a critical framework of understanding and reference that is fundamental to a lot of the insights I aim to share throughout this journal.

When defining what I mean by higher or lower levels of

consciousness, I refer to the ground-breaking work of Dr. David Hawkins and his famous 'Map Of Consciousness' (MOC). This was highlighted in the 'must read' book mentioned earlier *Power vs. Force* which has sold over a million copies across twenty-seven languages. I won't go into details here other than to say that if you haven't read it yet, you are missing out on *so* much when it comes to understanding people.

MAP OF CONSCIOUSNESS

LEVEL NAME	CALIBRATED FREQUENCY	ASSOCIATED EMOTIONAL STATE	RESULTING PROCESS	VIEW ON LIFE	VIEW ON GOD
ENLIGHTENMENT	700-1000	INEFFABLE	PURE CONSCIOUSNESS	IS	SELF
PEACE (LEVEL OF SPONTANEOUS HEALING)	600	BLISS	ILLUMINATION	PERFECT	ALL-BEING
UNCONDITIONAL LOVE [JOY]	540	SERENITY	TRANSFIGURATION	COMPLETE	ONE
LOVE	500	REVERENCE	REVELATION	BENIGN	LOVING
REASON	400	UNDERSTANDING	ABSTRACTION	MEANINGFUL	WISE
ACCEPTANCE	350	FORGIVENESS	TRANSCENDENCE	HARMONIOUS	MERCIFUL
WILLINGNESS	310	OPTIMISM	INTENTION	HOPEFUL	INSPIRING
NEUTRALITY	250	TRUST	RELEASE	SATISFACTORY	ENABLING
COURAGE	200	AFFIRMATION	EMPOWERMENT	FEASIBLE	PERMITTING

LEVELS AT OR ABOVE 200 HAVE TRUTH, INTEGRITY AND SUPPORT LIFE — CREATIVE

LEVELS BELOW 200 ARE FALSE, LACK INTEGRITY, DO NOT SUPPORT LIFE — DESTRUCTIVE

PRIDE	175	SCORN	INFLATION	DEMANDING	INDIFFERENT
ANGER	150	HATE	AGGRESSION	ANTAGONISTIC	VENGEFUL
DESIRE	125	CRAVING	ENSLAVEMENT	DISAPPOINTING	DENYING
FEAR	100	ANXIETY	WITHDRAWL	FRIGHTENING	PUNITIVE
GRIEF	75	REGRET	DESPONDENCE	TRAGIC	DISDAINFUL
APATHY	50	DESPAIR	ABDICATION	HOPELESS	CONDEMNING
GUILT	30	BLAME	DESTRUCTION	EVIL	VINDICTIVE
SHAME	20	HUMILIATION	ELIMINATION	MISERABLE	DESPISING

(Left axis top: POWER, bottom: FORCE. Right axis top: STRONG, bottom: WEAK.)

POWER IS SELF-SUSTAINING, PERMANENT, STATIONARY AND INVINCIBLE.		
FORCE IS TEMPORARY, CONSUMES ENERGY AND MOVES FROM LOCATION TO LOCATION.		
ENERGY FIELD INCREASES LOGARITHMICALLY: 1 = (1) 2 = (10) 3 = (100) 4 = (1000) 5 = (10,000) 6 = (100,000) ...ETC		
ALL LEVELS BELOW 500 ARE "OBJECTIVE" (CONTENT BIASED) AND ALL LEVELS ABOVE 500 ARE "SUBJECTIVE" (CONTEXT BIASED)		

Credit: Dr. David R. Hawkins

The short version, for those not familiar with this model, is that there is a scale one can calibrate using the science of applied kinesiology. It starts at zero and climbs to 1000. Along the way are various stages that are defined by their characteristic tendencies, predominant emotional states and general view on life. As I will be making reference to it throughout, I have included a copy of it here, and also in Appendix C. It offers a useful guide and model to follow, especially when working with others. Incidentally, if you find the word 'consciousness' too ambiguous, then simply swap it for 'awareness'.

Contrast Frames

The next tool I want to share and that I'll be using here, is Contrast Frames. These are also one of the most powerful ways to re-contextualise experiences such as the one I am going through now. The basic premise is that meaning is only ever given in relation to other things. At least certainly at levels of consciousness below 600 which, on Hawkins' map, represents the dividing line between the experience of duality vs. non-duality.

When it comes to contrast, the wider the comparison, the bigger the shift in context. For example, if you get in a car and drive at 10 mph for a while and then suddenly accelerate to 50 mph, it will feel much faster. But if you are cruising at 100 mph and then drop to 50 mph, that same speed will now feel slower. A good example of this is a paper I wrote titled 'Lessons from my Skiing Accident' where I cried with happiness after breaking my face in 2007, because I realised it could have so easily been my neck. Having multiple fractures in my cheek and eye socket instead of being a quadriplegic for life, is a deal I would take *any* day of the week.

In here, the contrast frames have probably been the easiest part. For example, I once ran the Marathon des Sables - the toughest foot race in the world that stretches nearly 250 kilometres across the Sahara Desert. The conditions were extreme. In the day, temperatures climbed to 52°C (125°F) and at night they would drop to freezing. Lying in our sleeping bags, chilly and shivering and exhausted, we could often feel scorpions and camel spiders crawling over us (note, for squeamish people, *never* ever google 'camel spiders'). Oh man, what we would have given to have the kind of luxury of the building I'm in right now. The only pets we get are the resident mice and cockroaches - and yes, there are many of them in here. However, compared to my creepy crawly friends in the desert, these aren't even poisonous (yawn).

Next, we come on to some of my heroes. There are many, though three who immediately spring to mind include; Nelson Mandela, Gerald Coffee and Viktor Frankl. Take Mandela, twenty-seven years in prison labelled as a convicted terrorist, eighteen of which were on the notorious Robben Island. And all I get are a few months for contempt of court? Give me a break. Or Gerald Coffee who served seven years in a Vietnam prison in a cell that had the footprint of a coffin. Yet he's one of the nicest, happiest men I've met. Then there's Viktor Frankl, who wrote one of the most impactful and important books of the twentieth century, *Man's Search for Meaning*, which, if you have not read, is an absolute MUST and a game changer. In fact, I challenge anyone to read this and not burst into tears with gratitude at being lucky enough to even have the life I have in here. You get the idea.

My cell mate Mark was complaining at the fact that he got ten months for punching someone when he was drunk. I said "Imagine if he had fallen, hit his head on the pavement and died. It could easily happen and then you would be serving six years for manslaughter. Would you be grateful for 10 months instead?" He hasn't complained since. At least not to me but again, you get the picture.

OK, last one before I sign off (or my handwriting becomes too illegible).

Gratitude and Emotional Transformation Exercise

At the beginning of this letter, I gave a shout out to a module I teach to the Elite Mentorship Forum. This deals with Mastery of Emotions, and whilst I have not actually had a negative association to coming in here, I thought it would be a good opportunity to at least share with you the exercise, so I've included it here. It is a simple but also powerful exercise that helps transform negative associations and their triggers following any significant emotional event or trauma.

It consists of just three questions and one exercise. The key is to keep the answers as short as possible. This forces us to stay limited to the facts only and filters out the 'story'. Of course, it is the story we tell ourselves about what has happened that generates most of the negative emotions. Keeping the answers as factual and story-free as possible therefore helps us to be objective, without having our feelings hijacked.

Question 1: What *actually* happened?
Answer: I got an eighteen-month sentence for contempt of court. (Remember, facts only)

Question 2: Which means what?
Answer: Unless it's appealed, I will be away from home for nine months.

Question 3: What can I learn from this? (Give a *minimum* of five answers)

- I learned that in terms of law, it's not who is right or wrong but who can present the best story, i.e. fair play is not fair result, but of course it's not meant to be.
- I learned that when it comes to your (my) own convictions and values vs. society's rules and regulations, the current system will support society in a head to head. This seems irrespective of the common-sense nature of the challenge.

- I leaned that Indigo children (well, I guess adults now) will usually seek to disrupt and challenge the status quo of the existing system as a natural predisposition. This is not without consequences.
- The River of Life has a smarter and higher-level agenda than my left-brain.
- Theory will never cover the price of admission to the higher levels of consciousness.
- That no matter how hard the lesson or the exam appears or from how left-field it comes, I'll never be given more than I can handle.

Exercise:

List as many reasons as I can as to why I can be genuinely grateful that this experience or event has happened? (Note - this only works with at least ten to fifteen minimum. That can seem hard but go after them, they are there!)
Here are mine:

1. I get to work with and make a lasting difference to those in society who really need it. And from what I've seen so far, God knows, they need it!
2. I get to test my interpersonal and intervention skills in one of the toughest environments I've ever faced.
3. I get to be a real life Secret Agent of Change.
4. I not only get a chance to face the test of walking my talk but also the opportunity of gaining insights and distinctions over and above any planned learning in a classroom.
5. I get to really trust Life and the flow of the River, knowing it will always care for me as long as I practice non-resistance and focus on serving others and the greater good.
6. I'm grateful for being able to embrace uncertainty at a higher level than usual and to practice letting go of everything I fear to lose.

7. For the chance to grow through challenge so I can continue to contribute with the new emotional and spiritual muscles that will develop as a result.
8. That I get to practice joining the dots going forward instead of backwards and be grateful in advance for whatever amazing journey is lying in wait.
9. For the fact that Life is *so* smart, it found the *only* way in law that allowed me to be smuggled into jail without ever being accused of a crime and leave without being given a criminal record.
10. That I have the quiet quality time I've been looking for (and asking for) so I can focus on my own growth. This includes my next book and more quality content for my business school and my academy.
11. That after cancelling three meditation retreats I've been booked to attend over the last two years, due to schedule, commitments and time pressure, Life finally allows me to meditate in a place for several hours a day.
12. I get to deeply relax and unplug with no calls, no email, no messages or push notifications, no battery life, no schedule and none of the usual constraints to worry about.
13. That Thea and I get a chance to have our own space and a break in proximity before we get married and allow a real test of adversity to prove we can become stronger and lay an even deeper foundation on which to build our future together.
14. That Thea is finally able to prove how independent she is outside of my influence and shadow - something she knew was needed.
15. To see how well the Team members cope with me being away temporarily and see who steps up and walks their commitment and who bails at the change of circumstances. To see how the leadership team acts in terms of integrity vs. politics, power struggles, personal agendas, allowing me to come out and move forward with people of character, not conversations.

Alright ladies and gentlemen, that concludes Volume 1. Right now, I want to devote some time to my new prisoner induction story and to map out the education course. Hopefully I'll have them done by my next letter. However, before I go, I just want to say thank you so much for your energy, love and support. I also feel very blessed that I get to invite you to walk vicariously alongside me on this journey to help others. Just know I'm really proud of all of you and look forward to sharing more stories soon as well as hearing yours too. Keep shining your light and I'll be back soon.

Huge hugs and lots of love,

Peter X

Volume 2: Getting Focused (Week 4)

Volume two outlines Peter's views on the negative press and social media coverage, giving some profound insight into the mindset of the critic, along with ways to protect yourself by rising above the inherent drama that fuels it. He lays out his plan for helping the system, which he calls 'Operation Chrysalis', and completes his first piece; a story called 'Mud or Stars?'. This begins to have a big impact on inmates and later sees him nominated for a national award. On the syllabus side, he covers several more tools, including his personal affirmations and how he is using Sex Energy Transmutation. Readers are introduced to the incredible concept of 'egregores' that have a profound and negative effect on most people's psychology and behaviour. He finishes with an honest reflection of what it is like to be faced with the possibility of losing everything.

My dear and amazing family, students and friends

Before I begin, I first have to extend a HUGE wave of thanks to all of you. The number of letters, emails, love and support that has poured in here has been overwhelming. There are too many names to mention and unfortunately, my ability to reply individually is somewhat limited, but please know that I read every one of your letters and emails and each one fills me with positive energy. As I've often said, my role has only ever been to hold up a blind-spot mirror, so that you can see and recognize your own greatness and to remind you that you already are that which you seek.

I hope things are going great for all of you out there. Though know that in the context of achieving your goals, the term 'great' doesn't always mean comfortable. Nor is it meant to. An athlete is great because they embrace the discomfort of their training, not because they get to sit on the couch and get a medal.

Personally, I'm still doing well and enjoying this adventure. In no way am I saying this to 'put on a brave face' and nor would I. I am, in all honesty, having more fun and adventure in here than I've had in a long time. It's been good to get out of the theory of the classroom, roll up my sleeves and get my teeth into something real. In other words, to walk my talk. Especially in a place where there are no cameras or second takes, no script and no support. Just me, a testing environment and a lot of people who need help. For this part of my life, I see it as the perfect graduation event. Seriously, it's been a while since I got to play at this level and it's keeping me sharp and forcing me to step up my game. So, don't worry about me - some *amazing* things are happening in here as I'm sure we'll get onto, and I have never been more grateful for the opportunity. It also cements my belief that everything is unfolding according to a bigger plan. Honestly, I wouldn't change a thing.

Though, if there is one tough aspect, it is how sorry I am to anyone on the outside who has been inconvenienced in any way by me being in here. That, of course, was never my intention. Also, how much I miss Thea and the dogs, though that is part of the price of admission to the higher levels of growth, and I do connect to their energy constantly.

OK, on with the update. Aside from continuing with the learning syllabus outlined in my previous letter, I'll also aim to interweave insights and lessons throughout the content here, so as to try and give you as much value as I can for the time you are investing in reading this.

Let's start with what seems to have been a hot topic this week, which is the details about the case and the judgement (predictably) and some of the negative comments and drama that followed (inevitably). I don't want to spend too much time on this as, personally, I have nointerest. But there are lessons and angles here that are relevant enough to point out. For a start, remember that whenever it comes to matters of opinion, no matter how thin you slice something, there are always two sides. The fact that my barrister effectively failed to ask one meaningful question at all to elicit an advantage for our side or to advance any kind of compelling closing submission, despite all the evidence we had, left Thea and I looking at each other and wondering if he was actually batting for the other side. That simply left the other side unopposed and I was right in saying at the time that, if that were all the information I had at my disposal, I would have drawn the same conclusions as the judge. However, if you are ever inclined to hear my side one day, I promise you that it will balance your perspective. Also, it wouldn't surprise me at all if the original claims against me never even make it to court as, in my opinion, they have no legal basis, were instigated with false and misrepresented information, and were always intended to try and scare or pressure me into a quick financial settlement. Understanding the lessons I've learned about the legal industry is something I will share more of in future letters. Needless to say, a lot of it boils down to who has the most resources to hire the best lawyers.

That aside, let's look at some of the lessons in the dynamic above. Truthfully, while having more data points can be useful, and I'm happy to fill in blanks and provide clarification, I have little interest in other people's projection of judgement. If I did, I would not be able to do the work I do that has enabled the messages I share to have the global impact they've had. What's funny is that as a first-generation Indigo Child (born in 1972), the jokes about us have always been that, due to a penchant for non-conformity and an aversion to institutional authority, we'd either end up very successful or in jail. I guess as a throwback to my ego-driven over achiever days, I can now tick both boxes!

OK, so while I'm still chuckling at my own joke, let's focus on what we can learn. Here's a question for you: When it comes down to it, what has society (and especially the news and mainstream media) conditioned everyone's favourite pastime to be? Can you guess? The answer should be as obvious as it is prevalent: It's Drama! (add music for effect.)

Drama – the anthem of stress

Now, when I say everyone's favourite pastime, that of course is a gross generalization, but I am specifically talking about the 70% of the global population that calibrate below 200 on Dr. Hawkins's Map Of Consciousness. (Note - this map was introduced in my last letter and can also be found in Appendix C. It is also detailed extensively in the book *Power vs Force*.)

So, what is drama and why are people so addicted to it? Well, the dictionary states that drama is a part of our life that usually involves conflict and emotion. It also escalates by nature. Graduates of the Sage Business School will quickly recognise the ego-based needs of certainty and significance at work. Not surprisingly, the two driving needs of nature, which are growth and contribution, are nowhere to be found when it comes to drama. This is because drama has its basis in fear before love. Paradoxically, the need for connection also plays a role in fuelling drama. However, it's a poor cousin to the kind of fulfilling and heartfelt connection that lights you up. You have probably heard the saying; 'misery loves company.' This, my friends, is a lie. Misery loves *miserable* company. Case closed. I owe that quote to my dear mentor George Zalucki and it is 100% accurate.

Many of you will also notice the strong patterns of conformity and how fast drama hijacks the heart and mind. This subverts the intelligent part of our brain, or prefrontal cortex, and hands our decision making over to the rear, fear-based (limbic) part of our brain. This is typical of Pride, the level of consciousness that calibrates at 175 and is driven by Scorn as well as Inflation.

Advanced students will be able to identify the blatant role of the *egregore* here very well. I'll explain egregores later in this Volume for those who have not come across them before, but an important point to note is how egregores use drama as an escalation fuel. Some of you may have been hooked, or at least provoked, by other people's criticism of me. Though what I find interesting and even predictable to note, is that virtually all of the negative comments are from people who do not know me and have never met me. I also know that for those who do, it's easy to feel justified in trying to defend me when you think I'm in here and cannot answer for myself. Please be mindful, as it's still fuelling the fire. It is simply the flip side of the same argument-coin and an egregore doesn't care which side up it lands. In other words, even if you get involved in trying to stop the drama, you're still part of it.

So, what's the big lesson? Firstly, if you feed drama, it always begets more drama. The most likely and usual destination is that you end up in a battle of righteousness with both sides claiming the moral high ground and each insisting they are right. This is not only the classic starting point for most arguments but also for most wars. As such, it's worth asking the question: What actually IS drama?

When you unhook from the emotional fish-bait and put your offended or inflated ego aside, you realize that 95% of it is nothing more than our judgmental perception of what we think is going on inside someone else's head. It's not even noise. It's our buy-in to the *perception* of another person's noise!

It's distracting at best and highly destructive at worst. It usually leaves no winners other than a smug sense of emotional superiority, which is the ego's booby prize for giving up a ton of energy to what is essentially a meaningless exercise. Now you can probably understand why I have no time for it and zero interest in its participation. And of course, this whole lesson only relates to me, the court case, and nothing else that's going on in your lives…(hmm!)

The bottom line? Drama is like a fire. It goes out when people stop throwing fuel on it. The objective here is to stop (or at least drastically lower) the emotional rollercoaster in YOUR life. Forget anyone else, let them get hooked and play their fruitless game. You have bigger things to focus on.

Democritus vs. Plato – pick a side

Another aspect to be mindful of is our own level of perception. If we are trapped in a mindset rooted in materialism - i.e. thinking that the outer world is separate from us and can only respond to our direct physical input, then we tend to over-analyse the circumstances. We search for logic in the backstory to make sense of things by using the left side of the brain. This is the mind piecing things together in a way that tries to support its linear way of thinking. This model was first introduced by Democritus around 500BC and it is by far the most common belief system today. Not surprisingly, it's also the cause of most stress.

The alternative, and some would say competing way of looking at the world, follows more the teachings of Plato. This states that consciousness, not matter, is primary and that the outer world (what we perceive as the physical world) is always rearranging itself in accordance with a bigger picture than the basic cause and effect of materialism. Science now knows physical reality is impacted and influenced by our thoughts and forces beyond our current understanding. This has been demonstrated over and over again under the most stringent laboratory conditions. From the observer effect in the 1920's, through to the more recent iterations of the *delayed choice quantum eraser experiments*, such as the one performed at the Australian National University. I believe this is also why Einstein said: *"The most important question a person can answer in their lifetime is whether or not they live in a friendly universe"*. Materialists do not see a friendly universe. It is hostile by definition, as it exists separately from them and they have to fit into it through a Darwinian mentality (i.e. survival of the fittest). By contrast, those who choose to believe that they DO live in a friendly universe, find it much easier to chunk-up to a bigger (and smarter) reason for things happening. They also know that nature does not travel in straight lines.

You can already guess which camp I'm in. Though, as I said earlier, usually the easiest way you can tell is by the amount of stress someone has in fighting to control their circumstances. Losing what seemed an unlosable court case and having such an outlier of a result, means that there has to be (in my heart) a bigger reason and, of course, it didn't take my limited intelligence long to figure it out. Especially given my rather narrow skill set and abilities, as this is one of the few places I can use them. So, again, I don't care about how the outside / outer world moved things around in order to get me in here. Debating that is about as useful as debating why it rained last week. I'm just glad that I'm here. After all, steel is forged in a furnace, not an ice tray. And with the number of messages I've had, the outpouring of love and support, plus the work I'm doing in here, I don't think life has any plans for me to hang up my sword anytime soon. Not in this lifetime anyway.

Continuing on, would you like to know what is happening in here? There's never a dull moment in paradise, that I can tell you. Let's start with my cell buddy, Mark. As you may recall from my last update, he was very miserable and I got him all fired up on a health kick. I also wrote a letter for him to copy to his wife, Christine, who had refused to see him. Well, the good news is that Mark lost 4lbs the following week and not only that but (drum roll), Christine got the letter and came to visit with two of his five kids! He was over the moon. However, I'm afraid the good news ends there. As you probably recognised from my previous assessment, Mark's default state of consciousness was very much grouped into 'To-Me', or victim mode, and remember, misery loves miserable company. Well, when he realized I wouldn't play his game and support his low moods he'd get agitated and even threatening. His calibrated level of consciousness (in my opinion) bounced between 50 and 150 (that's Apathy and Anger as per the Map Of Consciousness).

Each time he would get angry, I'd break his pattern through the use of a reflective question tied to his issue (note - be careful trying to stop the train of anger, especially if it's already out of the station and gaining speed, as anger will usually escalate when challenged). I'd then go to my meditation space, increase my torus energy and send him love (I'll cover amplifying and projecting energy in the advanced section later in the update). That would normally calm him down four out of five times. Try it next time you're near a crying baby or a barking dog. It's a very real technique - similar to the highly published and successful experiments done on reducing crime in New York through group meditation. However, with Mark, it was becoming constant and draining. I even wrote to Thea and told her it was like babysitting a 210lb five-year-old. That left me with a dilemma but also the chance to share with you another valuable insight. Especially for those of you trying to help others. The question was; do I stay and continue to help Mark, or do I move on? I already knew the answer was to move, but there is always a tug of reluctance based on:

1. Not wanting to leave someone in pain (even of their own making).
2. Wondering if it's because you are not good enough to help and therefore the act of quitting triggers the primary fear that you are not enough, etc.

I knew I should go, but debated when, so I asked for a sign. It didn't take long before I had two of them. First, later that day, I got a beautiful and amazing letter from Tom Harvey, an amazing human being and a graduate of The Elite Mentorship Forum (EMF3). Tom not only said some wonderful things about how he used his learning from the EMF to help so many people, but he also said; and I quote: "Expect to have a whole rotation of new cell mates as the guards catch on that the most effective way to deal with the most troubled inmates is to put them in a cell with you for a few days!". I laughed out loud - thank you, Tom. I'm really proud of the work you are doing in your world too, my friend!

The second sign was more overt, which happened when Mark threatened to smash the TV in my face because the guards wouldn't entertain his 'I am a victim' story. It's the adult version of stamping your feet for an ice cream. So, I figured it was time to go. Not because I was worried for my safety. Having worked in crisis and psychotherapeutic intervention for years with drug addicts, emotional trauma, etc. (and thanks again to my training with Tony Robbins for that), this was just another day at the office, and I was always able (thankfully) to keep Mark from tipping over the edge. The key point here is I needed to remind myself that I can only go so far. Remember, you cannot change anyone and nor do you have the right to. You can only invite them by being the example and if they get too much of what we call *secondary gain* through their destructive patterns, such as self-importance, comfort of relinquished responsibility or plain old ego-based significance (as in Mark's case), then unless they are willing to let go of that, the behaviour will usually resurface and repeat.

A wonderful quote from the great John Milton: "The mind is its own place – it can make a hell of a heaven or a heaven of a hell." I have no right to be the gatekeeper to Mark's thoughts. I'm happy with what I was able to do during the time we were together, but my work there had reached its end.

It's worth sharing the parallel that a doctor or surgeon can never heal anyone. They can only facilitate the body to heal itself. The short lesson here, is that if you want something more for someone than they want it for themselves, you are usually wasting your time. There are occasional exceptions to this when it comes to forced intervention, but that's outside the scope of this letter. The sad end to the Mark story is that, the day after I left him, he had a full-on psychotic episode and it took five officers twenty minutes to get him out of the cell in restraints and into the mental healthcare wing where he is now being treated on a different program. Afterwards, one of the officers came to see me in my new cell and asked how I'd survived ten days with him and if he'd shown any warning signs of what just happened. I gave her a professional overview. The consensus from the staff was that he was a pressure cooker and I had acted as a damper or release valve and when I left, there was nothing to stop him boiling over. Poor guy. Had I gotten to him earlier I might have had a better chance (or not) but all I can do now is send him love.

So, guess what? I have a new cellmate. His name is Jinn and he is a 34-year-old Chinese guy and a nice cellmate to have. We've had some inspiring chats and he's enjoying learning some new perspectives on life and seems happy to have me here. Very different energy and mindset to Mark (obviously) and I didn't realize how drained I was becoming in there until I moved in with Jinn. Some of us have probably experienced this in a stagnant or even suffocating relationship, where the only reason we are with someone who drains our energy is because we were with them yesterday.

Incidentally, my *magic moments* list in here is now up to 42. Number 37 may make you smile. As you know, I was put into the business studies class and last week listened to the lesson on marketing. It was bad; I had to cringe. Nothing against the teacher but the syllabus she was forced to teach is SO academic that it has virtually no impact or relevance in the modern trenches of business. Seeing my obvious aversion, she asked me a question on marketing and within ten minutes had given me the floor. I gave a quick presentation on educational-based marketing and how to develop a core-story and everyone's mouths dropped. It certainly shifted some of the business plans in the room. When I walked in the next day, she told me she had a lot of marking to do and would I mind teaching again? I took the whole 3-hour class, covering Financial Creativity and how to start a business with no money. I wanted to do that as it gets people to think differently, and the way we are going to make any difference in here is through changing mindsets rather than trying to control behaviour. The head of department then came in for the last half an hour and has now asked if he could organise a talk / mini-seminar that I can teach in the library, which of course, I have agreed to do. I've also discussed my plans with him regarding the education program I intend to design as part of the initiative I outlined in my last letter. He is already on board and excited about the potential. I've now shared these plans with both officers and prisoners (selectively) to gauge feedback and see how on-point my initial thoughts were. The response has been overwhelmingly encouraging and nothing short of positive confirmation as to my role here.

It's now taken more shape since I first wrote and I am calling it *Operation Chrysalis, a Four-Phase Approach to Help Tackle Britain's Prison Crisis*. If you recall, this includes:

Phase 1: New Prisoner Welcome Booklet
Phase 2: Upgraded PowerPoint Induction
Phase 3: Personal Development-Based Education Course
Phase 4: In-Cell Edutainment Channel on the TV

I will share the outline of this as an appendix, together with a copy of the story I wrote for new prisoners, called *Mud or Stars?*. This is not just for those who are interested in what I'm creating in here, but also because the outline and format I lay out can be used as a template for many other kinds of projects. Sage Business School graduates will already be familiar with the difference between strategy and tactics and how strategic objectives play a crucial role in guiding the whole planning process.

My personal view is that any of the four phases would have a positive impact on their own. However, I feel the most urgent is the New Prisoner Welcome Booklet. So far, everyone who has read *Mud or Stars?* (including the Prison Officers) can see the potential impact. Not to everyone of course, that's just wishful thinking. Remember the doctor/surgeon example I gave earlier? The goal is not to change anyone and nor do I have a right to.

Instead, it is to help those who are open and, at the same time, also make people aware that there IS a choice on how to think. Unfortunately, this is currently only available to a VERY small number of people, who are both self-aware enough to realize it *and* have the mental fortitude to navigate the emotional minefield of negativity that is so pervasive in an environment like this. As I said, never a dull day in paradise.

The Learning Syllabus

So, that's the update on what I'm doing. Now let's move onto looking at some more of the tools I'm using in here to steer through this uncharted and unpredictable river.

If you recall in the last letter, we covered the following:

- Building a Solid Psychological Foundation
- The Role of Acceptance vs Resistance
- Using Contrast Frames
- Gratitude and Emotional Transformation

This time, I'd like to cover three more general topics and two advanced ones:

- Supportive and Go-To Affirmations
- Sex Energy Transmutation
- Ethnocentric Purpose
- Collapsing Powerful Egregores
- Energy Projection and Exponential Counterbalance

Supportive and Go-To Affirmations

Let's start with Supportive and Go-To Affirmations. Part of this falls under the umbrella of building a solid psychological foundation, but I want to address this specific topic separately as it's also a useful standalone tool.

The premise behind affirmations is pretty simple and I'm sure I don't have to explain it but there are pitfalls to avoid. When most people try to use positive affirmations, they rarely work and mainly because of one thing many people don't address. As you may have seen me reference on several of my YouTube videos, a basic but effective way of chunking down the human psyche, is by grouping it into two primary centres. A thinking centre (i.e. the mind) and a feeling centre (call it the heart). When the two are working separately and not linked, the impact is negligible (I'm talking here in the context of affirmations). An example may be the mind saying: "Oh, I'm in prison, it's OK, things will work out" but the heart is saying: "Are you kidding? This is terrible. I'm scared!" We call this 'putting on a brave face', precisely because we know it's the head speaking and not the heart. If you are in tune, you can pick this up straight away. Even if someone else's mind is trying to convince yours, your heart will sense the insincerity in their disunity. This is because, in order to convince, the mind uses language as its primary tool and it is exceptionally good at it.

However, the heart cannot be 'convinced' with either language or logic and neither can it manipulate or lie. It only *knows*. This is because the heart 'thinks', or rather communicates, in *feelings*, and no amount of volume or misdirection from the mind can change that. Alternatively, maybe the heart thinks (feels) "It's OK, I can handle this, it's not too bad" but then the mind starts panicking and inducing doubt by producing all kinds of negative 'what-if' scenarios.

In short, affirmations are only effective if the heart and mind are united. This is a state that neuro cardiologists call *coherence*. It occurs when the frequency of the electromagnetic pulse of the heart matches that of the brain and the two synchronise into a resonant state. When this happens, inner beliefs that are aligned with the message are strengthened and beliefs that do not match are far more susceptible to change. The classic example is the difference in thinking, "I can" vs. "I can't". If you are in a state of positive coherence and thinking "I can do this", your previous doubts become smaller. If your mind and heart are unified in thinking "I can't", then all positive resources, such as confidence or even past references, diminish. And here we see one of the biggest challenges with society today. Namely, that many people's heart and mind are far more frequently united in negativity and fear-based thinking than positive, upbeat, or love-based thinking. After all, the heart and mind can quickly agree on what they DON'T want.

The fall out to this is that many people just do not have a solid psychological foundation because the heart has been scared into a box by the mind's persistent fear-based conditioning. This is often due to repeated exposure to news, media, gossip, soaps, daytime TV, drama - you get the idea. (If you want a classic case study, look no further than Mark above!)

To coax the heart out of this box, one first has to use the mind to start loving it. Being nice to it, and not controlling it. Putting together your own personal inventory of awesomeness, instead of a compilation of self-criticism, is a wonderful and empowering place to start.

Incidentally, for the gentleman, as it's valentine's month, I'll draw a bonus analogy which may be useful in relationships. Women (feminine energy) are, in general, far more heart-based / feeling centred than masculine energy (remember, we all have both, so this relates more to characteristics than to gender). If you nurture and feed the flower of your woman's heart, it will not only come out of its box but blossom and open more beautifully than any rose. But if instead of using your heart to open hers, you use your mind to 'navigate the best and most logical route through the relationship', you cut off the source of nourishment to your woman's flower. And while she may still be with you mentally, her heart can only open to you fully if you pay attention to it with yours.

And guess what? It's the same with ourselves. If we don't love our *own* heart enough to get it out of the cold and grey box of negativity and into the sunshine of self-love, then the only beliefs you will have that are impactful, will be negative ones. But when your heart and mind are in a joyful union, a powerful shift takes place. New possibilities open up. Old beliefs that did not serve you start to have shallower foundations and create a gap for new ones. In short, when you start treating yourself like someone you love, life changes. Massively.

Another key set of ingredients that act as a cement between the bricks of any new beliefs, are new references. The good news about references is that they don't have to be yours. Plus, if your heart and mind are happily holding hands, your brain will notice more of them out of the vast amount of information it normally sweeps under the rug of your conscious awareness. We call this 'positive confirmation' and it becomes highly self-reinforcing. References also open up 'possibility thinking' which is another reason I want to include several of them in the New Prisoner Welcome Book I'm designing as part of Operation Chrysalis. These would be references of famous people who went to jail and then turned their lives around or who came out of prison only to make a huge and positive difference. People such as Mark Walberg, Muhammad Ali, Nelson Mandela or Lord Bird, etc. I know first-hand that giving people (including ourselves) positive references leads to thinking in terms of hope and possibility, not dead ends. You get my point, so back to the original one - what are some of MY key go-to phrases and affirmations that I fall back on when negativity knocks louder at the door?

Here are my top picks right now:

- Every adversity carries with it the seed of an equivalent or greater benefit.
- Life loves me, is smarter than me and everything is unfolding exactly as it should. In fact, everything is going according to plan!

- My outer world follows my inner world.
- Complaining about my current circumstances is the glue that keeps me tied to them.
- If Life were simple, it wouldn't be as fun!
- The light of love will always extinguish the darkness of fear.
- The river of Life may twist and bend but my destination is always assured.
- Theory doesn't cover the price of admission to the higher levels of growth and awareness. (I can't learn to swim on dry land.)
- The strongest trees grow in the strongest winds. If I want to be strong enough to reach my potential, pray for strong winds and don't bitch about them when they show up.
- According to the law of Quantum Mechanics, a new future is ALWAYS available.
- Train myself to let go of everything I fear to lose.

I left the final phrase until last for a reason I'll share later. The key point here is, do I use these? The answer is an emphatic YES! I know there is a tendency for some of my supporters and fans to think that I am somehow superhuman. I'm not. In fact, one of the many reasons I'm grateful for being in here, is that it helped neutralize the 'pedestal trap' that some of you have fallen into by elevating me too high. I've said many times, I'm just a normal guy, and you should always be very suspicious and wary of following false Gods or gurus. Sure, I may have a slightly more developed skill set when it comes to this kind of stuff but that's down to nearly thirty years of study, experience and a passion for helping people escape the prison (excuse the pun) of their own limited thinking. It's certainly not born of inherent genius, I can promise you that. The problem with putting someone on a pedestal, is that it automatically lowers your own greatness by contrast and that, my friends, goes against everything I'm trying to teach you.

So yes, another side bonus to this adventure I am on, is that it allows you to destroy the illusion that I'm any more perfect than you. Do I make mistakes? I bloody well hope so! Anyone who says they don't make mistakes is either lying or is too afraid to try anything new. Please don't be one of them. The travesty of the gift of Life, is wanting to live it fully but being afraid to do so by not having the courage to act. This is why courage is the tipping point between Power vs Force on the Map Of Consciousness, and probably why a master teacher, 2000 years ago, said: "Let he without sin cast the first stone". You see, it doesn't take courage to point fingers and criticize, which is why so many do it. As far as I am aware, in over a quarter of a century, no individual has been harmed or is less empowered as a result of me sharing my messages, and if there is anyone amongst the hundreds of thousands who have benefited, then I can only apologise as it was never my intent.

Out of the twenty-plus businesses I've had the courage to start, only one ever lost investors' money (and much more of my own), and that was only after we'd been hit with a deliberate bad debt. Do I look back and regret? Of course not. I look back and *learn* and then hope to make better choices moving forward. Though that's never guaranteed, especially with my Indigo tendency of butting heads with authority. What I can categorically state, is that anyone who has bought tickets to events or a product while I am in my current scenario, WILL receive it as soon as my mission here is done. That's a promise even HP won't prevent me from keeping.

So, do I make mistakes? Sure. Am I perfect? No, and thankfully never will be. (Oh, and in case you missed it, that gives you permission to stop trying). I recognize that society's version of perfection is unattainable at every level. Perfection and the perfect life, if there were ever such a thing, would be far better suited to the *direction of travel* than any kind of destination. In other words, it's infinitely more beneficial to learn and grow from our mistakes than trying to live some kind of utopian existence where we don't make any. And for those committed to walking their own journey of growth, know that when it comes to hacking through the jungle of mediocrity and conformity, cuts and bruises are to be expected along the way. It's par for the course and it's at these times that phrases like the above can significantly help.

Sex Energy Transmutation

This comes from the famous Chapter 11, in the classic book 'Think and Grow Rich' by the late great Napoleon Hill. (Incidentally, I had Thea send in several copies and I'm handing them out to those who I feel are ready to learn from it, along with some other books and resources that could help too). So rather than take the time here to go into a detailed discourse on the subject, I'd highly encourage you to go and read Hill's original work. But as a general summary, I'll highlight some key points and why I've included it as one of the tools I've been using.

The sex hormones act as one of the strongest innate drivers of human emotion and action. The urge is so strong that it can, and often does, override logic and intelligence. It can surpass fatigue, block out all distractions and even garner courage. Obviously, in prison, the natural expression of that with a partner (homosexuality aside) is somewhat tempered and many, I would assume, choose to waste this force through self-expression and in the escape of their own imagination. However, as it is a potent force and in the absence of being able to celebrate it with Thea, where one plus one equals eleven, it is far better utilised and harnessed by practicing the art of transmutation. In other words, channelling it into something else. There are several ways to do this through using breathing and focus. It's through using this energy that I can concentrate on creative ways to help people in here. To discipline myself to exercise in the cell each day. Not to let my mind get lazy but to hold a space for my meditation. To sit and write for hours, even when we are free to roam the wing or the pain in my hand is begging me to stop.

Sex Energy Transmutation is the difference between atrophy of desire and creativity, or the focusing of it! I fear I would not have had the impact in here I've already had if I had not been practicing this.

Ethnocentric Purpose

A key commonality in the lives of those who deal well with adversity, is the concept of an ethnocentric focus. In short, it means focusing on others more than ourselves. I've said before that the vast majority of people's stress is caused by them trying to fix the gap between what they want their life to look like (in terms of circumstances related to them) and what they perceive it currently looks like. In other words, their 'outer world' doesn't match the desired projections of what their 'inner world' says it wants.

This is a classic area that materialists constantly struggle with. Instead of accepting that the river of Life flows in a winding and non-linear way, they resist the bends, fight the current and try to carve out their own straight-line channel. I call this approach to life 'By-Me', also known as 'achiever mode'. This is because the mantra, having grabbed the world by the throat, is: "I'll make it happen By-Me". The challenge is that the world seems to be forever resisting, as would you or I if we were grabbed by the throat. The approach generally wastes a lot of energy and gives, at best, temporary results. Then, as soon as we stop applying force, it often springs back like a bent branch and slaps us in the face. 'By-Me' was the life I lived for most of my twenties which, I suppose, if you are going to fight life head-on and use force instead of power, your twenties are probably the best decade to do it in. It's pretty exhausting.

However, non-materialists (subscribers to Plato or the non-material spiritual-based model, virtual reality model, bio-centric model, etc.) have a different approach. They appreciate the complexity, beauty and even majesty of the winding river of Life. Rather than fight and resist the current, they concentrate their efforts on how to better position themselves IN the current. I call this approach being in 'Through-Me', as life tends to flow through you a lot easier than in 'By-Me'.

A word of warning here. Please note that when it comes to living in 'Through-Me', there is a distinct difference between going with the flow and giving up or not caring what happens or where the flow goes. The latter has its basis in apathy and is typical of the 'fate', or 'what will be, will be' model of the world. This approach lacks direction or purpose and simply reduces one's life to that of a leaf or piece of flotsam, aimlessly carried downstream at the mercy of tidal circumstance. As many of my students know and have experienced, living in 'Though-Me' is not about giving up. Nor is it about trying to control the river. Instead, first choose the river you wish to be in (i.e. set your goal) and then become a skillful sailor, purposefully navigating your boat downstream towards your goal. This way, you learn to accept and work with the bends, operating in harmony with the exciting and sometimes harrowing current. After all, learning to react to the curve-balls of life with graceful swings of the bat, rather than swear words or rushing for cover, is a far less stressful way to play the game.

Suicide - when the gap is too wide

An extreme example of an egocentric (self-centred) focus, where the gap between the desired reality and the actual reality is so big, is suicide. Suicidal people have chosen (consciously or otherwise) to focus, not just on the pain of how far apart the life they want is from the one they have now (emotionally more than circumstantially but their brain rarely makes that connection) but worse, they cannot see a way out of their pain at any point on their immediate horizon. Therefore, they have no compelling future and hence suicide presents itself as a viable painkiller.

Dealing effectively with suicide cases (and I've had my fair share), usually involves either:

A. Guiding them through a doorway to a compelling future, or at least the possibility of one.
B. Getting them to shift the focus off themselves and what they are missing in life and onto what they can give and contribute to others.

Usually with suicides, option 'A' is easier, as many, at least to begin with, have such a low self-worth that they question what they can offer to others. However, achieve either one or ideally tie the two together, and you no longer have someone who is suicidal. And up to this point, by the grace of God, I've not lost anyone yet. The good news is that both of these can usually be achieved with a shift in context rather than a shift in circumstance. In other words, by shifting their inner world in the right way, the pain of the outer world shifts itself (see third affirmation above).

My main point here, if you haven't guessed, is that an ethnocentric focus fuels us from a different place and is a huge antidote to the stress of what we think of as our own problems. Take Viktor Frankl on the classic and moving book *Man's Search for Meaning* (also mentioned in my previous letter when discussing contrast frames). He noticed the 0.3% of survivors in the concentration camps all had one thing in common; they had a reason not to give up. Something to live for, i.e. a compelling future. However, those who fared the strongest were those who focused on being there for others after it was over. There is a reason why this book has sold nine million copies and is one of the most impactful you'll ever read.

Before I wrap up this section, a word of caution. An ethnocentric focus should NOT be confused with the destructive 'Martyr' pattern, which I have covered extensively in other areas of my work but is worth touching on here. The Martyr mentality (slightly more common in women due to their more natural predisposition to nurture and to care), is where you give and give until empty. This is often driven by the forlorn or misguided hope that you are doing the right thing, either because you have to or that you can protect yourself from the fear of not being enough by 'proving' you are good enough through the 'vehicle' of helping others. The reason this doesn't work and keeps us feeling empty, is that it is a vehicle and not a natural or authentic expression. The difference is easy to spot by asking a question: Are we acting out of one or more of the following; fear, guilt, duty, obligation or a need for recognition? Or are we giving from the heart without any need for a measured return on our act of service.

Giving from our heart lights us up and leaves us feeling fuller. Giving from anywhere else, i.e., the mind, usually has a depleting effect which causes us to feel upset when the expectations of a return on our efforts (in the form of love, praise, recognition, approval, reciprocation, etc.) are not met. A true ethnocentric purpose transcends the insecurities of ego and comes from an authentic place of serving the greater good. It gives to both sides, instead of being offered as a horse trade. Another way of saying this is that, unless we are giving from our overflow, we are likely setting ourselves up for disappointment.

My focus in here is to use my time in a way to help others. Whether that is individual inmates (or even the guards I've cheered up), the system itself, you guys following along or the people you choose to share these letters or lessons with. ALL of that drives me. Lights me up. The intention, or even just the hope, that I might make a small difference, whether it's to one person in here or many I'll never meet, inspires me and extinguishes any semblance of hardship. Without an ethnocentric focus in here, I would have likely struggled to fight the large scale collective mindset of 'woe is me' and the pervasive victim mentality that smothers the prison like a suffocating shrink wrap. Doing the work I do punctures holes in that, which not only allows me to breathe deeply, but walk with vigour, a smile and a spring in my step. I love this work! It's also highly challenging, which allows me to grow and therefore helps me show up as a better version of myself.

This is what is missing in a Martyr pattern. You cannot do anyone any good if you are not first taking care of yourself at some level. That is why we are told to fix our own oxygen masks first *before* helping others. Do not be one of those who waste their entire life 'sacrificing themselves' rather than working on giving more of themselves. My heart truly hopes you can see the difference, as no matter how hard you try, you can never give that which you don't have.

Advanced Learning

Let's move into the advanced learning section. This is mainly a continuation of the syllabus I teach my students in the 'Masters Circle'. Speaking of which, I firstly want to say a huge thank you to all of the members. Many of you have already written to me, sharing your support. I understand that you have also stepped up and are not only continuing our weekly calls but taking them to a whole new level. Outstanding work; I'm so proud of you as this demonstrates that you can really fish for yourselves. If you keep going at this rate, I'll be out of a job! Though to be perfectly honest, I really wouldn't expect anything else from the level you all play at. Just as in Life, having the training is one thing, putting it into practice and seeing it all come together when it matters is another. Well done!

Another thing that makes me smile and is a positive anchor in here are the photographs Thea has sent in and that I have stuck on my wall. (To get resourceful, I use toothpaste which works as well as glue!). In amongst the ones she sent were several pictures from many of the Masters Circle Adventures we've taken together. From swimming with dolphins in the Bahamas, to nights at the casino in Monte Carlo and bike riding in Italy. I think of them often, along with many other *magic moments* we've shared such as husky racing across the Arctic to see the Northern Lights and being within jumping distance of wild lions in the African bush. And while this is a different kind of adventure, I know there are more to come as soon as I'm out.

OK, lesson time…

Collapsing and Dealing with Powerful Egregores and Exponential Energy Projections

Masters Circle members are familiar with the subject of Egregores, as they are covered in detail in Modules 3 and 4 of my Quantum Alignment Foundation Course. However, for many others they are likely to be an unknown subject. Therefore, allow me to offer some important context, and distinctions.

Wikipedia describes egregores as an 'energetic entity or thought form created by a collective or group mind'. Another common name for an egregore is a pendulum, coined by the Russian author and Quantum Physicist, Vadim Zeland in his outstanding book, Reality Transurfing. And, while they have been talked about throughout history in various guises, I believe the famous author and poet, Victor Hugo, was the first person to use the term egregore. The work of Dr. Rupert Sheldrake and his books on morphogenic fields, also tie-in heavily to the concept of egregores.

So, what are they?

An egregore is essentially a separate energetic entity that is created when two or more people think in a resonant frequency. Like when you share an idea or are discussing the same subject. When this happens, the egregore has the power to influence the thoughts and actions of the people that created it. Good examples are found in most organizations. Steve Jobs co-founded Apple, but at some point, Apple became bigger than the people who gave birth to it and an egregore was formed. At this stage, if anyone in the structure disagrees with, or opposes, what is felt to be the outcomes of the structure (company, organisation, club, etc.), it will turn against them or even throw them out.

What is the outcome of an egregore? To grow by recruiting more people who think along its resonant frequency. It is self-serving and nearly always creates an 'us vs. them' mentality as it jostles to attract more members at the expense of other egregores. Think Apple vs Microsoft, Republican vs Democrats, Manchester United vs. Chelsea or Christian vs Muslim. It's the same basic rules. The bottom line is that an egregore is created at the point where the structure, organisation or 'group mind' now puts its own agenda, survival, and interests above that of the individual members or followers. And, as we saw with Steve Jobs, it doesn't care if that includes the original founders.

Scarily, because its focus is always self-serving and fuelled by energy, it has a tendency to influence or even hijack our own thoughts and actions to support its goals. It is often destructive and frequently feeds off fear-based energy. In fact, one of the fastest ways to feed itself is through inciting conflict as that always releases immediate energy. That's why perfectly normal friends and families can become vehement enemies in moments when wearing different political colours or even football shirts. Have you ever wondered why one minute you can be engaged in a normal conversation and the next minute you find yourself in what afterwards seemed to be a completely pointless argument that appeared to come out of nowhere? Egregores are masters of engineering conflict in the moment by pushing your buttons and provoking retaliation in a way that makes you feel justified about doing so. I'm sure you are familiar with the pattern. Somebody says or does something that challenges your beliefs or opinions and we then set up to counterpoint. They then respond by pushing back harder and we respond by shoving. From there, if we don't recognise what is going on, things can rapidly escalate as the egregore gets us to push the energy pendulum from both sides. Each time harvesting the energy. What is critical to note is that it never cares who 'wins' the argument. In fact, it's not important. It just feeds off the energy of conflict. In the meantime, the poor players fall for the bait while being totally unaware of what game is actually going on. See any tie-ins to my earlier comments on social or mainstream media, drama and gossip?

What's the best way to collapse the structure? Simple. Stop swinging the pendulum. Step back, observe and watch it swing itself out while you stay detached from the game. Try it. You'll be amazed at what happens. There is, of course, a lot more on the subject and some far more advanced techniques but this is not the place to share it.

What I can confirm, is that when dealing with this type of energetic phenomena, the environment I am in right now provides a great case study and is why I've renamed Pentonville, somewhat tongue-in-cheek, to 'Pendulumville'.

Let's look at how it relates to being in here. First, let's go back to the Map Of Consciousness (Appendix C) and using the scale of 0-1000, calibrate the energy of the environment based on my own experience and observation. It's probably no surprise that I gauge the average energy level in here as Fear (100). This is augmented by a few ego-based expressions at Pride (175), as some of the peacocks fan their feathers. There are also many people operating between Shame (20) and Apathy (50). If we then trace the majority of emotions felt and expressed, starting at the bottom, we have Blame, rising to Despair, through Regret and into Anxiety. Craving then sets in (for what they miss or don't have) and finally, Hate or Scorn as the most powerful or should I say forceful and toxic.

I'll be honest and say in the small number of weeks that I've been here, I have yet to see ONE authentic expression of Courage (200) or anything higher. That's scary stuff (note - never confuse Courage for bravado, which is really Pride at 175). This all makes for a VERY strong Attractor Pattern / Morphic Field and in such a concentrated low-frequency environment, egregores thrive and there is little to stop them. Their main entry points for setting up a negative provocation oscillate between the emotions of disappointment and aggression, often using the first as a trigger for the second. Although, a point to note is that the majority of cases (circa 90%) are only expressed internally as silent turmoil, with the inevitable spillover of an external display at approximately 10%. As always, the velcro with which all provocations latch on to, is the level of importance attributed to something. For example, a common trigger for Mark was when he was looking forward to exercising outside, or going to education in class, only to have it all cancelled and the jail put on lockdown for the whole day due to short-staffing. This has happened about one day in every four so far and, as soon as he was hooked by the disappointment of unmet expectations, escalation always followed, or at least tried to if I wasn't there to check it. Even then, I certainly wasn't successful all of the time.

Protecting Myself Energetically

With such an insidious force in here, it's been essential for me to keep my own energy high. One of the benefits of evolving up the Map Of Consciousness, is that the scale is measured exponentially, not sequentially. Without getting too technical, this simply means that a loving thought is many times more powerful than a fearful or ego-based thought and therefore, one loving thought can counterbalance many fearful thoughts from the environment. An example we discussed in Volume 1, was the power of Acceptance, which calibrates at a massive 350, and which also operates at a high level of 'Through-Me'. This is because you accept the bends in the river as an inevitable part of the journey. However, I'm finding that the underlying energy my heart must beat at, for at least parts of the day, is Love (500) and even unconditional Love (540) which is more akin to radiating pure Joy. This seems to be the only thing that allows me to displace the enormous amount of fear and negativity that surrounds me in here.

I'll admit, it's not easy. Usually, the hardest time is early, when I wake up and it's dark and quiet. I've written about this in my private journal where I call it the 5am Pendulum. As I'm just waking, my energy is low and it's easy for my mind to be distracted by an onslaught of potential negative scenarios and doubts, such as; "Can I really trust the flow?", "What if I never recover?", "What if my messages never have any more impact?" or "Will I ever teach again?" etc., and it takes a real heart-based effort for it to shut up. Once I'm up, I'm fine, but it's a frequent reminder of how powerful the default Attractor Patterns and M-Fields are in here, and how fast they can wrap their energetic tentacles around you when your own energy is not strong.

Once I'm up, I activate my Torus, or energy field, and facilitate a three-level layer of energetic protection, taught by a good friend, Ed Strachar, plus an exercise he shared with me from a Taoist Master, Mantac Chia, that focuses on expanding an 'inner smile'. Once I reconnect back to the level of 350, I'm solid and pretty much glide through my morning practice. This is more than enough to be immune from the negativity, but I also know that I'm not just here for myself. A powerful part of my day is using meditation to connect to level 500 and 540. If you want something concrete to measure this by, try using the excellent Inner Balance app from the Heartmath Institute, which uses biofeedback to measure heart rate variability. I would say that being in a state of unconditional love, for example, would register at around the ten-plus mark on their app. It's easy to do but only with practice. I mention this only as a guide and if you want to try to benchmark it for yourselves. It's an excellent tool for training yourself to raise your state of consciousness and something I miss not having in here.

Once I achieve the state myself, I then project that love to everyone in here. Key distinction; I use the word *project* specifically. As science will tell you, everything is constantly in a state of vibration and always seeks its resonant frequency. The easiest way to connect or impact that, is through the feeling centre and not the thinking centre. This requires you to 'project', using will and intention, rather than using intellect, language (self-talk) or imagination. For me, I get a sense of it pouring out of my heart and connecting to all the hearts of the people in the cells up and down the prison. I then extend it as far as possible, especially to any potential emotional hooks or areas of potential vulnerability or disappointment that an egregore could use to latch onto.

Remember, when calibrating below 350 it's easy, or at least easier, for the mind to get very conditional and separatist. If this is not checked, it can quickly lead us below Courage (200) and into Righteousness (175), which is fuelled by Hate (150). And as a little green mentor once said· 'Hate leads to suffering' and at this level, it's almost natural to give in to the urge to blame. For me personally, it would be way too tempting to start climbing on my high horse about the injustice of what I thought the other side and their lawyers were doing, the courtroom smoke and mirrors, manipulated accusations they used to put me in here and all that yada yada bullshit. But it's the wrong game to play. By sending love to them instead, I acknowledge their part in the amazing master plan that's at work and that has enabled me to have this experience and adventure that I would never have had without them.

Incidentally, after the trial was finished, I went over to one of the opposing counsel, Mr Weekes, (yes, they had a whole team), and shook his hand and told him how impressed I was with his work. I also said I hoped he was able to get some well-earned rest now, after spending the entire previous night working on his closing argument (something which my counsel didn't do, despite me sending him several pages of key facts and material, which were not presented and that I was certain would win the case - again there is a bigger reason for this bend in the river). My comment to Mr Weekes was sincere and I have nothing but respect for him. The same goes for HP's lawyers, Mishcon de Reya. They are simply doing their job. Lawyers litigate, that is what they do, and expecting an alcoholic not to drink is futile.

Upon hearing that Brian Rose had pulled down my interviews on

London Real as a knee-jerk reaction to me being in here, despite them helping hundreds of thousands of people and being widely credited as the most impactful episodes he had ever broadcast, I was told he received an avalanche of backlash and negative comments, criticising him and slating him for what he'd done. Cut him some slack. Brian has every right to do whatever he wants to do and, like all of us, is clearly on his own journey. Try sending him love instead of judgement and see what appears in your own world.

No matter which way you slice it, the binary equation of life is always love or fear and it's *always* a choice. By raising our own level of energy, consciousness and love, we get to share it and in doing so, magnify our own impact on this journey down the river of Life.

Yoda Wisdom

Well, my dear family and friends, I suppose I'd better start closing off this Volume or I'll be out by the time you finish reading it! There's just one last thing I want to share and leave you with. A question I was asked recently was: Am I afraid of losing everything through what has happened?

Some of you astute readers will recall, I mentioned that I would circle back to the final go-to affirmation, out of the ones I listed earlier. For those of you who are familiar with my work in general, you'll recognise it as another of my favourite 'Yodaisms.' Namely:

'Train yourself to let go of everything you fear to lose'.

This also has its roots in Buddhism and those guys know a thing or two about dealing with stress. Essentially, it points to the fact that any major attachments we have form the basis of an emotional weak spot. Now, that doesn't mean to say or in any way imply that I don't care or am indifferent to anything and everything. That's called having an 'emotional-ectomy' and while that may be OK for robots, what makes us unique as humans is that we experience the world through feeling, not detachment.

No, what I'm unveiling here is something much deeper and eludes many people throughout their lives. In fact, unawareness at this level traps us in emotional bondage as fear and limitation keep us prisoner in our own minds. Freedom from this begins when we recognise that everything in the physical world is subject to the law of *impermanence*. Could I lose everything? Well, according to that law, it's guaranteed. At least at some point on the journey. All I can do is place one foot in front of the other in the best way I can, whilst trying to be the best version of myself as I go. And knowing, as I said earlier, that I'm also guaranteed to make mistakes.

Could I lose the business? Of course, and if I do, I'll start another one. If I lose my home, I'll find out who my friends are for a while and work to buy or build another one. Trust me, I'm sure it would be bigger than the one I'm sleeping in tonight. If Thea chooses to leave and follow a different path that was her new Truth, I'd have no choice but to send her love and positive energy for the next part of her journey. After all, ownership of another human being was outlawed long ago. If the dogs die, I'll cry, grieve and move on. In short, my friends, when you fully let go of everything you fear to lose, you gain something extraordinary. FREEDOM.

It's from this place, that I can give my all and not worry about what I can't control. It's from here that I can focus on adding value and not care about the gossip on social media. It's from here that I can give all of me to my partner from a place of strength, not neediness or fear (which paradoxically attracts them more to the relationship). It's from here that I can celebrate the time I've had with the dogs, rather than be paranoid about losing them. It's from here true freedom lives. And it's from this place that any one of us can make a difference to the world.

So, in closing, stay strong my friends and shine your light, as it's only the darkness of fear that can rob you of your greatness and potential.

I love you unconditionally and I'll write again soon,
Peter X

Volume 3: Behind the Door (Week 6)

In Volume three, Peter reveals what life is really like inside one of Britain's worst prisons. Be warned, he pulls no punches as he shares with us how he is coping with the conditions, the violence (including an attempted murder he narrowly misses), the drugs, 23+ hr a day lock-up and more. He answers questions about the most significant lessons he's learned so far and also what regrets he has, following what happened in court. He shares with us how he stays positive but also his lowest moments and the times he's cried. In the syllabus section, he gives an in-depth look into the concept of meditation, an area many people struggle with.

My dear and amazing family, students and friends

In this issue, I'm going to answer the three most common questions I'm asked, including; 'What's life inside Britain's toughest prison really like?' (Please note, the timid and squeamish may want to avoid this).

I also give an update on *Operation Chrysalis*, my personal initiative to help address some of the issues and fundamental challenges to the prison system that I'm conducting as part of my 'Secret Agent Of Change' mission from inside.

Finally, I'm going to continue the syllabus originally outlined in Volume 1 on what tools I'm using and how I'm using them to deal with the situation in here. This time I'm going to cover the often-misunderstood topic of meditation. Students of my work will uncover some deeper levels of distinction here, although there will be lessons and tips that all readers will be able to benefit from. Especially as meditation is one of the most frequent and misunderstood subjects I get asked about.

I'll keep it real and practical so that everything I cover can be tried and tested at home and in the real world.

As usual, the nature of my writing will likely go off-piste and skirt along and through the barriers of knowledge in ways that I hope are both entertaining but also highly useful. We will cover many insights as I make every effort to give you as much value as I can in exchange for your time and, hopefully, come full circle to various shifts and conclusions that will leave you better off having read this than not.

Let's begin with my answers to the three most common questions I'm asked:

1. What's life inside Britain's toughest prison really like?
2. What are the biggest lessons I've learned so far?
3. Do I have any regrets about what has happened?

I'll start from the top. What's life inside here really like? Well, for those under the illusion that it may be a holiday camp, I'm going to be as honest and objective as I can. Please note, before I begin, this is an OBJECTIVE overview and not my SUBJECTIVE experience, which obviously is going to be different from most prisoners, simply due to my background. In other words, no matter where you are, the environment is the environment. It's a constant. How you or I interpret meaning from and deal with that environment is always a matter for the individual. Hence, two men sat behind prison bars; one saw mud, the other saw stars.

I'll begin with a quick overview of Her Majesty's Prison Pentonville and then cover the following headings:

- The Cell
- The Violence
- The Food and Hygiene

There is obviously more but this should give you a reasonable feel. Let's start with the jail itself.

Pentonville was built in the 1800's and with the exception of minor improvements, has never been modernised. It is a high-security prison in North London, designed to contain what is known as 'Category B' prisoners. This category includes; those convicted of violence, drugs, armed robbery, gangs, sex offenders, aggravated assault and organised crime, to name but a few. The facilities are poor, harsh and treatment is draconian by any modern prison standards.

Many prisoners who are transferred here from other Category B prisons, or even Maximum-Security Category A prisons (due to being near to the end of their sentence), are shocked by how much worse this place is compared to where they came from. This is universal feedback. Personally, as I'm the lowest risk or 'D Category' and as far as I can tell, the only civil (i.e. non-criminal) prisoner in the jail, I shouldn't even be here at all – but more on that later. Not to mention that many of the prisoners I've met who are in here for violence and drugs received much shorter sentences than I did. You have to laugh.

I was doing some research in the library and came across a news article about a prisoner who was murdered here a few weeks ago. What struck me the most was not the violence aspect, as I'll get into that later, but the comments from the former Justice Secretary, Michael Gove, who singled out Pentonville as *'The most dramatic example of failure within the [prison] system'.* After now spending several weeks in here, I haven't seen anything to challenge his opinion.

The Cell (Home Sweet Home)

The cells are tiny. A total of twelve-feet long by six-feet wide (4m x 2m) and originally built for one person. Put in a narrow six-foot bunk bed, a small table (that I use to write on), a chair, two people, all of their clothes and personal belongings, wash gear, eating utensils, a small TV and you start to get the idea. I'm a top bunk guy and luckily don't move much, unlike a poor fellow who recently rolled out in his sleep, hit the concrete floor and broke his pelvis on impact. (Many beds have no safety rail). There is another and much smaller room, three-feet by nine-feet (1m x 3m), which has a toilet and a small sink (no plugs), which I also use as my meditation room. In the main room, there is a small window that lets in some natural light, together with a thin strip of metal either side that have a few match head-size holes in it to allow a faint trickle of air. There are also many days, where due to short staffing, we spend twenty-four hours in the cell. This is minus the five minutes it takes us to go downstairs at 5pm to collect our one cooked meal of the day.

Within the prison, there are lots of 'cell pets'. Namely, rats, mice and many cockroaches. This is partly because it's such an old building and also because many prisoners do not have the discipline to keep their cells clean. Jinn and I do a full mop and clean down every few days. This takes most of the time out of our occasional forty-minute social time and we have to request and return the equipment, but it is worth it. However, there are many stains on the walls (including body fluid - use your imagination), that we just can't shift. We also keep all food and rubbish off the floor, so it's rare that we get any pets. It also helps that we are on the fourth floor of the wing (also known as 'The Fours'), though I have seen 'pets' on every floor. Just as you don't need to send an invitation for depression to a negative mind, you don't need to send rodents or insects an invitation to a dirty cell. The environment does it for you. Keep the environment clean and you have a far better chance to avoid any unwanted visitors.

The Violence

There's a reason Pentonville has its reputation for being one of the most violent prisons in Europe. Violence here is not just common; it is epidemic and a multiple daily occurrence. One can never be complacent. Aside from the frequent fights and officers in riot gear rushing into cells, there was an attempted murder here last week in the showers that I narrowly missed. Unfortunately, Jinn, my cellmate, wasn't so lucky. We both left the cell together to go to the showers. I went upstairs to the fives, as it's my old landing where I shared the cell with Mark and the showers there are usually less busy. Jinn walked down our landing on the fours to the showers on our floor. As he waited, three guys came in. Two blocked the door and the other pulled out a weapon. It was a toothbrush with the handle sharpened to a point, usually done by scraping it against the concrete wall in the cell. There were also razor blades glued to the head with the bristles. Crude but very effective. They were not after Jinn but another guy who had walked in. What happened next was gruesome as the guy with the weapon didn't waste time.

I didn't witness the attack, but the river of blood pouring out of the showers was like a horror movie. I got back to my cell and Jinn was on the bed, shaking. He told me he'd been trapped in there while it happened and had hid behind one of the shower curtains. He's a quiet, unassuming and very pleasant guy but since then, he will not go out of the cell for any social time or exercise and to be honest, I've not had the inclination to talk him out of it, as the cell is the only place he feels safe. I called Thea straight away after the attack and left a message about what happened – in hindsight not the best move to keep your partner calm but I was still a little in shock myself.

Then, two days ago, all of us on the landing had a questionnaire put under our door, asking for anonymous feedback on the violence here and what we think causes it. We were given options of gang issues, drugs, debt, outside issues, etc. I'll share with you what I wrote, as it serves as an example of looking beyond symptoms and assessing the cause. Those familiar with my work, will recognise the analogy I often use of going to a doctor because you have pain in your knee. At first glance, a traditional allopathically trained Doctor would assume the inflammation in the knee is the problem. After all, that is what hurts, and he would most likely administer anti-inflammatories, painkillers and rest. However, a more holistic Doctor would take a broader look. He might find that there is a tight shoulder that is causing one of the hips to be out of balance. This, in turn, could be creating more stress on the opposite knee which is then becoming inflamed as it carries a disproportionate amount of bodyweight. He therefore, treats the shoulder and as a result, the knee gets better. It's the same difference between constantly rescuing people out of the river, which is exhausting, and going upstream to find out and stop whoever is throwing them in. You get my point. Most of the time we run the same patterns because we get distracted by what grabs our immediate attention, rather than focusing on what may be the cause of it. So, what's causing the violence?

It's a fact here that drug use is absolutely rife. More so in here per head than outside. Much more. Not just your basic cannabis-based stuff, but more psychotropic and synthetic drugs collectively labelled 'spice' or 'mamba'. It's smuggled in from the outside in many different ways. From being thrown over the wall, to being delivered by drones and by visits. It's also estimated that as many as one in thirty prison officers supplement their income by bringing in contraband to order. The BBC alone states that the prison drug market is worth over £1m a week! Not surprisingly, a lot of people see this as a major cause of violence. I disagree. It certainly can be a factor but just like the knee, it is way more of a symptom than a cause. For a start, cannabis doesn't cause aggression but instead has a calming effect. It turns people into slow, docile, and unmotivated individuals. And from what I have seen of people on Spice, they are more like zombies than fighters, although they are probably going hungry as there doesn't seem to be that many large brains in here to eat. OK, forgive the humour on such a serious subject, but it's a good way of trying to keep my own energy high, particularly in here. And especially with zombies around.

Debt, on the other hand, is a big issue and is definitely connected with violence but again, this is more symptomatic than causal. The question is, why do people buy more drugs and tobacco than they can afford and then suffer the consequences of the black-market jungle economy with its super-high interest rates?

A lot of it has to do with the length of time that prisoners are kept in their cells (affectionately known as 'Bang-up'). Remember what I said about chronic short-staffing, leading to virtually twenty-four-hour lock-up days? Well, part of the problem is whenever the forty-minute social time, education or exercise is cancelled without notice, the disappointment of unmet expectations is high. If you recall, I also sighted this as a big trigger for Mark's mood swings in my last update. When this happens, which can be as often as three to four times a week, the prisoners' frustration builds. This is then compounded by an inability, through lack of tools and skill sets, to deal with the boredom, stress and cramped solitude. The knock-on effect is that many then smoke far more than they normally would for standard recreation and instead, are now using smoking and drugs as a method of coping and dealing with their situation. This is one root cause of why people, who can normally manage a basic budget outside of prison, get drawn into borrowing more than they can pay back. It's not because they are unintelligent. It's because immediate gratification and the desire to avoid pain, override their rational process, paradoxically causing more pain (and not just financial), later on. Oh, and notice any similarities? This phenomenon is relied upon by most modern marketing campaigns and is the driver behind why we often buy what we buy when we buy it and then regret it afterwards.

I could go on about the violence but at the risk of sounding like the nightly news or morning papers (with the exception that this account is actually true), I'll assume you get the picture.

Fear Factor

Interestingly, a few people have asked if I'm afraid. The absolute and honest answer is no. Not at all. Not even a bit. But not for the reasons you may be thinking (note - the shock when I called Thea after the attempted murder was more to do with the 'in your face reminder' of the reality of the place I'm in, lest I drop my awareness or forget). No, the reason I don't have any fear is not through bravado (which is nothing more than false confidence) or naivety. That's a fast track to a sharpened toothbrush sticking out of your chest or a quick razor blade across your throat. No, it's from a deeper understanding of the role fear plays and, much harder, being conscious enough to rise above it.

You see, in life, and certainly in this place, fear is a massive disadvantage. People often say that fear is useful in situations such as, avoiding walking down a dark alley at night or going on holiday to a war zone. Not true. *Intelligence* is useful in deciding to avoid those situations, not fear! As I'm sure we have all experienced to our detriment, when fear rises, intelligence plummets. That's not a choice; it's a biological certainty, as the blood is squeezed out of the frontal lobe and neocortex and is redirected to the rear brain. That's why we've all made poor and dumb decisions when in a fear-based state, only to think afterwards, "what the hell was I doing?". The evolutionary logic is that it's far better to fight on reflex (rear brain), than to stop and engage in critical thinking about which move to make. And while reflexive thinking may be useful in blocking a punch before your front brain knows it's been thrown, it is certainly not useful in making decisions that could be critical in avoiding the fight in the first place. In other words, if three guys approach me on the landing with a menacing intent, intelligence is going to give me a far better chance than fear. It's not because I'm some sort of Braveheart. Far from it. It's because being relaxed and smart is the safest choice. Again, easy to talk about, harder to live, which is why I'm grateful for the opportunity to practice this for real and not in the classroom. Remember, my friends, theory does not cover the price of admission to the higher levels of growth and awareness. Luckily, using a combination of rapport skills, intelligence and directed energy, also known as focused intent, I get on with virtually everyone. In fact, many of the prisoners now come to my cell for either advice or coaching.

One example was a prisoner on my wing who was out on cleaning duties and who knocked on my cell door to ask if I'd help him write a letter. He was trying to offset an extra twenty-eight days added to his sentence for attacking his prison psychiatrist three years ago, due to a mix up with his anti-psychotic medication. I know, another day in the office – you really couldn't make this stuff up! Now, after three years of good behaviour, which had earned him his D Category rating, he now wanted to find a way to apologise but wasn't very literate. He'd asked around and was sent straight to me. After a ten-minute chat through the small glass window in my door, I went and drafted a letter for him. I then slid it to him under my door and he literally beamed reading it, he was so happy and grateful; it was heart-warming. He was transferred four days later.

This is just one example of many I could give (and if I get time in the personal update section, I may share some more) but it has helped a lot in positioning me as someone who is both neutral and a useful resource. I think another big part is that people can tell it's because I care, rather than because I have any other self-serving agenda. Especially as I never ask for anything in return. Why would I? I'm here to help and make a difference, not barter. The same is true in our own lives outside. I learned a long time ago, that if you come from a place of authentic contribution, where you do things because it's the right thing to do, you'll be amazed at how people treat you. This is in stark contrast to the horse-trading many of us engage in, with its rules and hidden agendas. It's a sad fact that most communication on a global basis is usually designed to get someone to behave (or buy) in a way that serves those who are doing the talking, rather than those with whom we are talking to. This is also what's known as Level-2 Relationship. Though one thing I'm certain of, is that knowing how to build rapport and foster relationships from a place of genuine intent, is a critical life-skill. And especially in prison.

The Food

Now the food is amazing! In fact, it's the one area that this place has got nailed. Part of that is because we have an ex Michelin-starred chef working in the kitchen. Plus, I also get live fresh juice brought to my cell each morning and… oh hang on, erm sorry, dreaming.

Damn. Nearly had myself fooled there for a second (mmm… fresh juice…)

Well, what can I say? Of course, those familiar with my Straight Talk Volume 10 on Health & Vitality will understand that everything food-wise is always assessed in the context of 'compared to what?'. So, compared to what I would normally feed my dogs – prison food would be a second choice. Compared to starving to death – it's OK. Remember, prisons are run on a budget and food is a line-item that has its selection criteria based on costs before nutritional quality or quantity. Not to mention that the government's guidelines on the subject are decades out of date and are largely responsible for the current cancer, diabetes and heart disease epidemics that rob so many people of the life they could otherwise enjoy. This is the same for many places, not just prisons. Hospitals are sadly the most ironic example. This is why, when my mother was dying of cancer, I had to smuggle in live vegetable juices and special vitamins against the doctor's recommendations, but I was fighting a losing battle. As every oncologist knows (or should know), cancer is fed and grows faster on a diet of highly processed foods and hospital diets contain little in the way of live nutrition. What I find even more shocking is that they don't even make a distinction between cancer wards and others when it comes to serving food. Anyway, Rest in Peace, Mum, I love you. Sorry guys, I wandered off track there for a minute and got a little emotional but as many of you know, health is a subject I am passionate about for obvious and personal reasons.

Luckily, when it comes to coping with the poor health environment in here, there are three things in my favour:

One is the condition I arrived in. Whilst I'm no Olympic athlete, I do have a lifetime of good habits to fall back on which are grounded in good information and through placing health and vitality as a very high value. The second is that I'm not here for long and certainly not in progressive body degeneration terms. And thirdly, this is one area of the system that I do have a little control over. Each week, we get to fill out a sheet on which we can order some basic items (known as the canteen sheet, not that we ever get to visit a canteen). This is where I get to spend the £2 a day I earn in class (woohoo!) and money that Thea can send into my account, up to a maximum of around £50 a week or so. My usual order is £20 for phone credit (Thea is the only number I'm allowed to call), 10 pears, 3kgs of bananas, 2 lemons, a bag of ginger, 3 tins of coconut milk, oats, peanut butter, peppermint and camomile tea bags, and 10 litre and a half-sized bottles of water. This leaves a small amount for personal items, such as toiletries - soap, shaving gear, toothpaste (I buy non-fluoride), etc. All cooking is done in the kettle which, whilst very small, is good for heating the coconut milk, which I mix with oats, chopped banana and peanut butter. I rarely eat the lunch (a sandwich delivered at around 11am and which would not sell well in a deli).

It's by supplementing with the above that I can at least prevent the poor quality of food from leading to a steep drop in energy levels or degeneration over time. Something that is easy to spot in people who have been here for a while. Anyone who has attended one of my annual health and vitality seminars will know many other methods I use too.

Hygiene

Hygiene management is paramount. One of the challenges is that sometimes, due to staff shortages, we get only three showers a week. Many of them either don't work or just dribble and even if you get to go, sometimes you are waiting too long for a cubicle. It's a common place for violence and a favourite place for your kit (towel, gel, clothes, etc.) to go missing. I know, I know, anyone would think there's a bunch of criminals in here! On the day we arrive, we are given one plastic plate, a bowl, a plastic knife, fork and spoon, and we have to wash those each time we use them in the little sink next to the toilet and with no provided detergent. Jinn and I take weekly turns in using one of our issued T-Shirts as a combined dishcloth and tea towel. There is black mould in many corners and little air circulation. This means that maintaining a positive attitude in here is not just good for your morale (and is rarer than my mythical cell-delivered fruit juice), but it is also critical for your immune system. In terms of bedding, we get two sheets and a very thin blanket (more like a tablecloth) that we can exchange once a week. However, the mattresses are never changed and likely play host to a large number of parasites who are happy with their rent-free accommodation and all you can eat nocturnal buffet. Oh, and some days, the toilet doesn't flush due to 'pipe work'.

But apart from all that, life is good and you are welcome to visit anytime!

Seriously, remember the pre-frame I gave about the difference between objective environment and subjective experience? One of these you have limited control over. The other you have total control over. I'll explain more when answering the next question, which asks what I've learned. Members of the Elite Mentorship Forum will understand *exactly* why I am able to have a very different subjective experience here than most. It's not luck or intellect that allows me to live (or at least strive towards living) in these conditions cheerfully while demonstrating, to the best of my abilities; grace, humility, compassion and love, along with a deep and authentic desire to help and make a difference. It's a learned and practised technique that now becomes automatic. Am I suffering in these conditions? No. I'm having a blast in spite of them! Would I prefer to be at home with Thea and the dogs, or on a stage or on a podcast helping others? Of course! However, I don't get to do that until after I've finished school and learned what I'm here to learn or demonstrate whatever I'm here to demonstrate - but I'm getting ahead of myself. Though it does lead nicely to the next question:

What Have I Learned And What Are The Biggest Lessons So Far?

As with most of my answers, there are various levels of awareness from which to view them.

For ease, let's simply split basic and advanced. I'll start with the basic level first, as if we start with an advanced perspective, it tends to invalidate the basic one (actually supersede is a better word than invalidate). There are always good lessons from both, however, I find that most of society is myopically hypnotised into only focusing on the basic levels of awareness and almost always by conditioning and conformity, rather than a lack of ability. If you are getting lost or confused, I'll give a quick parallel. Earlier, I mentioned about the health and vitality seminars that I teach once a year. We start by focusing on the basic level of physical health. This is also the sole area that over 95% of the health and fitness / wellness industry focuses on. It's also the least effective in terms of return on time and energy investment because we are dealing solely with the physical world which, when compared to the non-physical in energy terms, is slow and dense.

We then progress to the level of mental and emotional health. Once this is understood and factored in, we see immediate and significant *same-day improvements* in strength, flexibility and endurance. Why?

Because as every top-level coach knows, your mind is either your best or your worst training partner, depending on how you have been conditioned to use it.

We then progress to the advanced level where we learn how to work with and direct energy. This *always* produces the biggest increase in measurable results. In fact, we promise a minimum of a 20% strength increase in five days. Something that no personal trainer working at the basic level of just the physical could ever deliver on. But if you talk to anyone who has completed that event, you'll discover that 20% is usually the low end of the results that occur.

However, and here's my point: If I started teaching the advanced level first and how to direct energy, the results would be poor because there would be no basic foundation on which to build. There are valuable lessons to learn on each level but it's usually our ego that gets offended by starting at the bottom, even though it's a requirement of growth. As far as I can tell, none of us are born enlightened. Neither do we start college on our first day of school. We start kindergarten. It's the same here. If I want to write these updates in a way that adds the most value to you, I need to demonstrate there are different levels of awareness and learning, and that each will resonate with you depending on where you are on your own journey. It doesn't matter if we don't get every lesson on every level, or if you agree with what I say or not – what is important is that we get what we need individually.

I'll give you a real example. From a basic perspective, me being in here has provided the perfect opportunity for those who follow my work to decide if they wish to continue. Some will see this as the perfect opportunity and positive confirmation that I'm genuine. That I don't just talk a good and positive game, but I can also demonstrate it when tested under tough and real-world conditions. That what I teach, I live. You'll put the situation into context. For example, one of the main reasons I'm here (circumstantially, not bigger picture) is because my former CEO, Carolyn, was paid money that she was owed and allowed to be paid under the terms of a freezing order. An order I assert was illegally obtained through false pretences by HP. It seemed obvious to me that they fabricated a fake loss that clearly never happened on a series of business deals we did years ago that they profited handsomely from and then retrospectively tried to apply terms that I was never bound by. All so that they could claim more profit on the very deals they already made a profit on (not loss) and helped set up. It's a classic chess move, and they are skilled players. That's all. It's nothing sinister and doesn't change who I am or what I teach.

You'll realise things like this happen and that even Sir Richard Branson went to jail for a deliberate VAT fraud. Does that stop me wanting to learn from him or think less of him? Of course not. He made a mistake, learned from it and moved on. Personally, I'll study him, learn from him and even appreciate him any chance I get, regardless of the mistakes he's made. More importantly, you'll weigh up in your own mind the value my work has to you. That's all that really counts at the end of the day.

For others, they may see this as a perfect opportunity and positive confirmation that I am not genuine. They will focus on their own selective aspects and use it to justify why they are right and I am wrong. And, hopefully, they will seek out helpful information to improve their life from somewhere else. Both answers are perfect from the relative perspective of whatever level the person is at and I have no issues with either of them. I will simply continue to add value and love you all regardless. Whether the glass is half full or half empty doesn't change the volume of the glass, it only reflects your perspective of it. We are all on our own journey and trying to do the best we can. In my last update, I also warned you about what happens when we create false gurus or put people on pedestals. We become smaller by contrast. This is one of the big problems with the personal development industry, which is full of people who position themselves as 'better than' those they preach and sell to. Something that I have been very focused on and vocal about trying to change.

From an advanced perspective, I'm very grateful for what has happened. How this situation has been orchestrated at a higher level of intelligence is irrelevant. It has given me a huge amount already. Apart from a complete break from what was becoming an incessant bombardment of emails, calls, texts, WhatsApps, social media, meetings, engagements, and more. I mean, think about it. Short of booking myself on a several-week meditation retreat back in the mountains of 'South Korea' (which I've been trying to get back to for three years) or a total societal meltdown, which could be a possibility at some point in the next ten to twenty years, due to the global reliance on a finite supply of cheap oil, where else or how else could I possibly get the (head) space needed to have some long overdue time-out and self-reflection?

One of the many benefits of being here is that it has reconnected me with my passion for writing (although not so much with a pen!). This is something I've been trying to carve time out for, for nearly four years! As mentioned earlier, it's also given me a practical classroom rather than a theoretical one to operate from. The chance to see if I can really cope when the chips are down; whether I pass or fail my current exam in practising what I preach. Will I succeed? That's not for you to decide. It's MY test. Just as you will (and are) attracting yours. It's what a basic level of awareness calls problems. The challenge is that most of us are too busy judging other people's tests to focus on passing our own. This may provide a welcome distraction for the ego, but it does little to raise our own game.

For some of you, the test is dealing with me being in here. Think about it. If this has inconvenienced you, are you using it as a way to justify being a victim? Or a way to embrace (rather than avoid) your own lessons in the most empowering way you can? Only you can decide, and you probably wouldn't want to swap classrooms. My only advice is that if you fail any of your own tests, learning opportunities, graduation events or whatever else you want to call your challenges, then life will simply have you re-sit the same exams with different circumstances. Don't take my word for it. Your own history is the only place you need to look. The sad fact is many of us have spent years repeating the same class over and over in 'Life School' and wonder why National Stress Day teams up with Slow Progress Day to form Groundhog Day. No wonder entertainment, media, drugs, drink and leisure travel (collectively known as distraction) have become the dominant industries they have, and in the meantime, we continue to believe that we can actually get fit in life's gym without picking up the weights.

If you want to see evidence of this, look at what happens when people get unearned income, specifically state benefits, lottery winnings or inheritance (yes, where there's a will, there's a relative!). When it comes to receiving benefits, statistics show a continuous drop in resourcefulness and motivation. After an initial euphoria, many lottery winners suffer from long-term unhappiness. And when it comes to inheritance, nearly all of us know families and siblings that have fallen out, leaving lifelong blood-based relationships torn apart and irreparably damaged. All because we wanted to shortcut the growth process and get something for nothing. The elusive magic pill that would make us lose weight without changing our dietary habits. Am I mixing too many metaphors? The main point being here guys, and thanks for bearing with me, is this: *We don't get what we want in life – we get what we need in order to grow.* That's my biggest lesson here. Along with the following rule that goes with it – please listen carefully: The control over *which* lessons are delivered in the classroom of Life, is determined at the local level by the choices we make. If we choose to be egocentric in a relationship, then we'll likely get the lesson pertinent to that. However, the control over *how* those lessons are delivered and under what circumstances is handled at a higher level. Why? Because if it were left up to us, we would choose the lessons and circumstances we *want* and not the lessons we need or that would cause us the most growth. That's why they have to be chosen for us. Remember, the tree may not like the storm, but the strongest trees grow in the strongest winds, not the best soil.

There is also another critical aspect to this that many people forget. The very definition of learning in the classroom setting of life means that we must be able to give the wrong answer as well as the right one. Or there would be no point in the lesson. After all, if you are the smartest money in the room, then find a smarter room. Anything preventing that is ego. In other words, by having the ability to choose the answers we give (also known as free will), we get a better opportunity to learn. In fact, wrong answers (decisions, choices, etc.) can be, and usually are, more powerful teachers than right ones. Providing, of course, that we do learn, which brings me to my final question in this part of the update.

Do I Have Any Regrets About What Has Happened?

I'm probably going to disappoint some of you now and answer with an honest *no*. However, before your judgement machines kick in, bear with me as this could be one of the most profound insights so far if you are open to seeing it. Of course, I certainly and absolutely have empathy for others who have been affected in any way by my previous decisions or poor answers given in class. I fully appreciate there have been repercussions that have both inconvenienced and tested others whose lives overlap. This includes all of my coaching groups. All people who bought tickets to the upcoming Sage Business School that has had to be rescheduled and, of course, my staff (team), family, loyal fans and followers, etc. And to those of you who have inadvertently suffered (i.e. got dragged along to the gym), I want you to know that it's been one of the toughest parts of my workout to deal with and I'm genuinely sorry for whatever knock-on effect this has had. Helping people and not hindering them is the backbone of the purpose of my life and something I couldn't change, even if I wanted to. Hurting anyone is never my intention. Giving and doing what I can to help *is*. It's also from that level of understanding that I'm going to ask you to please listen to the next sentence from the place I'm trying to deliver it. I genuinely do not have any regrets about what has happened. Now, this may seem in contrast to what I just said or even invalidate the empathy I'm conveying to you and for those who have been thrown a curve ball by me being here. So why do I say that? Simple. Regretting *anything* in life is not only useless but also highly destructive. This is because regret has its roots in grief and commonly leads to guilt. And if there is one emotion that is equivalent to cancer in the human psyche, then guilt is it!

Many of you have heard my teachings on guilt. I've even had one lady, Kate, write to me in here only last week, telling me how her life has changed since being able to transcend the guilt she'd been carrying for years (thank you, Kate – give your radiance fearlessly!). Guilt is one emotion where you stand alone, cast as the victim of your own judgement. It is self-defeating and traps you in an inescapable loop, anchored in a fictional past (hence inescapable). When I say fictional past, I don't mean it didn't happen (obviously), I mean that it no longer exists from the perspective of 'now'. It's also worth noting that there's a fair amount of credible research that suggests much of what we 'think' we remember didn't actually happen, at least not in the way we claim to remember it. If you want to let go of some of that, instead of carrying around a story, then remembering my definition of the past may be helpful: *The past is nothing more than a 'present time memory of our <u>perception</u> of a previous event, with the imagination filling in most of the blanks and <u>all</u> of the meaning'.* And yes, if I had a keyboard instead of a pen, I'd say that again!

In a similar way to fear, regrets serve no useful purpose. None. Don't kid yourself by thinking otherwise. Like my good friend, Prosper, says: "The past can be a useful place of reference, but it's a poor place of residence!" Unfortunately, many people fail to heed that distinction. We cannot change the past – period. But by looking intelligently and objectively at the poor choices we've made and analysing previous decisions, we can make better choices that serve the greater good and not just our ego. This is what Dr Joe Dispenza, a gifted scientist and consciousness researcher (and whose work I am a big fan of), would call 'turning your past to wisdom'. It is also an absolute prerequisite to a better life where the term 'better' is defined as one where we don't stay at the same level in 'Life School' year after year.

A far more powerful question to ask ourselves is not 'Do I have any regrets?' but instead, 'Would I do anything different in the same situation today?' And the answer to that, my friends, is a resounding Yes! To explain more would take us briefly into the details of the civil action that HP threw at me, which is not my intention even though a few of you have asked, but it will serve to share some lessons that I think we may all benefit from. In short, knowing what I now know, I wouldn't have gotten involved with the HP deals all those years ago. I had my reasons at the time - a separate profit centre and revenue stream to keep my company, Space Energy, going. This was after I'd invested my own fortune, along with other investors, over a number of years. It seemed a complete win-win with all parties, including HP, making a profit. (Note - HP will not disclose their profit, despite numerous requests to do so, as it would completely undermine their claim to a fabricated loss, even though it is extremely likely that they made much more than anyone else involved in the deal).

I mean, step into my common-sense corner for a moment. HP sells me $12.5 million worth of goods and is paid in full. They know openly and at various levels that it was being resold at a very small margin to other resellers, some of whom pay HP directly. HP themselves provide no contract or *any* written terms and conditions that prevent me or my company from reselling any of the equipment I buy. Then, several years later and in a different country, they sue me out of the blue claiming a "loss" of $17.5 million which, they say, is the difference between the wholesale price they sold it to me at and the retail price in store. In short, they subtracted the $12.5m I paid at wholesale from the $30m retail price and tried to charge me the $17.5m difference. This is irrespective of the fact that HP didn't provide any contract preventing resale and that nobody in the history of buying from Hewlett Packard has (or ever would) buy $30m of goods at a retail store. It's absurd to even think so. They then turn around within an hour of serving me a freezing order and state they'd be happy to settle out of court for a minute fraction of that, amounting to about half the profit I'd made on the deal. They also then try to twist the terms of the freezing order to state they could take my fiancée's engagement ring when it clearly belonged to her, she wasn't named in the order and she didn't even know me when HP and I were doing business together.

At the time, I viewed this as blatant and legalised extortion. Playground bullying with the size of the bully being the size of the legal muscles that could be flexed. They were wrong and I was going to prove it. And that, ladies & gentleman, was my biggest problem - an attachment to how right I thought I was.

Never Fight with a Pig (especially a huge one)

Upon reflection, and when searching for the lessons, it's been easy to see that the above created a huge ego-trap and I fell right into it. What I should have done is see this for what it was. A lesson I learned many years ago from Dan Pena, one of my three business mentors, was that in the business world, litigation is little more than a tool. It's a chess move, that's all. It has virtually zero to do with who's wrong or who's right, which incidentally, is *always* a subjective interpretation of the 'perceived' objective facts (which is why, in the courtroom arena, it's who can tell the best story of *their version* of the facts). If facts were purely objective, there would be no need for a court of appeal. In other words, most litigation is theatre with the best actors taking the prize. Forget ethics and morality for a second. They may play a role, but it is usually secondary to the main agendas. When Apple sued Samsung over patent infringements in Germany, the reality was it had less to do with patent infringements per se and everything to do with the timing of Apple trying to block sales of Samsung's products at the Berlin electronics fair, causing them to lose up to half a million unit sales and allowing Apple a head start in the market.

Are you getting the picture? The patent argument was the vehicle for the chess move. HP wasn't suing me over a real $17.5 million loss. It was merely a vehicle designed to pressure me into a settlement, knowing that I would (and have) spent more in legal costs to fight it. 'Check', your move. In order to get the upper hand and obtain the freezing order ex-parte (i.e. without me knowing), they had to construct the premise and present to the judge that Space Energy was fake. Without which it would likely never have been granted and I would have rebutted their argument from the outset. The fact I have since delivered over 2000 (yes two thousand) pages verifying the years of work and effort and investment (from myself and many others) to show the nature, credibility and efforts of Space Energy is proof of that. Also, it is important to note that, as part of the transparency, those pages are available to anyone who wants to see them at www.petersage.com/space-energy. However, all of this misses the point that *I completely missed the point*! My ego was so caught up in the need to prove that I was right, that I let *my* contempt for what I thought *they* were doing, land me in contempt of court. And I didn't even see it coming.

What I should have done was let go of my need to be right by sitting down with HP and listening to their side. Only then could I have made an objective and intelligent evaluation, in order to assess the best outcome for both sides.

Here are lessons from my two other business mentors. First from Errol Abramson; He often states that ego is expensive. I guess I needed an experiential lesson of this rather than an intellectual one. My other mentor, Peter Thomas, wrote a book called Never Fight with a Pig. In other words, choose your battles. Some just aren't worth it. It would have been a lot easier to read that than pick a fight with a hundred-billion-dollar company, backed by a hundred-million-dollar ruthless law firm. Oops.

My only hope is that in some way this example may help you with your own lessons, either now or at some point in the future. Though it probably falls short of making amends to those of you I've let down. Sorry guys.

In addition, much has been said in regards to the judge's comments. Again, my mistake was venting my frustration at the other side, rather than calmly explaining my side to Justice Jay. Instead, I made him a witness to a 'he said, she said' game of who's right and wrong. And with the (total) absence of an equivalent quality of professional representation on my side, it was evident that he viewed me as an indignant, unremorseful bad guy and wrote what amounted to a character assassination. Do I blame him? Of course not. He actually seems to be a really decent and fair-minded Judge. He was simply doing his job and drew his own conclusions based on the information he had, albeit heavily influenced by HP's proficient Silk level QC who was also doing his job; to paint the worst possible picture of me they could. 'Checkmate'.

Does the Judge really know me? Of course not. How can he? He can only know me as much as I know him, i.e. very little. I don't know if he's fun at parties or goes to pub quizzes, if he goes out at night and anonymously helps the homeless or if he has a mistress (which, for the avoidance of doubt, I am not suggesting). My point being, it takes a lot more than a few questions in a contrived and emotionally charged setting to know someone. A fact every parent is blatantly aware of is that even a five-year-old can make you look stupid with the right questions, so I'm not concerned with the perception that came out of that, and I'm deeply touched that many of you have sent in messages of support agreeing on the same. After all, most followers of my work are infinitely more qualified to make a more accurate assessment.

In summary, yes there are things I would do differently. But that, my friends, is the nature of the classroom. Both poor and good choices *have* to be available and we don't always get it right. Hence, it would pay to remember that no one is as noble as their best deeds, nor anyone as lowly as their worst.

Of course, the above is another analysis of the basic level on the material side. I've covered my thoughts on the more advanced level reasons as to why I am here in the previous updates. However, *both* levels of awareness offer valuable lessons and insight that I believe are designed to help steer us towards a path of growth. Remember what I said earlier? We don't get to choose *how* our lessons are delivered (neither the classroom setting nor the circumstances of our challenges). We only get to influence *which* are the most appropriate lessons we need to learn, based on the choices we make and how we show up. Physics and metaphysics work in harmony with the agenda of shepherding our growth towards less ego and higher awareness (ultimately Love). You may want to read these last two (or more) paragraphs again to really get the significance of what was just said. Do the lessons ever stop? No, but when we realise that *Life is a growth-centric experience*, then we can start to see our challenges in a different light. Our job is not to pass every single test first time but rather, it's to avoid being trapped in a repeating pattern of the same lessons over and over. What causes most people to get stuck? Glad you asked.

There are many things that trap us in a repetitive cycle of negative thinking but the most common, in my opinion, is an addiction to our 'why I am a victim' story. This keeps us trapped because, as we repeat the story, it affirms and reaffirms who we believe we are. This robs us of our ability to change because it fails to recognise that, although who we are today is a result of our previous decisions, who we are *becoming* is a result of the choices we make now. Make choices as a victim, stay a victim. Let go of the story and start making choices from a better place and watch life get better. It may not happen instantly, but what most people miss is that it's the direction of travel that is important. Not sitting and failing the same exam time after time, nor beating ourselves up for failing to get a 100% test score.

My final gift I'll leave you with before moving on will hopefully help you deal with and avoid any regrets you have. I know many people are not happy with parts of their life, in some form or another. This is the first step on the path of unhappiness and a fertile ground for regret and guilt, as we endlessly and pointlessly run scenarios in our head that start with 'what if I'd done this' or 'if only I'd done that'. How do we shift this? Well, the answer is counterintuitive but bear with me.

Many of you may be familiar with one of my most quoted phrases on the web that states: *'Complaining about our current circumstances is the glue that keeps us tied to them'*. And while it is natural for most people to complain about what they don't like or want, it usually traps us on a hamster wheel of more of the same. The key to stepping off the wheel is to see the perfection in what things are and not judge them for what we don't want them to be. If that sounds confusing, let me demonstrate.

We do not look at a baby and judge it for being an imperfect adult. We see it as a perfect baby. We do not look at an acorn and judge it for being an imperfect oak tree. We see it as a perfect acorn. Likewise, when it is a sapling, we see it as a perfect sapling. So the next time you look at your empty bank balance, do not judge it for being an imperfect full one. It's simply a perfectly empty one. When we see it this way, there's much less negative charge around it and we can let go of the energy we were putting into complaining and instead start focusing on the actions required to fill it up.

Are you getting the picture? The answer to the question 'What's wrong with right now?' is always *nothing*. Everything else is a fear-based projection based on what our ego wants the present to look like. Is it starting to make sense? Why can I be in here and still be happy? This prison is a perfect example of exactly what is. Not in spite of the description I gave but *because* of it! (I gave an insight into this in Volume 1 where I describe my experience on the bus looking at the alley). From this place, there is no resistance. From this place there are no complaints and therefore, not only do you unglue yourself energetically from what you thought you didn't want, but you now have more energy freed up to make (hopefully) better choices with. This is how to develop an empowering inner world where the weeds of regret that normally blossom into guilt cannot take root. It also allows you to take strides forward to where it is you *do* want to go, i.e. a more loving relationship, better job, higher bank balance, etc. All of which is much easier when you are not tripping yourself up, by focusing on what you think is an imperfect 'now'.

Personal Update

I'll try to keep this section brief as I've already gone on way longer in previous sections than I intended, although I hope it has offered some useful insights and perspectives. Also, in the interests of keeping this as real as I can, I thought instead of sharing the things I've done and the inmates I've helped (and I'm blessed by the fact there has already been so many), I'd share with you my lowest times. The times I've struggled and the times I've cried.

The outer environment is what it is and not much can be done with it. The inner world, however, is far more easily managed with the right tools than most people realise. In writing these letters, my wish has been to show you how I apply those tools, so you can too. Just like a fly banging against a window when there is an open one next to it, it only takes a slight adjustment to make a big difference. But if you are not aware, you can die still banging your head against the glass.

For example, being in the cell may sound bad but it is a real palace compared to some places I've willingly been. I remember an orphanage in Bungoma, rural Kenya, that I spent some time teaching at. I also did a magic show for the entire kids and staff. It was fun and rewarding, but the basic standard of living was poor. Electricity was available for less than one hour a day, and in our tiny mud huts, cockroaches didn't worry us, but deadly puff adders, scorpions and soldier ants certainly did. Remember the contrast frame technique I spoke of in Volume 1? Perspective changes everything and rather than complain, it's easy to be grateful that there are no snakes, scorpions or soldier ants in Pentonville.

Another point to note, is that humans are not meant to be happy all of the time. Happiness, despite how hard many chase it, is a transient emotion that is nothing more than the result of thinking happy thoughts. That's it. It's just that many of us have rules around how the outer world must look before we give ourselves permission to think those happy thoughts and so go on a quest to find it. But happiness is still just an emotion and, as humans, we are designed to experience a range of emotions. I didn't want to be happy at my mother's funeral. I wanted to grieve. However, I was content. I was OK. There were no unfinished conversations. She was out of pain and I understood that it's every parent's wish that their children outlive them. Happiness is not something that we are meant to feel all the time. Just as we are not meant to get the right answers in class all of the time. And, especially when it comes to emotions, we are designed to feel and experience them all. The main question is not 'do you experience happiness rather than sadness?', but 'which do you experience most or least?' In other words, where do you live and where do you visit? If you live in stress and occasionally visit joy, that's a very different life than say, living in peace and occasionally visiting fear. You get the idea. For me, I aim to live at the happier end of the spectrum but that does not mean I don't visit the other side too. The lowest moments I've had, unsurprisingly, were to do with missing Thea. The first time I felt my lowest moment was when she came for her second visit. A 200-mile round trip that she's only allowed to make twice a month (standard for a B-Cat prison). As you can imagine, I was SO looking forward to seeing her you have no idea. We spoke that morning before she boarded the train to London, so I knew she was coming. Visits are strictly 2-4pm and often shorter, as it can take up to an hour for them to process and search the visitors. They take place in a big school-hall type room with bolted down plastic seats and around forty or so inmates under constant supervision. When the time neared 2pm, they failed to collect me from my cell. I remember watching the little clock we have tick past 2pm, then 2.30pm, then 3pm, wondering why they weren't coming and what had gone wrong.

It turns out that one of the people she was meant to be coming with and who was due to meet her at the prison, had changed his mind and had cancelled the visit online without telling her. With the visit officially cancelled, they turned her away at the gate and I was left in the cell. At this point, my heart sank to its rock bottom. I like to think I can handle anything in here but man, that was a low blow.

Eventually, a combination of me banging on the door and convincing an officer to escort me to the visit hall (thank God for rapport) plus an amazing effort from Pa Joof, who was a surprise guest with Thea and did the convincing on the other side, we managed to catch the last 20-30 minutes of visit time. Although, as they let her in, it counted as a full visit and means at the time of writing this, I have been here for six weeks and the total face time I've had with her has been two and a half hours.

I've cried since then. The first, surprisingly enough, was while speaking to Thea on the phone when the dogs came in and she put me on speakerphone, so they could hear my voice. (Dog owners would understand). I just broke down. Thea asked me why I cried for the dogs but not for her. Reflecting, I responded that I get to speak to her most days. She knows where I am and what's happening. I feel more than ever that we are a team. The dogs have no clue. They just know that I'm missing. That I went out one day and never came back. You may not get that or what it means to me, but dogs have always been a big part of my life and are the best example I know of unconditional love. It's a fact that the two hardest talks I ever did were the closing eulogy at both my mother's and father's funerals. Especially my mum's as she was the last living close relative (I have no brothers, sisters, grandparents, etc.). However, holding my previous dog, Jack, as he was put down by the vet was the hardest thing I've ever done. Those who know me, know my connection and affinity to dogs (sometimes to the annoyance of Thea).

This started when I was three years old and my dad would take me to work with him. He owned a scrap yard in the days way before health and safety. So, to keep me safe in a dangerous environment, he would lock me in the cage with the guard dog, Sandy, who would look after me. She was a big German Shepherd and an ex-police dog. Since then, I've always had a special connection with dogs. I really do see them as the epitome of unconditional love, more so than we humans who have many rules that govern and restrict our willingness to demonstrate it. And in that moment on the phone with Thea, I realised how much I missed that and how it contrasted massively to life in here. There is no love in here, virtually no compassion and very few smiles. And the rarest sound you will hear is laughter.

The only other time I cried was when Thea and I had an argument on the phone. She's doing such a great job of trying to hold things together out there and has been put into a position she didn't ask for. Talk about being dragged along to the gym for her own workout and she's taking a lot of abuse from people who are taking a one-sided view of what has happened. I feel like a caged tiger for not being able to help her or take on the role I normally do as leader. Frustrations were high and by the time my minutes ran out (you only get a short amount of time allowed per call with no re-dial), I didn't have time to say sorry. It was a massive low moment and probably the lowest so far. However, the problem with crying on the phone is that it shows weakness and vulnerability to the other inmates and singles you out right away as a target for bullying and extortion. The phones are at the end of the landing and it gives the term 'walk of shame' a sinister new meaning.

Why am I sharing all this? Firstly, to be real with you and show you it's not all roses. Just as in your lives outside there are challenges we all face and like you, I'm trying to do the best I can with what I have. I also know that each of our own hero's journey has a dark night of the soul. What this has showed me is that the darkest nights do not come from losing anything material, such as money, reputation or work but instead, are connected to the perceptual absence of love. Do you think life is trying to teach us something?

On to more positive things…

Prison Initiative (AKA Operation Chrysalis)

There have been great things happening since my last update with some good progress to report. Having outlined my proposal in a detailed letter to the Governor, I received a very enthusiastic reply. So far so good.

Now, if you recall, phase one of my four phase plan to help the prison system was centred on creating a New Prisoner Welcome Booklet which would help new prisoners cope with the environment, give them tools to improve their mindset and generally set them up to win.

This includes the story I wrote and shared with you last issue called, *'Mud or Stars?'*. To see if it would actually have an impact, I decided to run a little test. During a rare and opportune moment in the education section, I found myself unsupervised near a print terminal. You didn't need to ask me twice and I quickly managed to run off about fifty copies before I heard someone coming and had to pull the plug. I then 'secretly' distributed them all over the prison, when and wherever I got the chance. I did this at various times, when walking to and from education, on what we call free-flow or going to the Sunday church service. You get the idea. I left them on tables and on noticeboards in other wings as I passed by. I even slid them under cell doors like a secret mailman.

At the top of each one it said: 'Mud or Stars? – A Prisoner's Story. Read, Enjoy and Pass On'. That seems to have been taken to heart, and the response has blown me away. So many people are talking about it and saying how much it helped make a difference. I'm not looking for credit and although I wrote it anonymously, I still get many people coming to the cell to say thank you. It was even mentioned in the weekly Christian church service by the Reverend 'Roc' who also read it and is recommending to everyone that they get hold of a copy. Not only that but it has also been put forward as the lead feature in the prison magazine, 'Voice of the Ville'.

However, the most humbling aspect for me is that the staff asked if it could be submitted for something called the 'Koestler Awards', a National Prison Competition and Exhibition. This is exciting because it has the potential to reach many more people and in many more places than just Pentonville. I agreed to do so (again, anonymously) and I'm sharing this with you guys as I'm thrilled about the potential numbers it could help.

The only other news to update you on in here, is the drama that happened as a result of the seminar I mentioned in the last issue that I was asked to deliver in the library. I called it, 'The Ultimate Inmate Workshop – How to turn your boredom into brilliance'. I designed a powerful three-hour event, created a poster and started enrolling people. However, I soon ran into a challenge. In fact, it was the one problem area I was kind of expecting to show up at some point, though it is still disappointing when it does. It also acts like Kryptonite to creative or entrepreneurial thinking. Yes, welcome to red tape and organisational politics, known universally as bureaucracy.

What happened? Well, when one of the Wing Governors found out I was running a seminar, he flipped his lid and put an immediate halt to the initiative. This was despite the fact that I'd been encouraged to do this by the staff and had already signed up the maximum number of people in less than a day. In other words, I had demonstrated serious interest. Part of the reason for his reaction, I was told, was that he just doesn't want people to better themselves inside but prefers instead to induce a sheep-like conformity of low-level thinking. Not too dissimilar to a former Justice Secretary who ridiculously decided that all books in prison should be banned.

Another reason I found out the workshop was cancelled could only be labelled as comical. On the poster advertising the event, I mentioned all attendees would get a free gift. This was going to be a copy of 'Mud or Stars?'. I also stated that there were prizes for participation and here's where things get silly. Rewarding participation is a basic teaching technique that encourages interactivity. The 'prizes' I planned to use were sweets and biscuits bought with my own money on my weekly canteen sheet and that I intended to give away. In addition, I had two copies of 'Think and Grow Rich' left from the five that Thea had sent in. OK, so it wasn't a new car, cuddly toy or a holiday but as a prison 'prize fund', it was the best I could do. However, when the Governor saw I was giving away 'prizes', he thought I was planning to distribute drugs, not books or biscuits. I know, you couldn't make it up but that's what he thought! So, with the Ultimate Inmate Workshop taking a bureaucratic setback, I need to get creative on how else I can deliver it. However, I do have a plan...stay tuned.

The Syllabus – Meditation

OK, let's move on to the final part of this update as we switch gears and go into the syllabus and learning. In this section, I want to cover a subject many have written to me about and attempt to engage in but also struggle to get to grips with, and that is Meditation. And while there are some useful videos on the subject on my YouTube channel, I want to offer some insights here that may really help those of you who are either new to the practice or are struggling to understand it.

At home, I have my own purpose designed meditation room. This makes it easier because it creates a supportive environment. There are candles, statues, incense and other objects which help set the scene. In my cell, I meditate next to the toilet and there are always multiple distractions, from shouting to screaming and from banging doors to second-hand drug smoke. It's a tough environment to meditate in by usual standards but I've learned over the years to calm my mind virtually anywhere.

Before I share one of the keys to doing that, I want to make an important distinction between two types and approaches to meditation, both of which serve different purposes and need to be viewed and understood separately. I'm talking about Passive Meditation and Active Meditation. In this Volume I'll cover Passive Mediation, as it is the starting point and where most people get stuck. In Volume 4, I will go into depth on Active Meditation which can get really sexy and blends the latest science of quantum mechanics with some powerful traditional insights. As usual, I'll try to keep it as simple and real as I can while throwing in some metaphors to try and simplify things. But buckle up, as what I want to share here and in the next Volume can be life-changing for those who are interested and have the intention and discipline to apply it.

Let's start with what most people associate with meditation or what I call 'Passive Meditation'. This centres on turning down the volume of data that is streaming in from our physical and mental channels. Most people are familiar with getting into a quiet place and closing their eyes and this does a good job of reducing the data from the senses or physical channel. But then they tend to struggle with information still coming in from the mental channel. Part of this happens precisely because we lessen the noise coming in via our physical senses. Just like wearing a blindfold during intimacy, taking one sense away can cause the others to become heightened. But when we take all physical senses away, the mind finds it easier to fill the gap and this is where people struggle.

The way that I approach Passive Meditation is by maintaining conscious awareness, while at the same time separating myself from the identity of the body and mind. Notice I didn't say stop trying to think. Where most people go wrong, is by trying to use the mind to stop the mind. An organising principle here is to realise that who you are is not your mind. You HAVE a mind. Just as who you are is not your body. You HAVE a body. This is easily demonstrated by acknowledging the fact that, if you were to lose an arm, you might have around 15% less body but you would still be 100% 'You'. There wouldn't be a sudden loss of 15% of your personality, vocabulary or your memories. The body from this perspective can be seen as a tool or a vehicle for 'You' (which is conscious awareness) to ride around in and experience physical reality.

The mind, as we will demonstrate, is also a tool for 'You' to use. Though it's easier to confuse the mind with the real 'You' because, unlike the body, both the mind and consciousness are based in the non-physical. The fact that the mind cannot be 'You' is easily demonstrated because if it were, then the times you didn't think, your sense of self would disappear. In fact, what happens is the opposite. When the mind is put into silence or left speechless, say by the beauty of a sunset or when deeply connected to making love with your partner, you feel even more alive. That's because the real 'You' is way beyond the mind. However, so the mind can try and identify that part (i.e. the real 'You'), under the rules of its perpetual labelling, we give it one. It's called 'Consciousness'.

The problem begins when the mind thinks it's in charge or worse, thinks it IS consciousness. This is a nail in the meditation coffin because if the mind identifies itself *as* consciousness (i.e. 'You') then no separation can take place. I'll give you a parallel example. If someone goes to the doctors and is told they are diabetic, and they choose to believe that and adopt that identity, they become stuck as it is now who they *are* and they can only manage the symptoms. If, instead, they don't see themselves as a diabetic but rather a person whose body is suffering from the condition known as diabetes, they stand a far better chance of treating and curing it successfully, as many thousands of people have. It is this sense of separation between your identity and the disease that creates a gap, allowing a greater possibility of healing to enter. It is also the sense of separation between your sense of self and your mind and body that allows for greater and deeper meditations.

Therefore, the first question is how do you pull the rug out from under the mind? The answer is found in taking away its primary need: Significance. Also known as the Ego.

By standing on a foundation of its own importance, the mind is quick to jump up and be in charge. This is largely conditioned by modern education which rewards the logical part of the mind for giving the right answers. It also, inadvertently, sets up a life-long habit of doing so.

Sitting back and analysing what the mind does most of the time is quite revealing. When we do, we discover majority function is nothing more than a second-rate commentary. Unless the mind is directed by an intelligent or useful purpose, it delivers a useless and incessant stream of poor quality jibber jabber which amounts to nothing more than biased opinion, vanity, rationalisations (which lead to all kinds of judgements) and a fixation with playing and re-playing old data, so as to justify and re-justify current moods, feelings and emotions. Many of which then become addictive at a biochemical level. In short, we become attached to and start defining ourselves by our 'story'.

Of course, because the ego hijacks the ownership of all thoughts, labelling them as 'mine', letting go of them undermines its primary need, i.e. Significance. This is why it rarely, if ever, looks in the mirror of honest self-reflection. If it did, it would come to the sobering realisation that, unless it is serving a specific and useful purpose (like solving a problem), all of its standard dribble is both unnecessary and largely irrelevant. When faced and confronted with this awareness, the pedestal of grandeur it stands on is brought down to earth and the mind is humbled by its own gaucheness. This is similar to a two-year-old learning for the first time, that the world does not revolve around them.

In other words, showing the mind the *in*significance of its childish ramblings, creates a space for it to be given permission to be quiet as humility, not ego, fills the gap. This causes consciousness to naturally rise and helps with passive meditation as the mind is now shown to be separate from the larger sense of Self. The mind can now be 'observed' rather than identified with. This also allows you to give up the 'goose chase' of running after the state of 'no thought' and actually sit as if you have already arrived at the state you were 'seeking'. Even if the mind does (predictably) throw its rattle out of the crib and start streaming thoughts, you, as the parent, are still in the perfect place of just observing it. This way, as the mind learns respect for the Self, you will adjust to the peace and joy of silence, out of which thought arises, rather than pandering to the neediness tantrums of the mind/ego demanding attention.

As with anything, it takes practice and a willingness to let go of the addictions of thought. This is why it is far better not to engage in the battle but instead, rise above the noise by separating one's identity from the childish justifications of the mind. This way it becomes easier to relate to it in the same way a loving parent relates to a grumpy toddler. With compassion and understanding but ultimately disassociation from the drama and noise.

Well my dear and amazing friends, I think that should probably bring our time together to a close for this issue.

Thank you SO much for reading. Hopefully, I will have been transferred to an open facility by the time you get my next update. The fact that I have been kept in Pentonville for so long, amongst some of the most vicious and hardened criminals in the UK, only serves to deepen my belief that I am exactly where I need to be, in order to help the people who need it most. Like Oliver, who I will tell you more about next time. A crack and heroin addict for fifteen years who got six months for robbing somebody with a knife at a cashpoint. He's never been shown a way out of his past until he befriended me a couple of weeks ago. That story will continue next time but needless to say, there are lessons for all of us to learn from the most unlikely places. I have certainly been a student in here as much as a teacher, and it has been a massively humbling and inspiring experience.

Until next time,

Big Hug,

Peter X

Volume 4: Against the Tide (Week 8)

In Volume four, Peter shares his thoughts on how the power of entrepreneurial thinking can be harnessed to improve the prison system. We are introduced to some of the many prisoners he's now working with and coaching. He also shares a secret on how to get your Cardio workout done in sixty seconds with a powerful health hack. In the syllabus section, he continues on from Volume 3, delving into the intriguing aspect of Active Meditation. Be prepared to learn some fascinating insights which blend philosophy, quantum mechanics, manifestation and the ageless practice of mindfulness.

My dear and amazing family, students and friends

Welcome to Volume 4 of my adventures inside. Yesterday was my two-month anniversary and after much deliberation, I decided to celebrate with a quiet night in.

At present, I am still checked into 'Hotel Pentonville' and as such, I still have to handwrite everything. The challenge now is that I can only write for short periods as I'm getting a lot of pain in my hand and joints from the sixty hours of writing so far. Hopefully, as soon as I'm transferred to where I should be, i.e. an open prison, I'll have access to a keyboard.

Speaking of transfers, since I had heard nothing, I managed to persuade an officer from the OMU department (those in charge of transfers), to check the computer and find out what the status was. I was subsequently informed that, despite over a dozen written and formal applications over the last two months, there was no record of any of my transfer requests. To be honest, from what I've seen and experienced here, it's no surprise. The system is so archaically flawed and inefficient, it is appalling. The fact that someone who hasn't even been charged with a crime, is locked up in a High-Security Cat-B prison amongst some of the most hardened and dangerous criminals in the country, is a constant source of amusement to me. The irony of being here because of contempt of a system which clearly has contempt for its own rules, makes me chuckle.

I'm sure it will resolve itself and I'll be moved at some point, but until then I'll continue to help the people here as best I can. However, even that has taken a small setback as my available time out of the cell has been drastically cut. Do you recall my comments last issue about one of the Governors not supporting the workshop that my teacher encouraged me to set up? Well, they took it a step further and subsequently banned me from all education, in-prison employment and even going to the library. All without telling me, questioning me or seeking feedback in any way. In doing so, they breached several Prison Service regulations and contravened European Law and the upshot is, they just don't care. It's as if they operate as their own little fiefdom with arrogance, impunity and with each of the many left hands not knowing what the right hands are doing. In energetic terms, it's a classic case of apathetic allegiance to the status quo. We see this in companies who fall in love with their own dominance rather than embrace innovation, and the result is commercial suicide. Just think of examples such as; Kodak, Nokia, Myspace or Blockbuster. The impact is worse when it applies to an entity like a prison because there is less accountability and therefore little incentive to do anything other than the minimum required. In the syllabus section later, I'll cover a law of nature which shows the difference between entities that decay by default, rather than consciously express energy into growing (improving) and contributing. The prison system in its current form is decaying rapidly and, to many on the outside, the scale of the rot is invisible. The sad fact is, instead of commercial suicide, it's the inmates who are ten times more likely to kill themselves.

To me, it's obvious where the major flaws are and how the system could fix them. Not overnight, clearly, but it only takes someone to remove the current blinkers and replace them with some fresh and intelligent thinking. You never know, they may even hire me when I'm out. Now *that* would be ironic. I won't hold my breath. As a result of trying to help reform inmates, which included sending the Governor a written plan on how they can save over five million pounds a year in this prison alone, I've already been banned from all activities and education. In real terms, this means for the last few weeks, I've been locked up over twenty-three hours a day for five days a week and at twenty-four hours a day (minus five minutes to collect dinner) for at least two days a week. One thing you learn fast here is that nothing in the system is based on fairness. Fairness is possible (though not guaranteed) in functional systems (organisations/people/etc.) but not decaying ones. Unfortunately, at this stage, it does not look as if Operation Chrysalis is going to become a butterfly. However, as I am sure you would expect, that doesn't mean I've been lazy. After all, I still get an hour out of the cell five days a week, plus an extra hour on Sunday for church. In fact, the church service is becoming a useful vehicle for me to have an impact as I have managed to get myself selected to do the Bible reading each week. Naturally, I am using this as an opportunity to subtly weave in some of my own philosophy on top and this already appears to be having a positive impact.

You may be asking, with all this time on my hands, what am I focusing on? This is always a great question to ask ourselves. Otherwise our attention drifts and it's easy to get caught up in unproductive habits we become so used to that we fail to see their damage, until it's too late. It may sound strange but many of us numbingly accept second best (or worse) as standard. This is usually for no other reason than it's what we're used to and therefore what we expect, which then becomes what we are OK to justify ourselves settling for. This state of living below our potential can then develop into a chronic pain for the soul. If you recall our Valentine segue in Volume 2, I state that the reason many people stay together unhappily is simply because they were unhappy together yesterday. The biggest problem is not the actual problem itself. It's becoming seduced by a cancerous comfort zone of familiarity and certainty and then thinking the problem is normal. This is what stops many from embracing the temporary emotional discomfort of stepping out of their comfort zone and declaring fulfilment as their birthright.

The starting point of that journey for all of us, is always courage. If you refer back to the Map Of Consciousness (Appendix C), it is no coincidence that courage represents the crossing point between the temporary expression of force and permanent owning of power. As has been emphatically demonstrated inside here, there is a distinct lack of courage in a decaying system (or a relationship). It takes courage to fix a broken system. Not apathy. It takes courage to mend or even leave a broken relationship. Not excuses.

Modern politics is another example of a decaying system, where instead of courage being the main driver of decisions (as demonstrated by people, such as; Mandela, Gandhi, Martin Luther King Jr, etc.), we find self-preservation (i.e. re-election) being the primary filter through which most decisions, statements and even policy are made. But don't get me started on politics or I'll permanently damage my hand running out of ink.

Back to where I am focusing my energy. Well, I'm not spending too much time trying to help the system from the inside. The disappointing revelation is, it just does not want help from that angle and has tried hard to shut me down. However, helping individuals is another matter, one which I am super busy with. Here are some updates on a few of the people I've already introduced you to. Do you remember Dell's son from Volume 1 who started training again? Well, according to Dell, he's back in the ring and not only won his last fight, but also got a 'box of the night' award. See what happens when we let go of our fears (in this case, of not being good enough if we lose)? We find ourselves with more energy to channel productively into our goals. Also, Ali, who I wrote the letter for to get his days reduced via articulating his remorse, was transferred to a D-Cat open prison just three days after they received the letter. Damn, maybe I should write myself one. Oh, hang on, I have - in the form of nine applications, none of which mysteriously happened to have been entered into the system. Hmm, maybe I should attack my psychotherapist, just as he did. Oh wait, I *am* my psychotherapist!

Sadly, I've heard nothing else from Mark since he was taken to mental health care as they have never released him. I just hope he is getting care that amounts to more than pills.

In the last update, I also mentioned Oli, a self-confessed crack and heroin addict for over fifteen years. I spend at least an hour a week with Oli and I am so pleased with his progress. He's gotten himself a job cleaning the chapel, which gets him out of the cell. He trains in the gym and is now focused on a reason and purpose. Remember, if your 'Why' is big enough, the how will show up. Oli's big 'Why' is to make himself a better example for his young kids. This is a big driver as, due to his addiction, his wife has refused to let him see them. It's still early but he is becoming motivated to show himself and others that, no matter what life throws at you or how many mistakes you make, it's never too late to turn your life around and step up to be an example, not a warning. In short, he's starting to realise that a new future is always available.

Then there is Edgar, who has been here for eleven years. Wow, I can only imagine what it's like being institutionalised for a third of your life. As I'm sure you can guess, he was pretty numb inside, just going through the motions. There was no spark in his eye and no life in his soul. Edgar's first tipping point was reading *'Mud or Stars?'*, which caused a big shift in his way of thinking. He was also the first to accept the rowing challenge which I set up in the gym (more on that later). He's become, hmm, what's the best word to use? Intrigued. Yes, he's become intrigued again with life. He's starting to believe that possibility may just be possible. There's a long way to go but there is definitely a small spark coming back. You can hear it in his voice and in his questions, which are now driven by a hopeful curiosity, rather than an apathetic resignation. There are still low moments for him, and I'm only able to see him a small amount each week, but the mental and emotional direction of travel has certainly changed. As I said, it's early in the process, but I'll keep you in the loop.

Next, we have Mo. Mo is from Bangladesh and is actually a big supporter of my work. He even recognised me from my videos. He's in here for working on a student visa. His family put their life savings into sending him to college here in the UK and then the school shut down after his first term/semester. He lost his education and his family lost their money. This led him to feel both desperate and guilty. He knew he couldn't afford to pay his family back by working in Bangladesh, especially without an education, so he started working illegally in the UK, even though he only had a student visa. The irony is that I may be partly responsible. I'm not kidding when I say I think he's seen every one of my YouTube videos. They were the reason his mindset shifted from being a victim, to allowing him to get resourceful and committed enough to figure a way out of his predicament. He started following his dream of being an entrepreneur instead of a student and figured out a way to start earning good money. He's even found a way, before being sentenced, of generating a passive income so he could have money sent back to his family while he's inside.

When he first approached me, he said he'd spotted me two weeks earlier on the wing but didn't have the courage to come up and ask if it was really me. Bless him. Remember the pedestal trap I spoke of in Volume 3 and how limiting it makes you? Don't fall for it! I could have already been working with him for the last two weeks. After our first chat, he asked if I could coach him on a big problem. It was fun to see the look on his face when I looked him in the eye and said, "Of course! It's probably the reason I'm here!". It turns out that Mo's big problem was that he still desperately wants to become an entrepreneur but thinks because of what has happened, he's failed. I'm sharing this because there is a lesson for us all. I asked the question: "Why do you think you are not an entrepreneur now?". His answer was typical: "I don't have the money; I don't have my own successful business; I'm in prison, etc.". You may be starting to see the problem.

The Entrepreneurs Secret

Mo's problem is that his rules for what an entrepreneur is and does are preventing him from accepting it as an identity. Nothing more. I asked him to list the character traits of an entrepreneur. Not the *results*. Results, by their very nature, are always temporary and transient. Character traits, which are always the necessary pre-requisites to any entrepreneurial 'trappings' of so-called success, are not. We went through the usual suspects, such as; the ability to handle uncertainty, resourcefulness, courage, focused determination, a willingness to take calculated risks – even against the odds and putting everything you have on the line. Once we had this down, I said: "OK, let's look at how this applies to you." I then showed him how he had already demonstrated all the traits of being an entrepreneur. From leaving everything behind to come to a foreign country where he didn't know anyone, didn't speak the language well, had no fall-back position, very few resources and yet still managed to survive, in spite of the college going bankrupt through no fault of his own. In short, I showed him how he was far more of an entrepreneur than I was. That I would never have had the courage to face what he had and make the decisions he'd made and, therefore, could he please give me some tips on being an entrepreneur. He was floored. He'd never even considered it from that perspective. I told him that if he could figure all that out, then the business stuff, by comparison, was easy and got even easier with experience. However, his problem wasn't that he didn't have a business, it was that he believed he needed one in order to be an entrepreneur.

It's a common trap for a lot of people I meet or who come to my Business School. I call them the wantreprenuers. Always thinking they need to prove to themselves or to the world and its dog, that they can make it. This is why they take the next course, read the next book and do everything they can to try to 'get' to a place where they can finally call themselves an entrepreneur.

What's the secret to breaking that pattern, if it relates to you? It's simple but very effective. Instead of waiting until you have a successful business before calling yourself an entrepreneur, take on the identity NOW. Why is this so powerful? Because by recognising yourself as an entrepreneur today, you will start thinking like one. You will also go out and build a business when you find the right idea, because that's what entrepreneurs <u>do</u>. It is NOT a qualification which has to happen first in order for you to become one! Is this making sense? My point here my friends, is this: Most of the time it is not our abilities which prevent us from becoming a 'fill in the blank' (entrepreneur, successful coach, athlete, musician, artist, trainer, accountant, etc.). *It is our rules for what has to happen, before we allow ourselves to wear the label.*

I asked Mo the following question: If I were to lose my business tomorrow, which has happened several times before, would you think in your wildest dreams that it would stop me from thinking of myself as an entrepreneur? The answer was *never in a million years*. Why? Because who I AM leads what I do – win or lose. Never the other way around!

For those of you coming to the next Sage Business School, I will proudly introduce you to a good friend of mine. He's a great entrepreneur. His name is Mo.

Diffusing A Time Bomb

I could go on but I want to respect your time and so will share one final scenario with you. A gentleman called Aziz. I met Aziz a few weeks ago when I overheard him and another two guys arguing over religion. Aziz is a Muslim and very quick to defend and attack when it comes to the view of his faith. Gatecrashing a conversation like that is not without its dangers. Especially in here and especially when the force of the dialogue between the three parties seemed to be escalating towards anger, fuelled by rules that say, in order to be right, we have to prove that others are wrong. Not exactly live and let live.

I took a quick register of the situation. This includes a subtle yet rapid assessment of critical factors such as; body language, facial expressions, language patterns, energetic distribution of aggression, control and more. Having read this, I felt it could easily turn violent, so I decided to step in and see if I could diffuse the potential time bomb before it exploded. To do this effectively and without setting it off, there were specific strategies and techniques I could use. To begin with, I needed to break their pattern and interrupt the flow. I would then need to build rapport and gauge when the energy had shifted, so as to pick the best opening for them to invite me into their conversation. Once invited, it would give me the opportunity to attempt to elegantly hijack the debate and hopefully re-frame or re-contextualise the foundations of the argument, so that it lost its emotional charge. And I needed to do all of this while maintaining everybody's illusion of power so that they wouldn't start defending their beliefs, in order to retain their sense of significance. How would I start? Well, a seemingly casual, non-threatening and unrelated question should act as a pattern break. I moved closer, smiled and took a breath.

'Hey guys, sorry to butt in, but does anyone know if we are going to get exercise today?' They stopped mid-flow and looked at me blank for a second (that was the pattern break). One of the guys said he wasn't sure and another said he hoped so as it had been cancelled for the last two days. Then Aziz started complaining about how they keep us locked up like animals and the others agreed. This mutual agreement meant the energy was less charged which was the gauge I was looking for. 'Yeah tell me about it', I said to everyone, though I kept my non-verbal communication directed at Aziz. (Note - getting this agreement frame was important as it also helps build rapport.)

I allowed a tiny pause before I followed up with 'What's up? What are you guys chatting about?' This was my opening. Aziz immediately took over and proceeded to outline his argument in support of Islam and why people who don't understand it are wrong. I let him talk for long enough to think I had heard enough to understand, but not too much as to just provide a platform for him to vent and project his entire model of the world. He seemed an auditory guy, so I responded with 'I totally hear you', followed by 'I've never really been smart enough to understand the different religions but from my limited knowledge, it seems they all teach the same thing at their core. Kind of like how different school teachers will teach the same curriculum in different ways. Teachers such as Jesus, Buddha, Krishna and Allah etc., all taught us to walk a path where we grow out of hate, anger, fear and selfish desires, and replace it with love, compassion, kindness, humility and forgiveness. Usually through personal discipline, linked to ritual'.

They all stopped and stared for a moment as their brain registered what I had just said. I followed with 'My personal view is that the biggest travesty of humanity is that we argue and even kill each other over who our favourite school teacher is, as if they were the only ones allowed to teach. Doesn't make much sense to me, especially as there are so many classrooms in the school of life – way too many for one teacher. You'd think they'd be glad to share the load, especially if the lessons are basically the same. It would make sense to me to just find who you like, start studying and, in line with what they are teaching you, wish all the other students well. After all, if you think you have a better teacher than them, then you should really feel grateful about that, rather than judge them for not being as lucky as you'. It was as though their tongues had stopped working. I then said, 'To me, people who are smart enough to study under a spiritual teacher, probably wouldn't be unintelligent enough to waste time on that kind of argument'. This helps me turn their own need for significance to my advantage, by linking insignificance, i.e. being unintelligent, to the continuation of the debate. The silence and 'deer in the headlights' look from the three guys told me everything, at which point a guard shouted: 'Exercise!'

While outside for our forty-minute walk around the small yard, Aziz and I continued the conversation and by the end had become good friends. He and I have had many conversations since then, and I like the way his open-minded scepticism allows him to see things in a different light. It's as if he's OK with others having a different viewpoint and, instead of trying to prove them wrong, he's now curious as to why they think that way. He's an intelligent guy and keen to learn. He's also a fellow D-Cat who's been waiting to transfer with zero feedback. Although he's now much smarter at playing the hand he's been dealt, rather than spending energy bitching at the dealer or how the pack was shuffled. You'd also put your head in your hands if you understood the petty-mindedness of the authorities that convicted him and why. I won't go into it but he really shouldn't be here and doesn't deserve it. Another of the many examples of a failed system.

Solutions Not Problems

Does that mean I'm giving up on the system? Of course not. Though dealing with and helping an individual prisoner is treating the symptom of a failed structure – it would obviously be more efficient to address the cause. Going back to my earlier metaphor, it's a waste of time and energy rescuing drowning people in the river instead of going upstream to see if you can stop whoever is throwing them in. Is it really that difficult or complicated to address the issues of the prison system? Well, it seems to have eluded countless politicians and justice Ministers for successive terms. One can only conclude they are either unwilling to address it or unable to think of ways to do so.

Are there ways to help? Sure, and they are fairly obvious to me. In fact, they would be fairly obvious to anyone with a basic understanding of human behaviour, a commercial mind and uncommon sense. I'll share one insight so that you can see.

At the present time, the UK Government has privatised several prisons and has plans to privatise many more. Publicly, they state that this is a way to help solve the issues, though from the ever-present political perspective of PR and damage control, it is more likely a way to shift the blame from themselves to the private sector. Especially as right now the problems are getting worse, not better. This was highlighted in a recent documentary by Panorama for the BBC called 'Behind Bars'. It involved an undercover reporter who spent two months working as an officer at Northumberland Prison. During the documentary, you'll see exactly the same issues I talked about in Volume 3 and that I've personally witnessed here. The drugs, violence, disorder, forceful containment, etc. with virtually no chance and little focus on rehabilitation. In fact, current figures show just the opposite. Immediate reoffending rates are over 40%, and prison, in many cases, makes people better criminals. So, if the government is now bringing in business to run prisons and wants them to make a positive difference, let's ask ourselves a question: what is business good at? To be fair, it's a subject I have some experience in. The answer, obviously, is 'making a profit'. Let's face it, if they are not good at this, they die. OK, next question: how are contracts for running prisons awarded? It's the answer to this question where we can see things starting to go wrong.

Contracts are primarily awarded to those who can do the required job for the least amount of money. For example, the firm which won the contract to run the Northumberland Prison did so by promising the government that it would do it for £130 million cheaper over fifteen years. What's the easiest way for a business to save money? Invest in being more efficient? Sadly no, that's the smart long-term view. The easiest short-term view is to cut costs and the first thing the firm did was sack 200 people, nearly half of which were the prison officers. Remember, businesses do not have the same luxury as the public-sector which is immune from bankruptcy, even if they are mismanaged or go over budget. Instead, companies are driven by the commercial imperative to be profitable in order to survive. Let's now include the fact their 'customers' are prisoners. Private prisons get tens of thousands of pounds a year per prisoner and with no shortage of supply. So, let's look at this. They get rewarded for having more prisoners and for spending less money on looking after them. Hmm, can anyone spot an issue here? Talk about predictable. Incentivising both overcrowding *and* under-resourcing, while putting the needs of the client last. Tell me one business on the High Street which would survive five minutes with *that* model? So, I hear you ask, what is the solution? Well, as successive Justice Ministers have found out to their detriment, you cannot fix a rotten tooth with a veneer. In other words, there is no 'one' answer or magic pill and as history has shown us, throwing money at a problem rarely solves the problem. Neither, as in this case, does trying to do it cheaper. However, I am a great believer that the ultimate resource is resourceful*ness*, and that starts with taking an inventory of what you already have. Luckily, I think the Government already has an incredible resource in their current model – they are just using it against themselves – kind of like buying a cannon to defend yourself and then pointing it at your head.

In short, the secret lies within the privatisation model. One of the best things about business is that it must find a way to adapt and innovate or it dies. Businesses by their very nature are creative, resourceful problem solvers. They figure out solutions and find a way to get things done, even if it means cooperating with rivals. Boeing planes have many parts made by Airbus and vice versa. Several car manufacturers share engines – you get the idea. In other words, business gets it done. Business finds a way. Not a way to get re-elected in four years, which leads to veneer-based decisions, but to survive, which means they must fix the tooth, so they can chew and not starve to death. The problem with the current model is that innovation is geared around how to reduce costs and continue to operate. Wrong Focus! Instead, let's start with the most important, the most obvious and in this case, the most ignored question: 'What is the ultimate outcome?' Is it getting your lifeguard badge or stopping people from falling in the river? The answer to the question in this instance is found in another question (remember questions direct focus) and that is, 'How do we use prisons as a more effective way to treat the problem of crime, rather than just try to temporarily contain the criminals?' When we ask that, rather than 'How can we save money?', we start to redirect the power that business has for creativity, innovation and survival onto a different focus. Instead of paying private prisons a service fee and a per-diem per prisoner, switch the model to financially incentivise the desired outcome which is non-reoffending.

A comparable model already works in schools. Schools in the UK have league tables and are ranked according to the results they deliver. In a state school (public model) they get 'given' pupils based on demographics or catchment areas. A poor rating means a poor career for the head teacher. The focus is therefore on performance first and not budget. It also ties back to the primary question of, 'What are we trying to achieve?' The answer here is obvious – to provide a good education.

In Private schools (commercial model), they have to compete in the marketplace for students based on results and *not* that they can do it for less money. And guess what? The better their results, the more money they can charge. Every parent appreciates this scoring system, public or private. In the private model, a lot of parents work harder to pay more for their children's education. They certainly don't look for ways to cut corners. This could obviously work in prisons. Not so much by naming and shaming in league tables (unless it's a public company, many private CEO's don't care that much and often value profit over reputation, within reason), but instead, by using the creative force of the commercial prime directive. Just imagine what the private sector could do with all of its entrepreneurial resources, innovation, creativity and problem-solving skills when focused on achieving the real goals that society is looking for.

By simply tying in and linking some of the profits to whether or not prisoners re-offend within say, eighteen months, or the number re-called back on licence (probation), etc., then business, ever hungry for profit, will find a way to access those bonuses and extra revenue streams. The bonuses could come, in part, from the money the government saves on fewer re-offenders going back to prison, with the added bonus of less people clogging up the courts, less strain on society and of course, fewer victims of crime. This works very similar to an affiliate programme in traditional business, where the affiliate gets paid from the money that would otherwise have been spent on marketing. In short, when rewards and profits are tied directly to the desired outcome of better-managed prisons and less reoffending, *business will find a way to make it happen.*

The government can also help by working with business to research and explore examples that have worked around the world and from a long-term quantifiable and practical basis, not an academic or short-term one. One that is aimed at shifting and redirecting behaviour by addressing the *cause* of the behaviour and the very thing that precedes it. What is that? It's the sixty-four-thousand-dollar question, and there is only one answer: Thinking!

It is a psychological fact that no deliberate behaviour can occur without the thought of doing the behaviour. This is where most rehabilitation attempts fall down, as they place more emphasis on shifting or controlling behaviour and not shifting the mindset that precedes and causes it. I remember my greatest mentor, George Zalucki, who also worked in the Criminal Justice System, once said: 'The criminal act is harboured in the mind long before the deed is actually done'. The fact remains, if the profitability of the business is linked to the result you want, business will find a way to make it happen and will always be looking to improve by finding a better way. It's the commercial prime directive.

Designing a way to ultimately help shift the criminal mindset, was the entire basis behind my Operation Chrysalis. Imagine that taken nationwide? Quick, someone tell the Justice Minister! Remember, it's not that politicians are not smart, they just have a very *different* prime directive. It's called re-election and self-preservation. I also believe that many people who could successfully run a country, never get into politics. I mean, think about it. We live in a world where the UK Financial Director / CFO, also known as the Chancellor of the Exchequer rarely, if ever, has a strongly qualified background in finance or accounting or has ever successfully run a commercial division of a large company, let alone a country. Could you ever imagine THAT in business? Oops, did we stray back to politics? My point is that the addiction to the status quo that most of the Prison Governors seem so committed to, is a death sentence for productivity, effectiveness and long-term results. Unfortunately, the metaphor doesn't stop there, as the poor families of those who take their own lives (one every three days) will testify. Let's hope for their sake that one day I can get an audience with those who could afford me the opportunity of drilling down much more than a pen, paper, and writer's cramp will allow. Trust me, I'm doing what I can in here guys. I've even been approached by prisoners who work at the induction wing, begging me for more copies of 'Mud or Stars?' as it helped so many people who've read it. Unfortunately, my hands are tied having been banned from the education wing and the library. Thankfully they did not lobotomise my resourcefulness. At least not yet, as I posted my last copy out to Thea, so she can scan it, print it and then post me a whole bunch of copies back in. I just hope they let them through.

MAKING A DIFFERENCE IN THE GYM

What else has been happening? Well, I have finally managed to get to the gym after two months. Having figured out the system, I'm averaging 1-2 workouts a week, although on many days the gym is cancelled. No reason is ever given, but it's likely short staffing. Even if it is open, there are a few challenges getting in. Firstly, D-wing (my wing) is only allowed access to the gym a maximum of three times a week although, as I just said, this rarely happens anyway. Next, access to the gym takes place during our precious social time. This means we use up most of our social time queuing up at the gym entrance and if the staff don't show up, it means we end up wasting nearly all of our social time crowding around a door wondering if it's going to open. Thirdly, there are only twenty or so places and always more people waiting to get in. This means that when the door opens it gets aggressive because no one wants to be left out. It's not a time to be polite and many of the prisoners are big 'meat heads' who aren't shy about getting to the front of the line. My height helps and I almost always get in if they open the door. But it's a mob mentality. Once in, I saw what I expected to see. Nearly everyone is lifting weights trying to get bigger arms or a bigger chest. It's what I call T-Shirt training, as many are driven by a huge need for significance rather than functionality. I can't blame them. The environment here is more akin to the animal kingdom than a civilised society and size is equated to protection and pecking order.

Thinking of how I could add value, I decided to see if I could organise a different focus, one that would not only play into their significance but also offer them some functionality as well as variety. Enter the 'One-Minute Max Challenge'. Also known as the 'Miracle Minute'.

The gym is poorly equipped but it does have three Concept-2 indoor rowing machines. The best overall fitness machine money can buy. However, in classic prison fashion, only one of them works because the other two don't have batteries. I keep mentioning it and even wrote to the Head of Physical Education, pointing out politely that they had £2000 worth of equipment sitting there unusable because of £5 worth of batteries. I even offered to pay for them myself. The response I got was . . . nothing. But at least one works. Now, for those interested, I'll share with you one of the physical hacks I teach on the Health and Vitality seminar and how to complete your whole cardio workout in sixty seconds. To begin with, you need a full compound machine that trains multiple body parts involving arms, legs, core, etc. The Concept-2 is perfect for this. Set it to a single time of sixty seconds at level 10 and see how many metres you can go. Simple, right?

Well, let me explain a little as this is based on cutting-edge sports science and only works under one condition. All out, full on, no holds barred 110% everything you have. For the full minute. Allow me to share what will happen. The first ten to fifteen seconds, you get in your stride as the body responds to the mind telling it to go go go! During the next ten to fifteen seconds, your body starts grabbing all the available oxygen and glycogen it can find in the bloodstream to convert to energy, in the form of a mollecule called ATP. The next ten to fifteen seconds, it starts scavenging as the oxygen and glycogen cannot be produced or reach the muscles in time to be converted to ATP in order to replenish what is being explosively used. This is why, if done correctly at 110%, the last ten to fifteen seconds is when you hit the wall. Similar to a marathon runner after three to four hours. The difference is you are doing it in SIXTY SECONDS. What happens next? Well, our bodies may be living in a modern era, but most of our biology is still hardwired for a primitive environment. One where you couldn't guarantee your next meal and the *only* reason you would expend *that* much effort in that short a time frame, would be to either run away from a threat or to catch food – in other words, a survival situation.

The fact you DID survive (which was by no means a guarantee

back then), sends a message to the brain which says something like 'geez, whatever that was must have been close. I need to get fitter, stronger and faster in case it happens again and pretty damn soon'. In short, it triggers a growth factor response which rapidly accelerates your results, but only if you give it everything. Ninety-nine percent won't work. Anyway, as I'm sure you can imagine, explaining this to the guys in the gym got their interest, not to mention, played to their macho competitive side. So, we now have a one-minute max challenge running. After all, what I believe people in here need health-wise is more functionality than strength. Many of them are trying to build big arms and shoulders but are placing them on top of a weak or dysfunctional core. This leads to posture issues, pain and injury. Just to add some incentive, I went first and offered a prize of £5 of my own canteen spend to the first person who beats my score. For those of you interested, today it was 359 metres. Go have fun!

Speaking of fun, several of you have asked how I'm doing and if I'm still enjoying myself, especially after the frankness of my last update. Of course, the environment itself is tough. Right now, it's nearly 1am, and as I write this, prisoners are banging their chairs against their doors and other prisoners are screaming abuse at them to be quiet, venting their anger and frustration in futile protest. Another night in the hotel. Not sure it would do too well on Trip Advisor. The guards do nothing so the banging and screaming just continues. Oh, for the silence of the lambs . . . So that's not fun but you tune it out and send them love. It's all you can do. Missing Thea and the dogs is still difficult. That's not fun, and today HP lawyers sent me a letter saying they'd put a charging order against my house for tens of thousands in legal fees, which I'm struggling to pay and could likely enforce it while I'm in here, so I could lose my home. So that wasn't fun either. But let's go back to the gym as a metaphor.

We go to the gym because we want to grow and we know we only grow through challenge. If you took the viewpoint of the muscle fibre in your bicep, just as you busted out the last and near impossible rep, your muscle is screaming, being broken down, wondering what the hell is happening out there and sending pain signals to the brain telling it to stop. But you have a different perspective. You know it's necessary and are quite happy, even pleased with yourself, for squeezing out that final burning rep. Similarly, if you hire a personal trainer and don't feel like throwing up at the end of your session, you'll be disappointed and want your money back. The secret to rolling with the punches of life, is to realise that life is your personal trainer and yes, even though the gym I'm in right now is challenging and even though there seems to be a heavy weight on the bar, I'm still going to approach and participate in this workout with the mind of a committed athlete, determined to give it everything I've got. To seek out the growth, not run from it. To come out of this stronger, despite the bruises, broken-down muscles and lactic acid.

But to get back to the original question, yes, there are plenty of parts to this workout I am really enjoying. It's not all the last burning rep of a particular set. I adore working with the prisoners and seeing them shift. I love writing to you guys and sharing my journey and lessons. I light up reading the letters and emails I get on a daily basis from so many of you around the world. Not only sharing your support but also YOUR journey and how you've applied some of the lessons and the difference it's made to your lives and the people you care about. Hearing your stories helps me through the tough times in here. You compel me to work. You give me the strength to lift the bar and for that, I'm exceptionally grateful.

THE SYLLABUS – THE GIFT OF ACTIVE MEDITATION

Let's move onto the syllabus. In the last volume, we covered the topic of 'passive' meditation. Do you remember the two essential takeaways? The first was the awareness that we are not our mind or body. We *have* a mind and body. The second was on how to quiet the mind by showing it how insignificant and meaningless 95% of its noise is. In short, passive meditation is about quietening the volume of the physical and mental channels and identifying yourself as the source or point of consciousness.

'Active' meditation gets way sexier. Though I must point out that passive meditation is a critical skill to develop and one that makes active meditation easier and more effective. Think of passive meditation as preparing the vehicle (checking oil, water, putting in fuel, checking tyre pressures, etc.) and active meditation as driving the vehicle to a specific destination. This is done by having strong intent. What is a strong intent? I personally think it is best described as a highly focused, yet unforced, concentration on a single and clarified objective.

Mind Over Matter

The reason we use active meditation is to influence the probability of something happening in the outer world. Can that really be done? You bet. In quantum physics, this is known as the uncertainty principle and is tied to the famous wave-particle duality effect and its relationship with the observer. Using intent to influence physical circumstance at a higher-level (non-physical) becomes easy to understand when you realise a few basic current facts. However, for those whose belief systems are still conditioned to a pre-21st century model of materialism, I'll give you a quick dart in the board with a brief and basic overview. I would also highly encourage you to get closer to the current bullseye of our scientific understanding by doing your own research. Aside from the thousands of papers published by renowned institutions, a good place to start would be Princeton Engineering and Anomalies Research Lab (yes, Princeton is where Einstein spent the last half of his life teaching – they are pretty good at doing top level science).

So, for all of you materialist left-brainers out there, listen up. What we know is that the physical (material) world is essentially virtual, i.e. there is nothing there when we drill down. Similar to how pictures on a high definition 2D television look real and 3D from a distance, but if you look closer, you see that it is not 3D. In fact, it's not even real. It is glass. Get closer still and we discover pixels. Even closer and it is LEDs. Get closer some more and we discover it is three primary coloured lights (photons) rapidly firing in a big and intelligently coordinated sequence. In other words, it's a 2D virtual reality made to look and sound real but only from a certain distance.

Now let's jump into our [own] 3D virtual reality. This is also made to appear real - but only from a distance. Using our arm as a parallel example to the screen, we can see at first glance, that it appears to be covered in 'skin'. But get closer and we find it's actually made up of billions of independent 'pixels' called cells. Each individual, yet working together. If we get closer still, we realise the cells are made up of billions of molecules performing hundreds of thousands of functions and communications a second. If we get closer to this 3D holographic television, we see the molecules are composed of billions of atoms and if we then get even closer, we find, to our amazement, the atoms are made up of 99.999999% empty space (in physical terms, not energetic) and 0.000001% condensed energy called 'matter'. Not only this, but the tiny piece of condensed energy only exists in physical terms when it's being observed or, to be more technically precise, measured. In other words, it is intrinsically linked to our own consciousness. The one part that traditional science has never been able to explain. This is because it is outside of the material paradigm. Yes, consciousness is primary. In other words, brain function does not produce consciousness any more than a television produces programs. The brain simply runs the current physical body that your consciousness temporarily inhabits.

It may also interest you to know, that another false paradigm of materialism is that atoms are solid shell-like structures with electrons whizzing around them in fixed patterns, like planets. The reality is this 'model' (still widely taught in education) is dogma which was, has, and never will be proven (because it does not exist) and was constructed to fill a gap in knowledge. This is known as matching assumption to the available data. The problem is we forgot it was an assumption and started believing it was fact. The model was chosen because, at the macro level, we understood the relationship between the sun, planets and moons and at the time it made sense to apply the same model to the micro level as a best guess. That is until Quantum Mechanics came along and screwed everything up, causing the data to no longer match the assumption.

Throw The Emperor A Towel

At this point, you may have thought traditional science would have looked for new answers. However, as this would have required someone to throw an apple at Sir Isaac Newton and knock him off of his pedestal, it didn't happen. Instead, many scientists clung tighter to their material-based model and simply ignored the data. Some even went as far as making up excuses and inventing loopholes to cover the inconsistencies. Why? Because such is the relationship between dogma and ego, which often culminates in an addiction to being right. A far better approach would have been to let go of the death-grip on how they thought the world worked and instead, embrace the healthier scientific perspective of open-minded scepticism in the pursuit of discovery. Closed mindedness is the death of discovery. Remember the story of the Emperor's new clothes? Heaven forbid he's actually naked. No, it must be your eyesight that's wrong. Hmm, should have gone to Specsavers. They would have told you your eyesight is fine but those thick dark-lensed belief glasses you're wearing could do with a modern upgrade. Oh, and while you're at it, throw the Emperor a towel. It also reminds me of the quote by Max Planck, of one of the great founders of quantum physics, who famously stated: 'Science makes progress one funeral at a time'.

Of course, this doesn't invalidate the use of the previous model to answer some of the questions being asked at the time about the relationship between atoms, electrons and material physics. There's no doubt that Sir Isaac was a brilliant man who certainly did know his apples from his calculus, but it doesn't change the fact that models are only useful to the extent that you realise they are a model.

What is ironic in the context of materialism, is that the model is backwards. The arm, and the body it's attached to, is nothing more than a car that allows consciousness (us) to drive around and experience this physical reality. And, just like a real car, it may look and feel solid but the part that actually makes it work, the part that makes decisions on where to go and how fast, is definitely non-physical. We call that consciousness.

Why is this not only relevant and useful but also critical when it comes to using active meditation as a tool to help steer your life?

Before we answer this question, there is one crucial yet often overlooked fact we must uncover, but to find it, I'm going to ask another interesting yet revealing question: why does water only flow downhill while you and I can walk uphill? See if you can come up with a response to that before reading ahead.

The answer I'm getting at divides the world into two halves. Both of which operate under different rules. The two halves are Sentient and Non-Sentient. Or, to put it in basic terms, living and non-living. The primary difference being that if something is sentient (alive) it has the ability to express conscious intent by various degrees. Whereas non-sentient objects can't. By that definition, a house, a rock face and a table are non-sentient. For example, a house which collapses cannot decide to rebuild itself. On the other hand, a sunflower, a bird and a human are sentient and the higher one climbs up the sentient ladder, the more choices there are to express conscious intent, also known as free will. A sunflower expresses its intent to get energy by choosing to turn towards and follow the sun. It has a low level of conscious awareness and is therefore mostly autonomous in its actions. Higher up the scale, we have a bird. It has more options and can choose things such as; where to fly, which worm to eat and who to mate with. Humans, on the other hand, are at the top of the evolutionary table as it relates to choices on how to express conscious intent. Lucky us. Though, as you will see, this comes at a price.

Why is the distinction between Sentient and Non-Sentient important? Put simply, Non-Sentient objects follow the path of *least resistance and energy conservation* as demonstrated in the classic second law of thermodynamics. This means that a house left to itself will always eventually crumble, as will a rock face. A table will rot and ultimately decay. And water can only flow downhill.

Sentient objects follow a different rule set, which is *energy consumption and expenditure in the service of growth and contribution.* In other words, we take in energy and then have a choice on how to use it. OK, that's enough open loops, let's close a few and see how this all ties together in active meditation, quantum physics, choice and the directive which covers sentient vs non-sentient beings.

Quantum mechanics states that a new future is always available, due to matter 'arising' out of a state of infinite possibilities known as 'The Field'. Before we go on, let me add a constraint to the word 'infinite' to keep our left brainers happy by clarifying that the possibilities are limited to, and governed by, the mechanics of relativity and the space-time rule set. In other words, I am not saying it's possible to have a future where you suddenly grow wings and fly or develop superpowers. But, within the realms of the rules that govern how physical matter behaves, the 'movie of your life' has countless available 'scripts'. Think of it as similar to the experiment Hollywood conducted, when they shot films with different endings and let the audience vote on what kind they wanted. What you may not have realised is that YOU have the ability to vote on and influence which scenes play out in the movie of your life. There are two ways to do this. The hardest and most common is where you storm onto the set and try to act the lines you want and try to force the other actors to play along while physically adjusting the set and the props to fit your script. I mentioned this approach to living earlier and called it living in 'By-Me', but not only is it damned hard work, it also makes for a lousy movie. Moreover, it's an acting technique many of us have to learn in order to one-day (hopefully), figure out what NOT to do.

The other way is to influence the actual script itself and allow the 'set designers' and other actors to work in harmony, supporting it. After all, there are an unlimited number of potential plots, scenes and storylines (minus flying people and X-ray vision). In this regard, the quantum field represents a blank pen and paper with every future scene still available to be written. In active meditation, you use *intent* to write, practice and rehearse the scenes you want. This has a scientifically proven and statistically significant impact on the probability of them showing up. However, in order for this to be effective, there are some rules. One relates to your rehearsal technique. Are you leading with your head, trying to be technically correct? Or are you leading with your feelings and emotions and thereby, in movie terms, capturing the hearts of the audience as they get swept up in the realism of your authentic performance? Of course, the heart and mind must work together, but *the heart must lead and steal the show*. The mind is just called upon to remember the lines. There are no Oscars in this movie for a safe or technically correct performance here. People want to be moved emotionally. Remember the famous line from Gladiator? 'You win the crowd – You win your freedom!'. When it comes to rehearsing the scenes that you want in the movie of your life, the crowd is the fifty-plus trillion cells which in unison make up your body. When every one of them believes and *feels* the performance, you can be sure the quantum pen is busy writing.

The second rule in getting your script authorised by the producer (which some people call God), is by asking yourself, 'does this serve my growth or my ego?' That's a personal question to answer, and I can only offer guidelines. To begin with, this is NOT the place to listen to your mind. As we discussed in the passive meditation section in Volume 3, your mind is exceptionally gifted and highly trained at one thing - justifying why you are right. At everything else, it has limited value unless directed from a deeper place. If the scene in the movie you are trying to select from The Field of infinite scripts is about you, what you can get and is all about you, then two things are likely to happen. Either a) It won't be sanctioned by the producer and you'll be left to forcibly try and fight to make it happen (back to 'by-me'), or b) the scene may present itself but will usually come with a sting in the tail downstream to give you a reflective lesson. (Note - this is partly what has been referred to throughout history as karma, but a full and deeper discussion on this is outside the scope of this update). The bottom line is it may seem fun and appropriate to stand and throw spit balls in the classroom of Life, and you may even get some short-term payoff, laughs or significance. Although sooner or later, a detention is coming. This can also apply if you want to use intention and quantum mechanics to take advantage of others. Or worse, hurt someone or settle a score.

However, there is also a caveat to the growth option. Even if you feel that it fits all the criteria for approval – if it interferes with the bigger picture of your overall script, then you are still swimming upstream. Remember what I said in my last update? We don't get to decide *how* the lessons we need are delivered. This is where the mind often gets stuck as it likes to try and figure out a straight line to its goal, only to find itself bumping into the nonlinear workings of the Quantum Field Movie Industry. The good news is, if you choose a scene which matched the right criteria and you followed all the rules (there's more to come) and your scene doesn't come true, then you can relax, knowing that the bigger plan ALWAYS takes precedent and is often delivering something much better.

This is why it's always important to flow with the river of life, rather than resist the way it bends and winds. Remember, there are no straight lines in nature. The fallacy of a straight line being the fastest way between two points is a linear construct which works well on paper but is not suited to non-linear life, powered by non-linear consciousness. This means that while the straight-line solution may appear to be the SHORTEST distance to our goals, it is almost never the quickest. If you doubt this, try leaving your front door and driving in a straight line to work. It may technically be the shortest way, but the first brick wall, ditch or field you encounter, will certainly not make it the fastest. The fact that your script goes sideways and doesn't fit your pictures (what we call a bend in the river), may cause upset to the mind and trigger massive resistance, but the truth from a non-linear and bigger picture perspective is likely that a) it's going perfectly according to plan, b) the river of Life is looking after you so as to avoid an unseen waterfall ahead or c) it's giving you the perfect opportunity to grow and develop the exact muscle you need to lift the goal you are after. And most likely, some combination of all three.

If you are able to surrender the vice-like grip the left brain has on how it thinks Life should be and start trusting the wisdom of the bigger picture of the current, then not only is life less stressful but things are far more likely to work out, as the intelligence of the river of Life reveals itself through the oncoming bends. This is another reason why I'm able to be OK with where I'm at. The short-term view here is not helpful. I'm in prison. I've had nearly everything I've worked for taken away from me. Some of the people I thought would never run for the fields or take advantage of me if I was here, have done exactly that. All in all, a tough scene. But I'm OK to act in this scene because I recognise I'm playing a longer game called a movie. And I know my movie is about raising the global consciousness of humanity in a way which can help millions of people help themselves by relating to life in a more empowering way. To help turn their own movies into an example, not a warning. And to do that requires bigger muscles and to obtain them requires a bigger gym. I still have many decades of potential acting and scenes to shoot, and I have zero doubt whatsoever that this present bend in the river will play a perfect role in the overall script. The only way I can screw it up is to lower my own perspective and consciousness and start resisting, bitching and complaining about the current scene, or start feeling sorry for myself as the ego seeks to wallow in its own self-pity. I know, no matter how hard the scene gets in here, as soon as I do begin to wallow in self-pity, they may as well throw away the key.

The third rule centres on time, effort and consistency. You do not win an academy award by showing up to acting class when you feel like it. As my late friend, Chet Holmes said, to get a PhD you need a PhD. Also known as Pig Headed Discipline. Why? Because every great achievement in history has been built upon the shoulders of persistence. Influencing the quantum field to affect the outcome of your own movie is no different. It is also not a magic pill which will do all the work for you. Think of yourself in partnership with it. You may be able to influence the producer to create intentional scenes in the movie but you still have to get on set (the physical world) and act your part. For example, if you are actively meditating on passing an exam and are feeling the joy and celebration of getting an 'A' but at the same time you are not willing to study, then don't expect the non-physical to help you. There are no free rides. Either you put in the work or you don't. This is where understanding the rules of sentient vs non-sentient show up and either help you up the ladder or send you crashing down.

If your goals are focused on growth and contribution (non-ego) and you work hard at your acting career with dedication and commitment, the river will take you towards your goals in ways which you cannot predict. Infallibly, and every time. There will, of course, be bends and opportunities to grow your muscles (like negotiating rapids), but if you know you are on the right river, do you care which way it bends? No, you relax and enjoy the excitement of the journey as, regardless of the twists and turns, your destination is assured.

However, if you do not follow the dictates of a sentient being (energy expenditure in the pursuit of growth and contribution), then by default, you fall under the clutches of the non-sentient directive. This appears as randomness and chaos but is simply following the rules of least energy expenditure and which always leads to decay.

The obvious question is, which class do you want to join? The problem with modern society is it has sold us the idea we can have an easy life (path of least resistance) by focusing on what we can get (ego) whilst avoiding the consequences of non-personal growth. This is why we see so many millions of people living in the most advanced time in human history, unhappy, stressed out and drugged up to their eyeballs on prescription and recreational drugs to cope with the consequences of missing this simple, yet costly distinction. Of course, I am not advocating self-imposed hardship or denial of comfort like some religions piously encourage in an effort to overcompensate. Our modern society has produced amazing things to help us advance and grow, and we should use them. But to use them exclusively for self-serving agendas is like using them to barricade ourselves into a comfort zone in an attempt to avoid the classroom of life. It's just not why we are here. It is also why those who follow that fake yet shiny star, feel empty and unfulfilled as they meander away from their own True North with its inherent purpose and meaning.

In short, it will always seem easier to open another beer than to lift the weights in the gym. But if that was the reason you are here then you would have been born a rock, not a human. The invitation of this entire section is for you to put down the Budweiser of seeking comfort and to embrace your calling to greatness. The good news is, you are not alone in your quest. Far from it. You have the entire conscious quantum field at your disposal, waiting, willing and *programmed* to help you. All you need to do is understand the rules and let's be honest, they are fairly simple. Going back to the car metaphor. You either embrace the challenge of learning to drive around this game of life by continuing to grow and give the best of who you are to the world. Or, you take your chances rolling aimlessly downhill trying your best to avoid obstacles.

One path rewards you with unlimited possibilities to express your gift along the freeways of life. The other usually results in your insurance premiums rising in the form of extra stress, frustration, fear, anger, resentment and the usual crowd of non-joyous states. I think we call it feedback.

The final rule for getting results with active meditation, is understanding the role of time. Both in terms of effort (consistency) and reward (results). Consistency is easy. Spend a minimum of ten minutes a day preparing your car for the road (passive meditation), as this leads to creating a foundational state we call coherence. Then spend a minimum of twenty minutes driving the car to where you want to go (active meditation).

Anything less than this and it's like going to the gym, lifting a couple of light weights and going home. It may look like it ticked the workout box on the to-do list but don't expect any visible results. The ideal time is double that, i.e. an hour, made up of twenty minutes of passive and forty minutes of active meditation every day. If you do this and follow the rules, you can expect 'unexpected' (non-linear) results, that some would call 'coincidence', to start showing up in anytime from a week to eight weeks. Why so long? It depends on three things: Firstly, the effectiveness and consistency of your practice. Second, how far away the probability is from the current likely scenarios (for example, if your intention is to be a successful concert pianist but your playing ability is only on grade six, it's going to take longer than if you have twenty years' experience). And third, the physics of the Quantum-to-Newtonian transition point. Let me explain this one a little more.

Imagine the quantum non-physical world running like the second hand of a clock. The physical world runs at a slower speed, like a minute or hour hand. Just because you cannot see the hour hand move, doesn't mean the clock is not working. Just like you cannot see your muscles grow but if you go to the gym and train them, you don't worry about if they will or not. You know if you put in the effort, you'll get the reward. And, as the atoms that make up the muscle tissue come from, and are largely made up of, the quantum field, why do we expect results from our meditations to suddenly produce immediate changes? We may get a few things that amount to a 'muscle pump' but growth requires commitment and consistency and those, my friends are usually the ONLY things which stop us from getting what we want. Whether it's learning to play the piano or manifesting from the quantum field. Therefore, let me help out with a viewpoint, which may help you invest one of those twenty-four hours we are given each day towards becoming an effective meditator and reality creator.

Whichever way you look at it, actions express priorities. If you want to see what's important to someone, see how they value and use their time. Someone who values a loving relationship will always find time to be with their partner, just as someone who values health will always find time to work out. If someone is unfit, it's not because they can't get to a gym, it's just that being fit is not a higher priority than the other things they do. If rich Uncle Albert left a million dollars in his will and all you had to do to claim it was complete a marathon in the next twelve months, your priorities would likely shift. What would it take for your priorities to shift in terms of committing time to your relationship to meditation and the quantum field of possibilities?

Well, while this may not be a completely accurate analogy statistically, it will serve the point for purposes of the exercise. As the non-physical operates at a higher frequency than the physical, we will assume one order of magnitude (i.e. x 10) is the difference between time and effectiveness. In other words, one hour spent influencing the quantum field with focused and conscious intent i.e. Through-Me, will often produce *at least* the same results as ten hours trying to 'make' it happen in the physical world by just getting busy and rolling up your sleeves in By-Me. Therefore, not making time for your daily meditation cycle because you are too 'busy' in the physical world is the same as saying you are too busy rushing to a meeting across town with only a rough idea of where the address is, and therefore you have no time to stop and program the Sat Nav / GPS.

The illusion is supported five minutes in with the 'kinda know where I'm going' guy, seemingly further ahead in the race. Of course, we both know what happens next as the GPS guy arrives at the meeting first. The reality is, saying we haven't got time to program the quantum Sat Nav is just hare brained logic which falls foul of the speedy tortoise every time. It's also a poor practitioner who engages as a result of needing to. Waiting until you're hungry is a bad time to plant seeds. Just as it's foolish to stop planting because you are full. You plant because you are a farmer and that is what you do. Like it or not, you are a sentient quantum practitioner who is *always* broadcasting your signal. You can never escape that because The Field is ALWAYS listening. Not taking conscious control of what you broadcast is like being given gills and webbed feet and choosing to live in a desert. Use your gift and your abilities wisely, and they will serve you well. But trying to influence the outcome of an inoperable brain tumour when you only have hours left to live is not the best time to start. That is not to say it cannot be done, but the existing probability of death is so high, it would take a much higher signal-strength to affect physicality within the time-frame available and within the parameters of the Quantum to Newtonian Transition Point. Not to mention, if the person involved had that level of developed skill, they would have probably used it when they first learned of the diagnosis and not waited until the eleventh hour. To quote a Chinese proverb – 'the best time to plant a tree was twenty years ago. The second-best time is now'.

Another common problem with short time-frames is that they tend to massively raise urgency and importance. This is always counterproductive as it encourages the mind to force things and try to impose its agenda on The Field. This drops you back into By-Me and leads to disharmony. It is ineffective at best and destructive at worst, as the heart and mind align in fear of the clock running out, rather than love and gratitude for the desired result. The power of The Field is always available but, as alluded to in the section on violence in the last issue, fear blocks your connection to that power. Fear not only slams the door shut on your desires but can often cause it to bounce back and hit you in the face. Whereas Love (high frequency), unblocks your connection and enables it to rise.

This is why letting go of the outcome is a big part, also known in many areas of spiritual growth as, 'the art of allowing'. However, it also brings up our final paradox. Resolving what I call the 'I want it, but I don't want it' issue. The way to resolve this is with a shift in awareness, as we bring all of the instructions full circle.

Summing Up

To practice what you have learned in this section effectively, begin with getting clarity on what you want for the right reasons. This means your intentions and outcomes are to be in alignment with your truth, not your fears, and serve your growth, not your ego. Next, relax and prepare the car for at least ten minutes, using passive meditation to quiet the mind and disconnect from the noise of the mental and physical-sense data. Then, when you're ready, switch to active meditation to take a minimum twenty-minute drive to the destination of where you experience your goals and desires as if they've already happened. While driving, use calm, unforced, yet focused intent. This provides the direction. To be effective, be sure to get associated to the feelings of what it is like to be at the place you want to be and flood the body with those feelings so that every single cell is left in no doubt what that experience 'tastes' like emotionally. Back this up with a solid willingness to do your part of the bargain and act appropriately in the physical world (i.e. pray, but move your feet) and listen for the strong and intuitive messages on which actions or directions to take. Finally, have patience and consistency, don't criticise yourself for not being perfect and know you will get better with practice.

Follow the above and soon you will develop trust and certainty that you are in the right river, as you notice small changes in your outer world for the better. At this point, you can relax and let go, knowing you no longer NEED your goal because you feel as if you already have it. It's simply a little further downstream in the physical world. Your heart and mind celebrate in harmony as you focus on being a good sailor, steering the ship responsibly and enjoying the river ride to your destination. In the meantime, the quantum field rearranges the outer world in a non-linear way to fit the new script you have written and the people around you, who are unconsciously playing the non-sentient game by default, look on in amazement at how your life progresses.

THAT, ladies and gentlemen, is the promise and gift of active meditation. However, before you give yourself four well-deserved gold stars for making it through all of that, there is one final tip to leave you with that will prevent you from undoing your efforts. Going to the gym is an unmissable part of the health plan, i.e. no workout, no results. But if you leave the health club and go supersize your meal at Burger King, you will sabotage your results. Investing time in your meditation and feeling your chosen future is your quantum workout. But feeding your mind the junk food of negative thoughts, doubts and fears throughout the rest of your day will cause you to spin your wheels. Instead, if you nourish yourself with good quality mind-food such as; love, gratitude, optimism, kindness, etc., then you can expect much better, faster and consistent results. Now go get those stars.

I Love you all,

Peter X

Volume 5: Rising Cramp (Week 10)

In this Volume, Peter breaks down his daily routine. From what time he awakes in the morning to his in-cell fitness and meditation routine. It's a short letter as the pain and cramp in his hand prevents him from writing for longer than a few minutes at a time.

My dear and amazing family, students and friends

Well, guess what? Yes, I'm *still* in Pentonville. And although I should have been moved weeks ago, I'm currently finding the thought of being transferred somewhat bittersweet. The reason is that I'm really enjoying the work I'm doing in here with the inmates. Some of which are in a bad way mentally and completely unsupported by the system. Also, I'm still very much enjoying the challenge of the environment. I think Winston Churchill called it 'cheerfulness in the face of adversity'. Though to be honest, it's not that difficult, and there are still a ton of things to be grateful for.

With the small time I get out of the cell to socialise, I'm busier than ever and there's always either a queue of people that want to see me one-on-one for personal issues, or a small group that gather for help and general advice. The feedback is humbling and the progress many are making, and the shift they are having, makes me so proud of them.

Just yesterday, a guy called Lee sought me out. He is a career criminal who's in his forties and been in and out of jail his whole life. A big, tough black guy, hardened by a life of crime and not someone to get on the wrong side of. I smiled as disarmingly as I could and saw both pain and sincerity in his eyes, albeit behind a veil of measured indifference. "Are you the guy that helps people?" he asked. It was direct and frank but with a clear undertone of hope. I replied, "It depends on what you need help with, my friend," hoping he wouldn't say an escape plan. What he said was heart-warming and in a way, it was an escape plan. Not one through or over a prison wall but out of a life of crime. He was currently awaiting sentence after being caught breaking into and robbing a Frankie and Benny's chain restaurant. He was an alarm specialist and his usual style was to go into commercial premises at night and crack the safe. He told me he hit corporations because he felt it was more 'victimless' to rob a faceless business owned by a multinational, than a mom and pop shop. However, he'd recently come to the awareness that this was simply a justification to make him feel less guilty. A commendable awareness, and one that had led him to want to apologise to the company. But he didn't know how to do so, who to approach or where to start. He wanted to know if I could help him write a letter and get his thoughts down on paper. I asked a few questions, essentially stress-testing the authenticity of his desire to 'go straight'. There were various hot buttons, including the fact his kids were now old enough to judge him for what he did and, as such, he wanted to give them a better example by becoming a better example. That in itself is a great lesson that many people never learn.

Another reason for his new-found conscience, was a result of him beginning to mature emotionally. Remember, most people's level of conscious awareness or emotional maturity is not correlated with their age. Some people stay in victim mode their entire lives as it's easier to blame (or in Lee's case justify), than it is to have the courage to grow up and raise your game. To take on the responsibility of personal growth. The fact that Lee was close to my age is no detriment to the fact that he was just starting to wake up.

It's a sad fact that society still contains a large number of emotional teenagers walking around in adult bodies. For Lee, it was a combination of conformity and poor choices that had led him to his life of crime. At an egocentric level of consciousness, it was easy for his mind to justify breaking the law. In fact, it's probably the most common misuse of free-will in society. People focus their efforts on finding shortcuts to fill desires by taking *from* the system, even if, like Lee, it means breaking the rules rather than working to add value *to* the system. Generally speaking, this is because society is geared more towards forceful control than responsible empowerment (i.e. the tendency to legislate rather than educate). But it's also because no one has ever really sat with the Lee's of the world (certainly not the ones in here) and ever helped them believe they were good enough to be able to offer something or recognise their own gifts. To believe in themselves enough. To feel validated, without the need to prove it through the amount of overpriced champagne you can buy in a nightclub. To understand that Life is a growth-centric experience. Not a money grab.

I translated Lee's thoughts into a letter he could use as a template for both the Judge and the company he robbed. I'll let you know if I hear back but the result is not nearly as important as his intention behind the message.

This is just one of many examples of how I'm trying to bring a small light into what is a vast and very dark abyss many people fall into here and one the government seem to want to sweep under the carpet and that society is largely oblivious to. Anyway, the bitter part of leaving here (if I ever do), will be leaving behind the people who most need help. Although, even from the inside and from what fraction of a difference I try to make, it seems to be a never-ending and bottomless pit of despair. However, I'm also sure you are aware of the starfish analogy where no matter how many thousands are washed up on the beach, you always make a big difference to the one you throw back into the ocean.

The sweet side of me moving to a D-Cat prison, which is where technically I belong, (although after the above it seems more selfish) is that it will allow me more opportunity to be out interacting, and I'm sure there will be no shortage of people that I can help, even in an open prison. A big challenge here is that for the last five weeks, I've been treated like an A-Cat maximum security prisoner locked in my cell for 23-24 hours a day and denied all access to education, jobs and even the library. I guess it's a good job I enjoy my own company. I think it was Eckhart Tolle who said that if you are happy with yourself, you can never feel alone.

I have filed several applications asking why I am being kept in the cell. Everyone has been ignored. So, I filed a formal complaint. This is a form that cannot be ignored and must be logged and responded to within five days. On the fifth day, I did receive a formal response. Whoever wrote it apologised, stating it must have been a mistake. The 'official' position was that there was no reason why I had been banned but that my privileges had now been restored. I immediately applied to get back to the education wing, as it gets me out of the house for an extra four hours a day. The result?

Education requests can take up to three days to process. This was ten days ago and I've still had no reply. I put a follow up in yesterday and in two days I will lodge a further complaint. To put this in perspective, for the last five weeks I've been treated far worse and with much more 'lockup' time than most of the murderers, rapists, armed robbers and drug dealers in here. Bearing in mind that, as someone who wasn't even accused, let alone charged, with any crime and with zero history of violence, drugs, or anything else that would pose a risk to society, I was automatically given my D-Category status within forty-eight hours of arriving. This is something most prisoners strive for throughout their whole sentence as it means a much, much easier route. D-Cat prisons are open, meaning there are no walls, gates or barbed wire. A friend in here I was previously helping, Bradley, was transferred within seven days (today is day seventy-four for me) and has written to me from his D-Cat saying that he even gets a key to his own cell. The guards say if you are going to escape (by simply walking out of the front gate), then please leave the key as it's a real bitch to change the locks. Of course, why would you escape, only to be caught and sent to a high-security place like here?

Anyway, Thea and my solicitor have a copy of all my formal transfer requests. All nine of them! My assigned supervisor, who is responsible for my transfer, went on sick leave three weeks ago. Before he left he promised me everything was in progress. Two weeks ago, I managed to talk my way out of the cell when Jinn was let out for his daily education and I made my way to the office where the people who control the transfers are. After a kind officer, who'd been working here for over twenty years, heard I'd been a D-Cat for over two months - he went to check. Now, bearing in mind this is a high-security B-Cat facility that is overcrowded by more than 300 past its capacity, you would assume they would want the D-Cats out to make room asap. Ah, silly me, that would be way too logical. As it happens, the officer came back and said he can't understand it, but there is NO record on ANY system that I have even requested a transfer. You couldn't make it up. He now assures me it's in progress, although that's what education told me when they said I could go back to class ten days ago. Oh well, if life was simple, it wouldn't be as fun! Seriously, you have to laugh at the absurdity. So, until then, I'll continue to do what I'm doing here, though it is getting harder to write by hand. What did we all do before keyboards?

Daily Routine

So, you may be wondering what I do all day in my tiny, I mean cosy, little cell? Well, as I'm kind of on a forced working holiday, I'm actually having a lie-in in the mornings until around 7am. I know, shock horror! Where's Pete's 5am morning routine gone? Well, to begin with, let's remind ourselves that the only place in the universe time even means anything is in the mind of a human. Nothing else obsesses over it or even keeps track. That aside, the practical application of getting up at 7am means I don't wake up Jinn. Each week, education and jobs rotate through morning and afternoon, meaning that this week he goes to class at 8am - 11.30am and next week it will be 1pm - 4.30pm. When we are on mornings, virtually all of the prisoners get out of bed around ten minutes before class. From what I've seen, even at 7am, I would be one of the very few members of the 'get up early' gang. I clean my teeth, have a wash and then do my stretching and yoga. I journal, and when Jinn leaves the cell, I meditate – usually for an hour, sometimes two. After which, I read and study. The books are mostly spiritual or personal development. I read and re-read the classics (my favourites, such as; Think and Grow Rich, Richest Man in Babylon, etc.) and much of the works by Dr David Hawkins.

The great thing about Hawkins is that each time you read or study his work, a deeper level of understanding reveals itself. Especially in books such as The Eye of the I, and Reality and Subjectivity. I also study different religious books, looking at the common threads and trying to gauge and appreciate both the minds of the masters and, more pertinent to today's world, their followers. After all, I feel understanding, empathy and tolerance will help us far more in addressing the challenges we currently face. Technology is not going to solve our problems as it is only ever a tool. It's the use of technology that will make the difference and that is driven by the very human aspect of intention, which is governed by the level of consciousness and emotional maturity it operates at. Much like a car, it's always the driver who makes the un-manifest potential manifest, based on their intention and character. A tank can still be used to take someone to the hospital, and an ambulance can still be used to run someone over and kill them. In other words, every action is preceded by a thought, which is driven by a combination of emotion in the short-term, or character and values (represented by the level of consciousness) in the long-term. Ultimately, the binary equation of Life lies at the point of discernment, and it is the plain and simple choice of choosing Love or Fear. At their core, this is something that all religions seem to agree on, with the overarching message being the invitation to grow up (emotionally and spiritually more than physically), by choosing Love over Fear in ever more challenging circumstances.

Back to the cell. Each cell has a small TV which I rarely watch. For years I called it the 'electronic income reducer', and to this day I have never in my life seen an episode of EastEnders, Coronation Street, General Hospital, Emmerdale, Hollyoaks or any of the other mind-fudge type programmes so prevalent in today's society. With the exception of The Big Bang Theory, which Jinn loves to watch and that I've grown to enjoy as a small daily escape from reality in here. Much to the amusement of Thea who is convinced I am the lead character, Sheldon, or at least related and hopefully with more developed people skills.

On the days I am let out - the wing is allowed around forty minutes to socialise - most of which is spent either waiting for a shower or waiting for the phone. This is also the time that many of my contemporaries seek me out. About half the time when we get 'social', as it's called, we also get exercise afterwards that involves another thirty-to-forty minutes of walking in a small circle around a small exercise yard. As this is a B-Cat prison, the exercise yard is in the centre of the prison with high fences, razor wires, cameras and at least two dog handlers. I'm also often asked to help many people during this time which I'm happy to do as at least outside I get to breathe fresher air and see the sky. In the evening we are let out for five minutes to go and collect dinner. Then it's lockup again until the next day.

Two hours after dinner (around 7pm) I train in the little room where the toilet is. I have to say, it's very versatile. With my pillow in there it becomes a meditation room. When empty, it's a bathroom and when I'm in there with my shorts, it becomes a gym. A jolly considerate room by most standards. My inspiration to train in the cell comes partly from the fact that health is one of my highest values, and partly from the example set by Mandela while he was incarcerated on Robben Island. In his youth, Mandela was a boxer and learned to prize health as well as use training as a way to work off stress. In prison he would do stationary running in his cell for up to forty-five minutes followed by one hundred fingertip push-ups, two hundred sit-ups and various other calisthenics. My current in-cell exercise routine consists of fifteen minutes of yoga, a five-minute plank, followed by a thirty-five minute sprint on the spot, where I visualise running around my favourite park. The route is six kilometres and I've done it so many times in real life that my imagination is accurate to within a couple of minutes of my usual finish time as I see each step in my mind's eye. Sometimes, I'm so engaged and associated to what I am visualising, that I nearly trip over the dogs as they run with me or shout hello to fellow runners and park dwellers. It's at this point that Jinn thinks I've lost my marbles. He's not an exercise guy at all.

Of course, some days I am lucky enough to get to the gym. This happens roughly once a week and on those days, I don't run in the cell. I used to do Virtual Workouts. This is a technique I teach the Masters Circle which allows you to grow muscles and increase strength, without doing any exercise and by just using your mind. This is something many universities have proven including, most recently, Harvard. I was also a resident expert on a clinically controlled study on this back in 2007. The challenge I found with the Virtual Workouts in here is that, while I can increase muscle mass and strength easily just by using my mind, I can't seem to circumvent the biology of eating the valueless food in here and not burning off the extra calories that my body isn't used to having. I lost my six-pack and became more lethargic, and that's when I knew I had to step up the physical side of burning off the junk they were feeding me.

After training, I have a strip wash as the gym becomes a bathroom again, put on my swanky PJ's (err, ok not swanky) and sit back at my desk, read, write and study until around midnight. Then I'll meditate again for around an hour before bed. Jinn is usually asleep around

10.30pm and I normally turn in around 1am. Of course, every night we have what I have affectionately called 'The Drummers'. Those who bang on their doors screaming abuse at the system, each other and whoever doesn't want to listen. It usually dies down by midnight, but not always.

Oh, that reminds me – in the last update, I was just finishing off when a particularly enthusiastic drummer kept banging hard and way past 1am, causing many frustrated inmates to scream abuse back. I know, just another happy day in the People Zoo. As expected, the next morning when the wing was unlocked for social, several inmates attempted to viscously assault him. He was immediately moved to another wing. However, it turns out that the guy who was his cellmate that night, and who was essentially trapped in there, was Oliver, one of the guys I mentioned and whom I've been helping here for several weeks. He found me at the first chance he got and told me it was him who'd been in with the loud drummer guy. He said that previously he would have screamed or gotten violent but now, after everything he'd been learning, he managed to keep his cool and even tried to use some of the techniques I'd taught him to calm the guy down. I was so overwhelmingly proud that I gave him a big hug. Not only for keeping his head together but more so for being mindful enough to help in a situation that was both dangerous and somewhat out of his depth. One Starfish at a time.

OK guys, I'm going to sign off on this update as I'm fighting a massive pain in the knuckle of my little finger which is causing my handwriting to become unreadable, even by myself. Big thanks to the fantastic Noorah and Anita who I believe get these typed up for you.

I'll write again soon and answer some of the questions you have written in with, including: 'What is an Indigo?', as I have referenced it a couple of times in previous updates. I'll elaborate next time, although for those interested in a preview, feel free to google the term 'Indigo Children' and you'll get a heads up. For some of you who really resonate with my work, it may even answer some of your own questions about why you feel different or out of place in society. Why nobody 'gets you', and why you have a strong and natural tendency to question authority and live by your own rules. Especially as it's clear to you that they are better-serving to society and make more sense than the traditional authoritarian crap heaped on you from birth. Some of you may even discover that you've finally found your tribe - and the others may finally understand why, those you know or care about and that fit the Indigo profile, behave the way they do.

Stay tuned. Stay cheerful in the face of adversity and above all, stay amazing!

I love you guys. Speak soon,

Peter X

Volume 6: Indigo Meets Black & White
(Week 12)

Volume six covers the intriguing topic of Indigo Children, along with their unique character traits. Peter also lays out the critical differences between content and context and how it affects everything from beliefs, to the criminal justice system. He shares a powerful lesson from Nelson Mandela and even answers the question of whether he still has contempt for the court. We are also introduced to a failed part of the prison service called I.P.P and the lives it is wrecking. Finally, he shares an enlightening moment in class, along with what he shows to be the single most effective way to foster rehabilitation and prevent reoffending.

My dear and amazing family, students and friends

Welcome to Volume 6 of Inside Track, and yes, I'm *still* in Pentonville. Three months as a D-Cat prisoner in a high-security B-Cat prison and still smiling. Part of that is this amazing and fascinating adventure I've been blessed to experience, and part of it is the overwhelming sense of love and support that continues to pour in daily through emails and letters. One piece of good news to start with, is that I've been promoted to 'enhanced' status for good behaviour and a few weeks earlier than one is usually eligible, due to receiving high praise from the guards. Being enhanced allows me three visits a month instead of two, plus one extra gym and social time a week. I'm happy about that as more time out of the cell is more time to help people and manage what is becoming quite the workflow. Seriously, this secret agent of change role is turning out to be a full-time deal!

In this issue, I promised to cover the topic of 'Indigo Children', as I've referred to the term several times in previous updates and some of you have asked what it means. I've also had several letters that follow up on Volume 4, where I offered insight on how to use the commercial strengths of the private-sector to help prisons achieve better rates of rehabilitation. (This is in contrast to how the system is set up now and that actually fosters reoffending.) Many have asked if I had any ideas and specifics on that and the answer is yes, absolutely. A short insight was given in detail in Volume 2 as 'Operation Chrysalis', but if time and pain in my hand permit, I'll update you based on my work and experience here since then. As ever, I'm mindful of your time and can promise you the lessons and insights I cover here will also offer much value in your everyday life as well. Please never doubt that my intention is always to serve you, as much as it is to share the journey from in here.

Introducing the Indigo

OK, let's start by covering a topic I feel many of you will resonate highly with. The phenomena known as the 'Indigos'. Rather than go into a deep dive, I'll cover it in a way similar to how I covered the topic of Sex Energy Transmutation Volume 2. I'll give you an overview, so you can get a feel and understanding, and at the same time offer some resources for those who wish to drill down.

There have been many books written on this subject, including one called 'Indigo Children' by Lee Carroll and Jan Tober. The original term was first used by a well-known clairvoyant called Nancy Ann Tappe who was studying the correlation between the colours in the bio-energy field of people (known by many as the 'aura') and their personality and behaviour. Bearing in mind, many police forces around the world hire and use psychics such as Nancy to great effect in cases such as locating missing persons.

(As a side, students of the Elite Mentorship Forum will be familiar with my overview of 'Remote Viewing', together with my own experience. This is covered in the advanced modules of the programme. For others interested

in this, I would recommend the book 'Psychic Warrior' by my friend and instructor, Dr David Morehouse. It's an excellent read.)

What Nancy discovered, beginning in the early 1970's, was a new colour she had never seen before and that started showing up in the auras of certain children. The colour was indigo, which is a mix of blue and violet. The interesting thing about these children is that they had very pronounced and different behavioural characteristics than so-called 'normal' children. The main characteristic they had in common was a strong and independent spirit that was very resistant to rules. In fact, Indigos are best known for having a complete aversion for institutional authority to the point of contempt. Hmm, does this sound familiar? This is not in a low-level, rebellious or teenage-type anarchistic way at all but quite the opposite. Indigo's question <u>all</u> rules and naturally resist those they do not feel are integrous at a higher level of consciousness, don't make sense or are outdated and contextually irrelevant in the bigger picture of how they see the world. In other words, they do not belong or fit into society's rigid framework, and they often feel this at a deep level. Like an undercurrent of discomfort, rather than an intellectual disagreement.

Other characteristics are as follows: -

They are sensitive to other's energy and feelings. They are also more sensitive than average to stimulants such as toxic food additives and chemicals. It is also common for many Indigo children to be misdiagnosed with labels such as ADD, ADHD, or Bipolar. This is due to a combination of agitation, caused by being forced into the strict and inflexible school structure, and being fed processed or altered foods. The tragic downside is that many are then forced to comply by being medicated (drugged) so they can fit back in. In other words, they are told their gift is not a gift but a malfunction. Of course, not all children who are diagnosed with the above are Indigos and vice versa, but I'm sure you are starting to build up a picture of their typical characteristics. Here are some more for those who feel they may be identifying themselves as an Indigo. For others, it may also help you to better relate to, or understand, some of the people you know who are. (There are many books on how to understand and relate to Indigo's if you are a parent or caregiver of one).

Indigos tend to be loners or are very selective of their friends (usually other Indigo's) and are comfortable with their own company. They have a very strong attraction to either healing, teaching, or being messengers that resonate at a higher level of awareness and understanding. They have little interest in other people's opinions unless they respect them, and that respect is gained by the quality of their truth or consciousness, not a job title.

They are usually drawn far more to spirituality than formal religion. This is due to having an affinity for the message of the great teachers such as; Jesus, Buddha, Allah, etc. but an aversion to the 'rules' religion then puts around the message, which historically has always had more connection to control and institutional agendas, than living the purity of the teachings. The rationale much of the time is that Indigo's feel such a strong connection to the recognition that they *are* children of God (as Jesus said and told the masses emphatically many times) and therefore, why do they need a mediator or a middleman to communicate with him? It doesn't make sense, and if it doesn't make sense to an Indigo then it's often not followed, irrespective of the law which can sometimes be seen to be archaic, oppressive, self-defeating and caters to the lowest common denominator.

You can probably see why these disruptive, yet aware and evolved souls could end up clashing with many aspects of society. A lot were born in the 70's and 80's. Although, Indigo energy has existed in smaller and more isolated examples and concentration throughout history and the character traits I outlined earlier are typical of many who have shaped the world in which we now live. Why the sudden influx? Simple. Evolution. In the 70's, the world was, and still is, in need of change. This is evidenced by looking around at the dysfunction and unsustainability of many of our systems. The amount of fear people experience in general, or just the realisation that we are currently on course to be the only species in history to create a mass extinction of ourselves and thousands of others. This is on top of the thousands we have already eliminated. Therefore, to counterbalance, evolution throws in a large bunch of 'change agents' and 'non-conformists' who won't stand by and just fall in line.

To understand this more, I'd like to revisit the Map Of Consciousness introduced in Volume 1 and that I refer to through this work. (Incidentally, the book Power vs Force which describes it in detail, is a book that every Indigo would resonate with.) If you recall, the map outlines a progressive and exponential scale of consciousness measured from 1 – 1000. However, the crossing point of where power begins is at the level of 200, also known as Courage. The levels that calibrate below 200 represent a life that is based on force, not power.

A simpler way to look at this, as it relates to the character traits of people, is that those who calibrate at 200 or over, operate from what could be called a higher mind. They are more ethnocentric (focused on others), less self-centred and are more solution-focused than problem focused. They are more givers than takers. But the reason they give is that it feels right. Not because they are banking brownie points to use later, (scorekeeping), or doing it to look good or to meet social expectations. Those who calibrate under 200 are generally more self-focused, egocentric, problem-orientated and probably far less likely to show an interest in reading a book like 'Power vs Force', let alone resonate with or even understand it.

Before we go any further, a word of caution. Please do not fall into the trap here of thinking this is a hierarchy of significance or superiority. That would be the temptation of what I call 'spiritual ego'. Instead, recognise this is simply a path outlining a progression of consciousness. The acorn is not worse or less important than the oak tree. It's simply not as far along in the development of its own potential.

And remember, when it comes to emotional and spiritual maturity, it has little to do with age or intellect. Why do I mention this? Because using the science of consciousness calibration (as demonstrated globally by Dr Hawkins, including at both Harvard and Oxford universities for those doubting academics), it showed the overall and aggregate level of consciousness for humanity, in general, had remained just below the critical threshold of 200 throughout history. Steadily rising but never crossing over. That is until the late 1980's. Coincidence? Hardly. Many Indigos, such as myself, are now grown up and you see evidence of their trying to express themselves everywhere. Either as activists, raising awareness against corporate greed or environmentally harmful practices, to social entrepreneurs, artists with a high social conscience, cause or theme or someone who helps out selflessly, making a difference to their local community or neighbourhood. All are in some way agents of positive social change. Positive being internally defined by choosing love instead of fear and by what they can give, not what they can take. By what difference they can make to the world, not just their own circumstances. This is largely irrespective of whatever society tries to tell them is the definition of positive. That is unless they've swallowed the pill of being told they were dysfunctional and found themselves conforming in some way to a rule based job they pretend to enjoy, while trying to ignore the splinter in their heart that won't go away.

Content vs Context – A Life Changing Distinction

Another huge aspect, certainly for me, that clashes with a large part of the existing framework of society (especially the criminal justice system, unfortunately) is the natural predisposition for Indigos to prioritise *context* over *content*, viewing life (or rather recognising life) as a far more subjective experience, rather than an objective one. Think about it. Even the belief that life is objective is, in itself, a purely subjective position and phrase.

The fact remains - and please tattoo this on the inside of your eyelids - *context is definitive*! If facts were solely objective, they'd be no court of appeal. The reality is, Life is not an objective experience and what we experience is describable but not provable. This means how we <u>perceive</u> and <u>interpret</u> the facts is always more significant than the facts themselves. Hence, two men sat behind prison bars one saw mud the other saw stars. Without context, facts become irrelevant at best and highly misleading at worst. Also, rather than blindly follow one set of interpretations (i.e. rules), it is far more empowering (and responsible) to recognise that each level of consciousness results in a different definition of 'truth', and one that is calibrated and attuned to that level. Please read that again.

Problems and disagreements in our lives don't happen as a result of what's right clashing with what is wrong, because at a higher level of understanding it's plain to see that everything simply 'is'. Friction occurs when interpretations and definitions of what is 'true' for me, conflicts with other levels of awareness that are 'not true' to the people at that level. Not only that, but even if there is agreement about the facts of the definition of 'truth', there are still variations and conflict as to what it means or signifies. Are you getting the picture? The fact that our court system places a higher value on content than context is simply evident of the need for it to also evolve. Especially as if context *is* brought to the table, it is (in my experience) always distorted from the truth and used to support a predetermined outcome in favour of those presenting and coordinating its distortion.

I personally fell victim to this in a classic example. In court, the prosecution found a personal document on my computer that was solely for my private use. It was printed and placed in my meditation room. It had not, nor would ever, be published or shared on any social platform. The document outlined a personal statement of how I aim to conduct my life. One of the sentences in that letter reads '…such as Mandela, to whom I've so graciously been compared…'. The reason

I wrote this, was due to a letter I received from a family in South Africa who I'd been working with to help. I was even honoured to write the foreword of the husband's book on overcoming diabetes. The wife wrote me a beautiful and touching letter (which I still have) comparing the work I was doing in helping South Africa to Madiba (the local name for Mandela). It is probably the most humbling thing anyone has ever written to - or about – me. I remember crying with gratitude when I read it. It was also deeply personal as I have been blessed to work with Mandela's family on various occasions. I spent the first ever 'Mandela Day', a year after his death, at Mandela House after spending the morning repairing gravestones in the township of Soweto. My Millionaire Business School had granted various scholarships to underprivileged teenagers, in partnership with the Mandela Legacy Foundation. An initiative that was highly praised by the Foundation and Mandela's family for the huge, lasting and positive impact it had on the kids who attended. One of whom, a 16-year-old who had been sexually abused, went on to start her own business that within a year was making 10,000 Rand a week. Of course, none of this was mentioned in the courtroom and instead, the opposing counsel twisted the phrase to try and tell the judge I was comparing myself to Mandela as I felt I was above the law. You can imagine how hurt I was, and my mistake (as outlined in Volume 3) was to allow that hurt to translate into indignation at the other side, which the judge then chose to see as evidence of ego and not contrition or apology. To me, it is yet more evidence of the smoke and mirrors of courtroom theatre that wilfully abuses context to distort facts and manipulate meaning.

Mandela himself was the quintessential Indigo who devoted his life to fighting social injustice in the form of Apartheid (which was happily declared legal and supported by the courts for many years). However, there is one lesson Mandela learned earlier in his life which I'll share with you, and one I wish I'd learned a little sooner.

Pick Your Battles!

Indigo energy will stand up to and against what it feels is forceful, manipulative or just plain wrong. Like corporate bullying. I felt what HP were trying to do to me was just plain wrong. To falsely claim and 'invent' a $17 million loss that was never incurred (nor could be), and then use it behind my back to get the upper hand in obtaining a freezing order in the hope that I would settle by giving them a quick hundred grand, instead of choosing to fight and spending at least that on legal costs. My Indigo nature said: "F**k you". My brain should have stepped back and picked my battles.

Mandela learned this lesson when he was at university. Being the adopted son of King Jongintaba, to whom Mandela was sent after his father died, he was able to have access to certain privileges many black South Africans didn't have. One of these was a good education, which the King valued as the mark of a leader, something the young Mandela was being groomed to be. As such, he was able to secure a place at the only black University in South Africa, Forte Hare. Mandela was popular and was put forward in the student elections for Student President. However, at the time of the vote, there was a call for a boycott of the elections as a protest over the quality of food. (Something I can empathise with in here!) Mandela was elected but refused to take the position, stating that it was not a true representation of the student body as many had not voted and therefore the result should not stand. The Dean of the University, an inflexible and rules-driven man called Alexander Kerr, demanded that Mandela take the position and gave him an ultimatum. Either do so or leave the University. Mandela, at that time, felt his integrity was more important than conceding to a bullying authority and walked away. On the surface, it may seem commendable and the right thing to do but, as the King pointed out afterwards, Mandela had traded a quality education for a relatively minor matter of refusing the vote result. In chess terms, he may have won a pawn, but he lost a queen.

The art of leadership is in taking the big picture into account and thinking several moves ahead. This helps win the war instead of trying to win every battle at all costs. The challenge here is always ego, which happily uses the mind to create and stand on seemingly solid rationale, so as to justify actions that lead to short-term wins and feelings of significance. It's worth noting that ego and long-term intelligence rarely go together. If you doubt that, look at how politicians avoid or misrepresent the truth in order to win short-term approval or avoid short-term criticism.

One of the other inherent characteristics of Indigo's, which can act as a two-edged sword in this instance, is the flame that gets lit when faced with the perceived misuse of authority. I've been asked if I actually do, or still have, contempt for the court. The honest answer is that it's almost impossible not to. However, to clarify that (before it's taken out of context by some status-seeking journalist), it's not in a defiant or anarchistic way. That's usually just uneducated and juvenile posturing. Instead, I have contempt of court in the same way many have contempt for the current education system which limits a child's sense of self-worth to their ability to remember answers to questions that have little to do with modern life, let alone developing their innate gifts.

Another parallel would be the healthcare system which isn't actually focused on health but instead illness management and perpetuation. This is due to the Big-Pharma profit-based mandate of a pill for every ill and an ill for every pill. One of the reasons I'll never go to a traditional doctor if I want to be healthy is simple. They've never studied health. Instead, they are experts in illness. Of course, if I want to be ill - then I'll talk to a doctor as they know all about it. Not to mention that, aside from the fact many are dedicated and hardworking, amazing and caring people who do genuinely want to make a positive difference, it's self-evident that many are not pictures of health themselves. Interestingly, they have a higher mortality rate than average (i.e. die younger), and every independent survey shows that a high percentage are addicted to their own drugs (do your research). Not altogether surprising when you appreciate the combination of their intent to serve, the limited tools they have which only treat symptoms and not causes, the stress of long hours, increased workload, paperwork and regulations, etc. and the unfortunate reality that society has promoted a culture of 'free money for being a victim'. This now shifts the centre of gravity from practising patient care over to practising 'defensive medicine'. In other words, doctors are ordering more tests, second opinions and unnecessary procedures. This is not because they care so much, but rather they are covering all bases to try and prevent lawsuits for negligence. This causes delays in treatment, clogs up waiting lists and spirals costs. Is it any wonder many are on drugs to cope? Contempt anyone? Err, you could say that. Not for the doctors, who are trying their best. They are hero's piloting a failing aircraft. It's just unfortunate, as even if you take away the legal parameters which restrict them by law to doing little more than prescribing drugs and recommending surgery, this mounting bureaucracy locks them into a mental and behavioural straightjacket that many of us would run from.

It's the same for the criminal justice system. I have already written about how much respect I have for the Judge and opposing counsel in previous updates. They are just doing their job. Hewlett Packard is just manipulating and trying to profit from the legal system just as a drug company tries to manipulate and profit from the health system. Like it or not, you cannot blame a leech for sucking blood as much as you can't blame an alcoholic for drinking. You may not like the outcome but blaming a mosquito for biting you and taking it personally is simply being ignorant of the inherent nature of nature itself, and anyone who tells you otherwise is either uneducated, a lobbyist or a lawyer looking for a fee. But back to the original point. One thing is certain. If I came in here due to contempt of court, having seen and experienced first-hand the total, blatant and utter injustice the criminal justice and the prison system perpetuate on a regular basis - I now have far more contempt for the entire process. For those on the outside who still believe or have faith in the system, being in here is like seeing your loved one dying in a cancer ward and still being told to believe in the illusion of healthcare rather than disease management.

No Way Out

A typical example is a gentleman I met in the library, Joseph Samuel. The conversation started when I was talking to another prisoner about how bad everyone says the conditions in Pentonville are. Joseph chimed in and said he'd just arrived from Hull prison where he suffered constant and open racial abuse from the staff (he's mixed race) but said, he'd rather go back there and suffer that than stay in Pentonville. I said that I hear that a lot about Pentonville from prisoners who had been to other jails. He then replied, saying it was true and that he should know as he's been inside forty-four prisons. Say what? I thought I'd misheard him but it was definitely forty-four. I said: "Wow, what did you do?" I was expecting some type of super criminal and my senses heightened and tuned in as I thought this could be a good opportunity to use my skills to help and work with what was clearly a pathological offender. I couldn't have been more wrong. Not about his ability or willingness to be helped, but by my initial and somewhat overzealous labelling. Joseph then shared his story.

At seventeen years old (still a minor in the eyes of the law), he was convicted of stabbing and mildly wounding a sex offender with a knife. There were no life-threatening injuries but it was inexcusable and Joseph was rightfully convicted. However, he was sent to prison under a sentence called a 'D.P.P.', which stands for 'Detained for Public Protection' and allows the prison to keep you for a maximum of ninety-nine years. There is a suggested minimum term, known as a tariff, which in Joseph's case was five years. At eighteen years old, the sentence was converted to the adult equivalent called 'I.P.P' (Imprisonment for Public Protection). Joseph was told that to be eligible for his five-year release date, he had to complete three courses in prison (he came in with no qualifications). That was twelve years ago. In that time, Joseph has obtained 158 qualifications inside prison covering everything you could think of from Barber, to Ford mechanic to Waste Recycling (plus over 150 others). He has a degree and is completing his second. He is also learning his third language. He has a certificate from the prison service confirming that he is the most qualified prisoner in the UK. He has been drug-free throughout his whole sentence and has no history of violence for over ten years. He's now twenty-nine and has been in prison since he was seventeen on a five-year tariff.

The obvious question is - Why? And to me, the answer is also obvious but that doesn't mean it's easily solvable. The problem mostly ties into what I was saying earlier about the way healthcare has degenerated into the practice of 'defensive medicine', as doctors juggle their focus on not being sued rather than just doing their best to help. It's the same in here. Welcome to 'defensive probation'. The reality is that no one in probation wants to be responsible for Josephs' release, in-case he re-offends and it reflects badly on them and their career. Each time he goes for parole, he's told that he either needs another course, as the one he's done or has taken has now changed names and is therefore not eligible, or often it is only available at another prison or he is moved before he has time to finish it. Now they are saying he has a personality disorder and is institutionalised (you don't say!?). At every parole hearing, he is also constantly reminded that the term is up to ninety-nine years, which is what he believes he will now serve (i.e. end up dying in prison). He has been moved on average every six weeks (hence forty-four prisons) so, sadly, he can never make long-term friends. Not only that, but due to the I.P.P. label (which he was never convicted for remember, just 'promoted' to at eighteen), he can only be sent to Double A-Category (Super Maximum), A-Category (Max Security) or B Category like here (High Security). His family never know where he is and have given up. He hasn't had a visit from the outside in ten years. He took his case to the High Court here in London, showing them a ruling from the European Court of Human Rights that stated his sentence is unlawful and he should be released. The High Court refused. Even Kenneth Clarke, the former Justice Secretary, said in the House of Commons that the I.P.P. sentence was "Inhumane, a stain on the British Justice System and should be abolished". He was replaced before he could do so. The I.P.P. sentence was finally abolished in 2012 BUT NOT FOR THOSE PREVIOUSLY CONVICTED. Many of which have served five-times their tariff!

Joseph has tried several times to commit suicide, as there is no light at the end of his tunnel (Remember what I said in Volume 2 about the link to suicide and no compelling future?). But here is the fact that should wake up every politician with a conscience: 50% OF PRISON SUICIDES ARE I.P.P. INMATES. In fact, over 300 of those sentenced have already killed themselves. I mean, can you imagine not having a release date? And then every time you go for parole and get your hopes up having jumped the hoops they told you to jump, they move the goalposts, give excuses and produce more hoops. Hence, we have the most qualified prisoner in the UK – twenty-nine years old who served his five-year sentence plus another seven with still no hope of release, kept in appalling conditions under an unlawful sentence that can keep him for ninety-nine years. A fact that probation officers hide behind so as to avoid taking the responsibility of freeing him. For two hours afterwards I couldn't even function as I felt I'd been punched in the stomach with a lead glove. I called Thea in a mix of shock, sadness and utter contempt. If he had committed the crime today (what's known as 'Section 18' – causing Grievous Bodily Harm with a weapon and intent), the maximum sentence would be five years. And that's for an adult. Joseph told me that the biggest irony was that the person he attacked went on to rape two other women, was convicted, and is already out walking free. And if you think Joseph's story is uncommon, you'd be wrong. I've attached a link to an article from this month's prison paper from a woman whose partner was also given an I.P.P. years ago, has served over double his tariff and can't find a way out. It's almost identical to Joseph's case – see for yourself by visiting https://insidetime.org/hes-given-up/

Joseph has written to many lawyers over the years, desperate to have someone take up his case but everyone has asked for fees. Justice, he keeps being told, comes at a price, but the tiny daily amount he earns inside (around £2 a day) goes towards minor comforts on the canteen. He's since stopped writing, as his hopes have been dashed so many times, but he's begging for help and doesn't know what to do. My friends, if you know of anyone who may be able to at least take up his case, please take action. Or visit him and see for yourself. That would make his year. His prison number is A0560AK. Personally, it's hard for me to engineer our paths crossing due to my own restrictions and being on a different wing. I managed to figure out his study times for his degree and try to sneak into the library on my way to class if I can, but the time window is tight and we've only managed two meetings so far. I can certainly work with his mindset as I don't want him to take another attempt on his own life, as it may be the last. Although I also need to be mindful of raising false hope which could then rebound and do more harm. I could give you a dozen more examples that would also make you shake your head in disbelief, but I think you get my point. Contempt? Don't ask me again.

An Enlightening Moment In School...

OK, let's switch gears and write about something more positive. After all, being part of the solution is infinitely better than just focusing on the problem. As some of you may have guessed from my 'on my way to class' reference above, I have finally been put back into education.

This followed seven weeks of 23–24 hours a day lockup due to what they claimed was an error. Want to hear the fun part? They've put me into a journalism class! This is for the guy who's never read a tabloid newspaper or watched a news bulletin for over fifteen years. Plus, my experience in how many so-called journalists operate, leaves me little time for their biased projections. Don't get me wrong, historically, journalists held themselves to a high standard and moral code, but as the industry became more competitive and cutthroat, standards dropped. Combined with the low barrier to entry and multiple outlets (from blogs to online rags and niche fields of every description, etc.) it became a common platform for many people who calibrate below 200 to stand on and voice their own opinions and agendas. This is usually supported by a carefully selected (or omitted) number of limited facts, positioned against a backdrop of either missing or distorted context. The overall opinion (which is almost always decided upon before writing the article) is then presented as fact and becomes pseudo-reality for those sucked into the premise. It is also a fact that the power of mass agreement hypnotises many people. In other words, they make the intellectually dumb mistake of confusing popularity for truth.

Another reason journalism and media attract many people below 200 (courage) is that it rarely takes courage to be a critic. Many of today's 'Keyboard Warriors' would lack the backbone to sit across from the people they write about and seek to ask objective questions, while being open to the possibility of being mistaken in their initial assumptions. Instead, they often seem more attached to imposing their own agenda and the status-seeking it provides. I am pretty certain that almost every article that has been written about me in a negative sense, has been selectively compiled by people who've never met me or studied my work. Playing devil's advocate, you could say the same about Mother Theresa or Adolf Hitler, but both of those were judged on the number of people they affected and in what way. Remember, it's always easy to cherry pick snapshots of what people have done, distort context, magnify or minimise whatever aspect you choose, and construct a convincing viewpoint. Just as a director of a movie can turn any scene into tragedy or a comedy, simply by adjusting the aspects of the set he wants you to focus on. I mention this as it's not without consequences. One particular journalist who seems to have taken delight in writing negative articles about me, and whose writings caused some podcast hosts to take down their interviews (including London Real), likely sat back in the naivety (or smugness) of genuinely thinking he was doing good. Not for a second did he consider the tens of thousands of people who had benefited or had their lives changed for the better, or how many lives that could have been helped had those interviews stayed up, but now won't be. All due to his personal interest in proving whatever point he wanted to make to satisfy his need to feel right and backed up by a moral sense of superiority under the guise of objective journalism. It's a classic and fundamental characteristic of what happens in the realms of consciousness below the level of 200. Of course, I'm not saying freedom of speech is wrong and nor should people's mistakes be swept under the carpet. Nevertheless, the clear, yet often missed reality about criticism, is that it is never a true reflection of the criticised but instead merely a projection of the criticiser, and one that often reveals more about their relationship to the world than the object of their judgement.

Personally, I think it's useful to accept that we all have blind spots. Not to mention that we're just not meant to get the answers right 100% of the time. Otherwise, how can we grow? I also feel that if and when I make mistakes, then that's for me to process, learn from and make any future adjustments in behaviour needed. Life gives you the best feedback. Not a social media gossip thread. The most empowering lesson I can give you in this regard, is to understand and see your mistakes of the past as your capital, not your regrets. The phrase 'look at what I've learned' instead of 'look at what I've lost' can literally be the difference between a life of growth, or a life of anti-depressants.

Anyway, back to the classroom as we've drifted a little off-track. That does tend to happen when I get on the subject of things like media or politics. So, here I was thrust into, of all places, journalism school. It certainly had the potential to be a red rag to an Indigo bull. Luckily, I had other ideas in mind. I've had five lessons so far, and by the second lesson, many classmates were reconsidering their view of the media (sorry, couldn't help it). In my third lesson, the teacher kept commenting on how quickly I was finishing the assignments. I explained it wasn't because I was smarter, but because I was able to read much faster and with better recall, having taught and practised the art of speed reading for many years. I showed that how we are taught to read in school was massively ineffective as we are not shown how to powerfully engage our brains. Worse still, we say the words to ourselves (either out loud or in our head) which means we process the meaning via the sound using our auditory sense, rather than the visual. We can therefore only ever read at the speed we can talk and which, for the average person, is between 150 – 200 words per minute.

The teacher was fascinated and, after a short discussion, agreed I could teach the skill to her and the class next day. I won't go into details, but after an hour (she'd initially permitted me twenty minutes), she'd taken more notes than most of the students, all of which were fully engaged and they all asked if I'd continue. It was like asking a fish to swim. At this point in my life, I resonate far more with the identity of a teacher (though always a student too) than a business guy. A big shift compared to my background, in which I always held the identity of a teacher second to that of an entrepreneur. I decided to find out what the most value I could add to the class would be in the remaining two hours, so started with an open frame where I asked what everyone's biggest pain points in prison were. As you can imagine, I got an avalanche of emotionally charged complaints about the conditions and how the lack of basic needs, combined with more lock-up time than many A-Cat prisons, was bordering on barbaric and inhuman. For example, the longest I've gone without a shower was ten days! (I know, don't ask, that's even longer than when I ran the Marathon Des Sables across the Sahara.) As expected, many of their complaints focused heavily on the surface issues. But when I started drilling down, I was able to re-contextualise their relationship to them and at which point, the entire conversation became a two-hour experience that raised the energy and consciousness level of the whole room. Here's what I shared:

One of the most significant problems in a 'faceless system' is that it's usually the front-line people who get the worst of the blame when things go wrong. For example, in a business that's poorly managed and is sending out, say, delayed or sub-standard products, it is the poor customer service staff that have to deal with the complaints. This is understandable as they provide an obvious scapegoat and outlet for frustration. In here, that frustration is expressed as anger most of the time, and it is the prison officers and staff who take the brunt of the attack. This, in turn, creates a hostile environment, which tends to attract more opportunity for hostile expression. Especially in Pentonville, as it is one of the most under-resourced and also violent prisons in Europe. That's not a coincidence. It's causal (as I explained in detail in Volume 4). However, the shift I wanted to make in my classmates was in understanding that, while nothing about how we are treated in here is fair (as evidenced in the extreme by Joseph's story), when you understand it is a by-product of a poorly managed, resource-starved, largely unaccountable (i.e. self-policing) system, and NOT because it has been purposely designed to be unfair - it opens up the doorway to a better contextual understanding.

This allowed my classmates to see the situation and the system as flawed instead of vindictive. That's a massive shift. It doesn't make it right, but once they stop taking it personally and see things for what they are, it's easier to stop blaming the guards and instead almost feel sorry for them. Like the doctors piloting a failing aircraft who are then also being blamed for the mechanical failure. Another way to understand it is to look at toothache. Toothache isn't trying to be vindictive. It's just the product of the environment. The tooth doesn't wait or plan for the ideal time to upset you, like on your birthday or a first date. It simply sends a pain signal as a by-product of decay. For my classmates, this was a hugely enlightening moment. By owning this one awareness, it's possible to quickly go from being an angry victim who seeks to blame and threaten the officers, into understanding and even compassion. This instantly raises your energy and levels of consciousness. What this also does at a higher level, for the more enlightened, is transcend the paradigm of victim vs perpetrator. Needless to say, this is something that can create and shift so many things, especially personal blocks and repeat patterns of self-sabotage.

The end result was a massive shift in class. The comments and transformations (including the teacher) made a paragraph on my Magic Moment list (currently at well over 100). Including one from a guy called Tyrone. He's thirty-six and has six children. It's his third time inside for drug-related offences and he is (or was) best described as bitter, non-conformist and opinionated. He's skinny and suffers from epilepsy. We sit next to each other in class. After that session, he touched my arm and said that he'd been expelled from every school he'd gone to. He hated education and all of his time there. But in the last four days and in particular that day, he'd learned more than his entire (although somewhat chequered) twelve years in traditional education. He kept saying over and over: "Something's shifted in me, man" and there was a deep understanding, almost wonder in his eyes. He also said: "You got me. For the first time ever in my life, I feel you got me," meaning I'd touched him at a deeper level. It was a hugely humbling moment.

It also underscores my conviction in the kind of education that is needed in here to make the biggest difference. This brings me (and this update) full circle to my last point and the answer to the question posed at the beginning about my thoughts on what kind of ideas I'd have on shifting the balance from reoffending, to rehabilitated. Of course, it's no surprise that it centres far more on raising consciousness than it does on the transfer of knowledge. Acquisition of knowledge without raising consciousness simply provides more tools with which to execute the same behaviours. That's why education in prison in its current form has virtually zero benefit or statistical impact on rehabilitation. However, those who have gone through any type of spiritual or church-based programme or received some kind of ministry, consistently show significant positive results when it comes to avoiding relapse. In some cases in America, it is close to 100%. The critical first step is to get people past the level of 200 on the Map Of Consciousness. This has proven to have more impact than any programme, initiative or scheme-based activity. Period. Here are some numbers that may shock you. (Calibrated in 'Truth vs Falsehood', 2005 David R. Hawkins M.D., Ph.D.)

	CALIBRATED LEVEL OF CONSCIOUSNESS	CORRESPONDING RATE OF UNEMPLOYMENT	CORRESPONDING RATE OF POVERTY	HAPPINESS RATE "LIFE AS OK"	CORRESPONDING RATE OF CRIMINALITY
	600 +	0%	0.0%	100%	0.0%
	500 – 600	0%	0.0%	98%	0.5%
	400 – 500	2%	0.5%	79%	2%
	300 – 400	7%	1.0%	70%	5%
ABOVE 200	200 – 300	8%	1.5%	60%	9%
BELOW 200	100 – 200	50%	22%	15%	50%
	50 – 100	75%	40%	2%	91%
	Under 50	97%	65%	0%	98%

The biggest awareness that jumps out from this is the massive rise in criminality from 9% to 50% as soon as one falls below the level of 200. Can you see the futility in just trying to 'educate' someone calibrating at, say, 100? It doesn't matter what they 'know'. They will simply channel that knowledge into committing more crime and avoiding detection. BEHAVIOUR IS A BY-PRODUCT OF THE LEVEL OF CONSCIOUSNESS YOU'RE AT. Case closed. So, therefore, a powerful question that arises and presents itself is: 'How can we help shift more prisoners past the threshold of 200?' Well, the fastest way I know of is to take responsibility for one's own actions and consequences (note - this is why working with and confronting their victims has had some useful success in various programmes). The main barrier to this is pride, and the main antidote to pride is humility.

Humility begins with self-acceptance of all of your supposed imperfections as OK and a normal part of being human, along with the realisation that everyone else's are as well. This opens the doorway to dropping pretence and therefore there is less need to defend or attack in order to protect an inflated sense of self. From here, authentic work can begin on one's own journey of growth. The obvious question is; would this work in here? Well, you can no longer tell me it can't as, for the last thirteen weeks, every person at every level I have worked with has responded positively in some way to the interactions we've had. Though remember, you or I can never raise anyone's level of consciousness. We can only position the stepping stones and invite them on the journey. Ultimately, it's their own decision. I would just dearly like to help them realise they have the choice.

Thank you for your time my friends and for being with me on this journey. Your strength, your support and your love touch many more lives in here than just my own.

Keep shining and I'll write soon,

Peter X

Volume 7: Reason to Live (Week 14)

A medical accident brings Peter to a potential suicide case where he proceeds straight into an intervention. What happens next is laid out step by step, allowing you to understand why, how and what goes on in the mind of someone who wants to kill themselves, and exactly what he did to change it. He also explains how he is teaching drug dealers to give up crime and start legitimate businesses through the concept of transferable skills.

My dear and amazing family, students and friends

It's now been over 100 days that I've been here in Pentonville awaiting transfer to an open jail. As a civil prisoner, that's around ninety days longer than I should have been here. The department that deals with transfers is called the OMU which stands for 'Offender Management Unit' and I have been trying what I can to build a relationship with them. This is nearly impossible due to the internal setup but there does seems to be a shard of light on the horizon thanks to an amazing man called Mr Daly who has intervened. He's been an officer here for twenty-seven years and is definitely a guy who gets things done. He even met with Thea on a visit and explained his plans for getting me moved. In essence, he has looked at my profile, behaviour and risk assessment and put me forward to be the first prisoner in Pentonville for twenty years to be released temporarily so I can make my own way to an open D-Cat facility. Quite the honour. Let's see what happens. As we know, things in this system move about as fast as an asthmatic snail with a heavy backpack.

Prison Break

Speaking of which, I'm moving a bit slower myself at the moment as

I think I may have broken my foot. I say this as I've been asking for an X-ray for the last ten days and have heard nothing. It happened as I carelessly tripped over the step on the top landing. My foot rolled as my body weight shifted onto it and I heard the bones break. This was immediately followed by searing pain, instant swelling and an inability to put any weight on it or walk. I then limped and struggled badly over to healthcare who gave me one anti-inflammatory tablet. They said they had no ice packs, no crutches and to this day I have never been given any painkillers. Or the X-ray. Welcome to Pentonville. Oh well, I guess it's life's way of slowing me down a little in order to get in sync with the system!

One thing that did blow me away, however, was the outpouring of care and support from the other inmates. On the first night, they brought my dinner to my cell as I couldn't manage to get down the stairs. Many have offered shoulders to lean on to help me get to education each day as I struggle to walk through the wing. Someone even brought a mop bucket to my cell with cold water and some healing oil, and after four days of the prison saying they couldn't find a spare crutch, one of the inmates made it his mission to find one and delivered it to my door as a surprise. Although, I did make him promise he hadn't beaten up or stolen it from someone with a bad leg!

Master Circle members will be familiar with the process of accelerated healing and which, in ideal circumstances, I've used twice before to mend broken bones in ten to fourteen days on X-ray. However, this is not an ideal environment but in the absence of resources (including painkillers), it's my primary tool. Well, that and not running upstairs.

What else was interesting, was that within an hour of the accident I must have had over ten people say "Claim! That's a claim – a few grand at least!" Remember my comment in the last issue (Volume 6) where I said society has created and conditioned the concept of 'free money for being a victim'? The strangest part was, they couldn't understand it when I responded saying how could, or would, I claim when it was my own fault? Even if it wasn't, why on earth would I trade off my sense of responsibility for everything that happens in my life for a few thousand pounds? It may as well be thirty pieces of silver. Owning your circumstances, both good and bad, rather than blaming others for them, will always lead to a much richer future. Trust me, a victim mentality at *any* level will cost you a lot more than what a compensation cheque can offer. This doesn't discount the fact that some people deserve and have a genuine entitlement to help, financially or otherwise, for certain situations, but the day I slip on a wet floor or walk in front of a car and then sue someone rather than own the fact I should have seen the hazard, is the day you never want to read another word I write.

A Wing and A Prayer

On the subject of victims, it's been a tough week here. Two days ago, a prisoner was slashed across the neck with a knife in a typical attempted murder, and since then two more prisoners have taken their own lives in successful suicide's. One happened yesterday morning at around 4am on E-Wing and another today on F-wing. Poor souls. I didn't know either of them as unfortunately I only have the ability to get to D, C and G wing. Incidentally, G Wing is nicknamed the 'Gaza Strip' and it is the largest and most violent wing in Europe. I spend time there as I have some students who I'm helping, but it's a bad place to hang out. Needless to say that during my meditations I send a lot of prayers that way.

I did do one suicide intervention this week and I want to share it with you. This is so you can see how fast you can shift someone through recontextualising the event or circumstances that are causing the pain. This is in contrast to trying to change the circumstances themselves – the inability of which is usually the biggest source of pain. Now, if you recall back in Volume 2, I give an overview of some of the commonalities that lead to suicide and how to address them, so I won't go into that here. But I do want to walk you through what happened, as it could serve as a way for you to help others or, at the very least, understand more about what is going on with them.

The event itself happened while I was lining up on C-Wing for my prescribed anti-inflammatories for my foot, having finally been given them a few days after my accident. I've never lined up for "meds" before as I obviously don't take any, but many here do. I was behind one guy in his mid-twenties. He seemed upset, so I built some rapport and asked him what he was collecting. He shared that his name was Gary and he was here to pick up some anti-depressants. However, he wanted a stronger dose as he didn't think they were working because he was constantly thinking of killing himself. My sensory acuity immediately switched to a higher gear. Many people use the term suicide as a cry for help, or to get attention or significance and it's the first thing to check for. Gary didn't say this for effect. It was more of a casual statement to himself, like a self-acknowledgement. His body language was congruent and resigned. I calibrated his emotional energy (reflected in his face and voice) between grief and despair. This is between levels 50 and 75 on the Map Of Consciousness and, in suicide terms, a dangerous sign. If someone is completely on rock bottom, with energy hovering down at the level of shame, or guilt or apathy, etc., then suicide may seem an option or avenue of escape, but taking one's own life usually requires a higher energy and commitment to get over the fear of doing it. This is why grief is a more common precursor than shame, even though shame usually feels worse or more painful than grief. It's also why a number of suicides involve taking alcohol first, as alcohol removes the inhibitions and blocks to higher levels of energy, allowing people to access states where they can now act on the thoughts. i.e. it's hard to kill yourself in apathy, but grief and fear carry far more energy to act. This same phenomenon accounts for why there have been many people who have killed themselves after taking anti-depressants or switching to a more powerful medication. (Robin Williams is a classic case). The families of the victims then blame the drugs but common-sense tells me to see it differently. Many anti-depressants artificially raise levels of hormones such as serotonin or block their inhibitors. If you were suicidal before but lacked the energy or motivation (including courage) to act on it, then paradoxically, anti-depressants in some cases can increase your mental strength to do so. Bearing in mind, they alter your brain chemistry, not the outer world circumstances being blamed for causing the depression in the first place. In other words, not having the will to live is not the same as having the will to kill yourself. It's like being too tired to go to bed. Once you're off the couch its easier. Stronger anti-depressants can sometimes be the energy that gets you off the couch and which allows you to act on your pain and put a rope around your neck.

This is why recontextualising the event or circumstances that people are depressed or suicidal about is usually, and quite often, a more powerful and permanent solution. This is what I did in the med line with Gary, though to begin with, I didn't want to allow him to get too into his 'story'. For a start, I didn't have time but, more importantly, it becomes self-reinforcing and a vehicle for those telling it to get connection and low levels of significance. Also, a lot of the time, the story becomes a method for them to seek agreement and justifications as to why they are a victim. This is why some charities and models of support in here that offer 'listener' type services can fall down. There's also a subtle difference in gender here that's worth noticing. As a gross generalization, feminine energy can actually release negativity and tension by sharing emotional pain. In this regard, listener services in female prisons can be a valuable resource. By contrast, masculine energy tends to use it as self-reinforcement of the position. This is why I didn't want Gary to get stuck into his own drama (which many will if you don't subtly control the conversation). Plus, as I said, we only had a few minutes in line before collecting our pills and being sent back to our cells. Therefore, in order to shift his mental relationship to whatever it was he was suicidal about, I needed some critical data points. In movie terms, I needed to elicit the general plot outline and not have him make me watch the whole film.

The reason Gary was so upset was due to it being the anniversary of his dad's death. This was accentuated by a large fist-sized tattoo on his neck of his dad's name, a gravestone and a date. His dad had been his best friend and since his death Gary felt alone. Some people can even feel abandoned by their parents dying, as if it were somehow their responsibility to be a parent forever. The vacuum was part-filled by his wife but, to add to the emotional pain, she wouldn't talk to him because she blamed him for being inside and abandoning her and their baby girl of two years old. To make matters worse, they had another baby girl due next month. Gary still had another twelve months to serve on his sentence which meant he would miss the birth and also the first year of her life. He couldn't get over the death of his dad and believed he was a failure as a son. And worse, that he was now a failure as a father himself. He hated prison and at least if he killed himself now, his daughters would never need to know or remember him. This underscored my initial assessment that this was not a suicidal wolf-cry for attention. This was a genuine possibility.

At this point of an intervention, rapport is critical or he'd likely discount whatever I said. Rapport can be quickly built through commonality and, as it happened, we did have something in common. I asked, "how long since your dad died?" He pointed to the date on his neck and said it was a year this week. I told him it had been nine years since my dad had died suddenly and I know how difficult it is. I also shared that it's every parents' primary wish that their children outlive them and that at least he had been granted that wish. Of course, the problem is we never get to choose when they go and it's always too soon. But by taking his own life now he would be ripping up his dad's most precious wish as, in effect, it would be his dad's death that killed his own son. I could see the cogs start to turn. I added that, as for his daughters, if ever there was a time to pick to go to jail as a parent (assuming you had to pick), then I'd pick a time they would never have a memory of and therefore they could not give any negative meaning to. This helped soften the lock on the door I really wanted to open. Bearing in mind, where kids are involved, it's far easier to question your own self-worth as a parent, than it is our own self-worth as a person, and if that identity is threatened (or in Gary's mind, rubber-stamped as failed), it can quickly compound feelings of worthlessness which is a close cousin of 'nothing to live for'.

It was clear that Gary had linked suicide, not only to escape from pain but also a form of redemption. To him, it was almost a statement of apology. I had to slam the door shut on that, and fast, as he was almost in line for his meds. I told him one of the greatest gifts a parent could ever give their children is that of self-esteem.

As a side note, this is especially true for girls who tend to have slightly more issues around self-image, thanks to societies fake projections of what they are told they 'should' look like. These projections are largely manufactured for the purposes of selling and marketing all kinds of crap they don't need, in order to fit false-stereotypes they then struggle to fit into. The sub-text is "I am not good enough the way I am, unless I look, smell or act a certain way." This kills self-esteem, enthusiasm and authenticity and instead breeds insecurity, self-consciousness and dependency on the good opinions of others. The irony is that studies often show that people who look the opposite of what society is conditioned to believe is 'attractive' but are enthusiastic and authentic (i.e. happy how they are, look, act, etc.) are far more attractive, accepted and appreciated (even looked up to) than those who have all the 'looks' but are not happy inside.

The question I asked Gary was "what message do you think your girls will likely get from you killing yourself?" (Note - this question was delivered with genuine connection, empathy and concern. Saying it in a challenging way would have broken rapport at this stage and he may have gone defensive and pushed back.) He paused, staring at me, water welling up in his eyes, and gave his answer almost like a question. "That I was sorry?" The doubt was already surfacing. I said "No, that's what you want to tell them, it's not what they will hear. What they will almost certainly hear is that their dad thought so little of them he chose to permanently abandon them. They will grow up knowing they were so unloved and not even worth sticking around for". It took two seconds for his jaw to drop as the awareness sank in. I continued "It doesn't stop there. Growing up with that kind of wound in their soul will likely cause them to feel worthless and end up with either someone who proves it by treating them like shit, or they'll end up on drugs to numb the pain. They will likely end up in prison themselves or worse, realise that no amount of heroin can heal their lack of self-esteem and the only way to escape would be to kill themselves. After all, that's the example you left so why not follow it? And could you blame them, as who would want to live if their own dad didn't care enough about them to even want to see them grow up? So, really killing yourself not only dishonours your dad but likely condemns your kids to a lifetime of misery and low self-esteem. It's probably the most hurtful thing you could ever do." He was now staring at me head on and the tears were giving way to anger. This is a good sign. Anger can be a useful emotion to illicit change – as long as it's directed. Angry people don't kill themselves – they take action. Both positive and negative (i.e. punching a wall or committing to change). I let the energy build for a second before opening a better door to channel it through. I said "Instead, right now, you have a once in a lifetime opportunity to show your dad and your daughters that even if you end up in prison for a short time, and let's face it, we all make mistakes, that you can come out stronger, wiser and an even better father. That no matter what life throws at you, you can handle it. That spring always follows winter. Now let me ask you, Gary, what kind of life do you think your girls could have if they learned THAT from their dad? Not to mention how proud your own father would be!"

I didn't need to say much more. The awareness hit him like a truck. His eyes were wide and I saw one of the most encouraging signs you could ever want to see in a suicide intervention: hope. Now it was time to finish by challenging him, as masculine energy responds and rises to challenge. "You think you've got what it takes to do that? Can you handle a little bit of prison time in order to give them that gift – because I sure as hell think you can and I've only known you for five minutes!" He took the bait instantly. "Fucking right I can!" In that moment, hope became positive determination and now we are well out of suicide territory. Neither is he likely to go back as the context for his whole issue had just been shifted into a different meaning. Instead of using suicide as a way out of the pain and as an apology, it was now more painful to end his life. Especially as he now had a pathway back to meaning and a reason to live, which included embracing the very circumstances he'd been resisting and using as justifications to end his life.

It doesn't take a PhD guys – or anti-depressants. Just a basic understanding of what's really going on without being distracted by the victim-story, which is usually the biggest part of the problem. If you recall in Mud or Stars (the story I wrote to help prisoners make a better mental adjustment), I state that it's easy to play the role of victim because it allows us to blame others and avoid responsibility. The downside is that it keeps us trapped in a closed circle of victim-based circumstances. The unfortunate fact for most of us is that we spend much of our lives blaming others for what our own egos have done to us, never learning the lessons we need to learn. We then wonder why the conditions of our lives perpetuate as we keep resitting the same exam in Earth School that Life wants us to pass.

Incidentally, I am very pleased to report Mud or Stars continues to have a big impact across the prison. Right now, I feel blessed to have people coming to me every day, either telling me the shifts they've had, or asking for more copies. One guy even wrote it out by hand before passing on the copy he had to someone else. One of the most incredible things that is happening is that people are shouting "stars!" when they see me. It's also been selected as the lead article in the prison magazine 'Voice of the Ville'. The impact and difference I've seen this one story have, means I HAVE to find a way of getting it into the hands of all new inmates. If I'm released tomorrow, I'd still make that my mission.

Money Matters

I've also written a few other articles this week in my journalism class. One is on the topic of finance. I titled it "Prison is your best chance to become a master of money!" The outcome was to show the prisoners the value of learning basic financial skills, such as budgeting, and tie it in with the ability to help them stay out of prison. It's no surprise that many crimes are money motivated, but learning how to more effectively manage the money you have is a big part of why people run out and then take shortcuts to get more (with the exceptions of addictions such as drugs or gambling, which will always bypass the rationale of money management to get the 'hit' the addictive behaviour gives them). The message I was trying to impart was simple: If you can't manage a budget of about a pound a day, with virtually all variables taken off the table (such as rent, council tax, petrol, food, insurance, etc.,) and only canteen and phone calls to spend it on, then what chance have you got on the outside? The other motivation for me to write this was the fact that a lot of violence in here comes from people borrowing money they can't pay back. I outlined this in detail in Volume 3. By encouraging some of them to learn to budget more effectively, by showing them this is their best opportunity to master a critical life skill, it may also help stop or prevent a little bit of the violence in here too.

I did a similar type of exercise with an article on health that was aimed at subtlety directing energy into a positive goal-orientated focus through challenging the ego. Hey, if there's that much ego in here, I may as well help them channel it in a positive way. I'd give far greater odds of being able to do that, than having them give it up in a sudden burst of spiritual enlightenment!

Freedom vs Liberty

As you can see, the basis of a lot of the teaching I am doing in here is two-fold. One mental, the other practical. On the mental side, the biggest shift is when someone understands the difference between Freedom versus Liberty. And that there is a difference. A big one. Liberty is what is restricted in prison. It's where your ability to go where you want is taken away. It's a matter of restricted confinement of varying degrees. A prison cell is one of the tightest. But a kid who's grounded can also feel locked up. A person with no passport can feel confined. Or someone without the means to go where they want to go, either financially, such as not being able to afford to get on a bus, or physically as they may have lost their legs and cannot run the marathon they always wanted to run. As I said, it's a matter of degree. Luckily, most liberty issues are temporary. Sentences come to an end, you can earn more money and technology can help you walk again. Freedom is a separate matter. Freedom is exclusively a state of mind. Anybody can be locked up, but only a mind can imprison itself. Either through belief or fear. One of the keys to mental freedom is the ability to find a positive in any situation. Of course, the precursor to this is the willingness to do so and that means giving up the victim/ blame model mentioned earlier. As for beliefs to support or empower you, rather than confine you to self-imposed limitations, one of mine comes straight from Napoleon Hill who stated: *"Every adversity carries with it the seed of equivalent or greater benefit"*. It was one of the first things I wrote as a sign when I came in and I read it every day. (See Appendix E). The challenge is most people are too busy complaining or worrying about the adversity to focus on watering the seed. A good starting point is always cultivating gratitude. This is why it's one of the many key skills I teach on day one of the Sage Business School. A lot of people are initially surprised at this, though by the end it's clear to see the world of business fares far better on a foundation of kind-heartedness, ethnocentric focus and having empathy, love and respect for the customer. All aspects of which are closely linked to gratitude. Cultivating easy access to this *one* state can be a game changer. For example, I think I've cried four times due to the authentic expression of emotional sadness (see Volume 3), and at least a dozen from overwhelming gratitude. This has been largely triggered by the, now hundreds, of letters of heart-warming support from the outside (thank you EVERYONE), and also because of the people I have worked with who society had completely given up on. Many of whom have also expressed their thanks in letters. Not that I need that, but these letters are now some of my most cherished possessions in here (a small selection appear in Appendix B). One thing for sure, when I put on the next Sage Business School, it is going to be a deeper and richer experience. After all, I've had a few months of the most incredible journey which has also provided an opportunity for focus, introspection, self-study and uninterrupted contemplation. Something I would never have been able to do at this level otherwise. There will also be a number of scholarships for those who I have worked with in here. Those who I feel have the potential, desire and willingness to change, but lack the guidance or resources to do so. That too, is one of the greatest things to come out of this. One of many.

Transferable Skills – Making It Real

I mentioned there were two aspects to my teaching in here. Mental adjustments are always primary as all actions are preceded by thought. Thought patterns are habitual, which is why trying to change someone's behaviour without changing their patterns of thinking is a great way to fail fast. However, unless there is a way to practically apply the new thinking in terms of behaviours, then the loop cannot close. The best way to do that in here is through the concept of "Transferable Skills". This is something we can all learn and benefit from. I'll give you a couple of examples of how I've shared it in here and you'll immediately see an opportunity for how you can too.

Let's start by recognising that this place provides a forced and unforgiving environment. To learn how to survive in a prison as bad as Pentonville, one quickly has to get resourceful. There is virtually nothing to guide new inmates on any aspect of life here. It is trial by fire. People have to learn quickly how the system works or they get bitten by it. Staying safe takes work and many learn to avoid trouble, or at least those who make it. Handling disappointment at things that were promised, or that you are entitled to, but don't happen, is a daily occurrence. But rather than be disillusioned (as many are, even the staff), I show people how they are building strong muscles in some of the most critical areas of life that even highly educated people on the outside rarely have.

Such as the ability to handle uncertainty – a critical life skill for everything from starting a business to becoming a new parent. Not being too reliant on what other people promise – a key skill for both avoiding being upset by things you can't control and for building self-reliance. Patience – if they can learn to deal with being locked up for twenty-three hours a day, they can easily wait an extra half an hour for their wife to get ready without starting the night off with an argument.

Pentonville is also a B-Category prison which means a lot of the prisoners are here for serious crimes. Either violence (from murder to vicious assault) or drugs (mainly supply), through to organised crime (all types) and robbery (from armed bank jobs to burglary). It's quite a laboratory for me to work in. One of the most common types of students I've worked with in here have been high-level drug dealers. Through the transferable skills model, I show them how talented and qualified they are (something many have never been told, especially in school) and how, as an entrepreneur, I respect their business skills. Of course, after they look at me like I've been taking too much of what they used to sell, I break it down. Running a successful drugs operation requires someone to master various things such as managing inventory, managing distribution, keeping in touch with the market in terms of pricing, dealing with competitors, product quality control, managing cash flow and credit and more. I show them how all of that can be a massive asset in the legal business world. That, if they didn't want to end up back in jail again, they didn't have to. They've already gotten a street MBA in business and could apply those skills in a legit enterprise selling something they were passionate about.

I also explain that in terms of drugs and crime, the game had shifted. It now wasn't a matter of 'if' they would get caught, but when. The fact is, the authorities are smarter, more resourced and with more access to information, equipment, manpower, technology and legal muscle than any time in history. No criminal, no matter how smart, can expect to get away with ongoing crime without being caught. It's like a roman solider battling Special Forces. Both brave, both fit and both intelligent, but one can kill you from two miles away with a sniper rifle which is a lot further than you can throw a spear! Notice what I've done here. I've not challenged their significance or threatened their pride (i.e. just as smart, brave, fit, etc.), which could be taken as an insult at best and a challenge to prove me wrong at worst. I've just laid it out that the scales on the battlefield are now more heavily tipped towards detecting and catching criminals than executing crime. So why do people still leave jail and go right back? Because they think they don't have a choice. Because selling drugs is all they know. But when they see that those skills are transferable, then that excuse goes away. Naturally, it's still their choice but the difference is they now know they have one. That can be quite an insight for some. One such inmate, Matthew, a big Jamaican lad from London, wrote me a beautiful letter about how his entire worldviews had shifted. Here's a direct quote from the letter "I've only sold drugs as a business, but I now have the confidence and understanding of how to use the same principle in something legitimate." He goes on to say he's never met another person like me in prison and that I've helped to open his eyes to a new way of thinking. I said earlier, I'm sure my being here was all part of a plan. How can I possibly complain about how I found myself in Pentonville when reading letters like that? It's all perspective. I said in a video I released before I came here that this was my opportunity to help those who would never normally get access to my work. The joy I've had in keeping to my word is only eclipsed by the joy of seeing the transformation in the prisoners themselves.

This, my friends, is something we can all do in our own lives. You don't need a trip to Pentonville to prove that. Leave that to weirdos like me. Nor do you need any special skills. The biggest difference you can make to those around you is by being the example, not the warning. By focusing on being the best version of you that you can be and in doing so, act as the invitation for others to follow while letting go of the need or expectation for them to do so. Loving and appreciating them for however they choose to walk their own path while you concentrate on being true to yours. Remember, the brighter you shine your candle, the more light you give for others to see their own greatness reflected in the mirror you become. And the better chance we have of preventing some of them ending up in the darkness of a place like this.

Thanks for reading guys, I love you all massively and I'll write again soon.

Big Hug,

Peter X

Volume 8: Date Night (Week 16)

In Volume 8, we get an update on the saga that surrounds Peter's transfer. We find out the result of his appeal, along with a further peak behind the curtain of the justice system. There is an inspiring lesson on how to use the mind to prevent our environment or circumstances from defining us, together with some surprising news on Operation Chrysalis. We also look at how Peter and Thea have managed to set up 'Date Night' in Prison and why.

My dear and amazing family, students and friends

Welcome to Volume 8 of Inside Track. As always, a big thank you for your continued letters, cards and emails which, even after sixteen weeks, continue to bring light and a nourishing smile to my world in here. You make it easier for me to continue my journey and mission and you have no idea how grateful I am for it, or the prisoners who you also affect vicariously.

Before we begin, many of you have written in asking about my foot which, as I shared in the last volume, I suspected was broken. Well, after weeks of repeatedly asking for an X-ray, I was finally sent to healthcare yesterday where I sat for three hours before seeing a nurse. Her first question was "So, why are you here?" I told her I thought it was for an X-ray, as I'd filed several applications for it. I was then told there was nothing on the system but she'd speak to someone later that day about referring me for another appointment. You couldn't make it up. It reminds me of Jin, my cellmate, who's had severe toothache for three months. It took two months for him to get an appointment with the prison dentist. I remember him being so happy that day as he went off to healthcare, only for a dentist to look in his mouth and say "Yes, that's bad, you will need to book an appointment for treatment." He came back disheartened and still in pain. Luckily, he did actually get his treatment appointment two weeks later. A minor miracle in prison terms. He walked in, was examined and told, "Don't brush as hard. Next!" No treatment, still in pain. I feel so sorry for the guy. Luckily, he only has two weeks left on his sentence.

The good news is that I am now walking without crutches and virtually pain-free, though it has been a month so if the bones haven't healed properly, then my only concern is they may need to be re-broken. However, with the work I've been doing on my own healing, I'm confident they'll be OK. Here's my hot tip of the week: Don't get sick or injured in prison. Or get toothache.

Managing Unmet Expectations

OK, moving on. Let's start with the transfer saga and some real tips I can offer. Namely around dealing with disappointment when our environment and circumstances don't match our expectations. Yep, you guessed it – I've still not been transferred. If you recall in the last issue, I shared that Mr Daly was putting me forward as the first prisoner in over twenty years to be released on a temporary licence and allowed to make my own way to a D-Cat prison. One of the excuses I've been given as to why I am still stuck here is because the open prison nearest to where I actually live is outside of the usual transfer zone of Pentonville and they have been struggling to find the budget to send me the extra distance. A few days ago, Mr Daly came to my cell at 8pm with an update. He said the temporary release route wouldn't work in time as, while I was the perfect candidate, it had been so long since the prison had authorised anyone to be released this way, that in order to get up to speed with the new procedures and paperwork, it would take three months. Despite that, there was good news. He'd pulled some strings and I was finally being transferred the following Wednesday. I was to be put on a bus that was taking prisoners back to Birmingham Prison. They had been shipped here a few months ago following a riot at that prison and were now being sent back. As such, Pentonville had authorized the extra budget to send me the thirty minutes or so further up the road to Derby after the Birmingham drop-off. I was told to be packed and ready to ship by 7am, which of course I was. And... nobody came. *Hmm...* I put in a written application to find out what had happened and was told that, during the Governor's meeting the day before, they had cancelled the extra budget that had previously been authorised in a bid to save money. The blatantly obvious point here is that it costs far more to keep me here (approximately £700 a week to the taxpayer) than the thirty minutes of diesel (call it an hour for the round trip) but hey, they don't seem to have taken that into account. I'm also thinking, maybe I should send them a ticket to the next Sage Business School.

Funnily enough, many prisoners I know have been transferred or released on parole recently. Remember Oliver? The crack and heroin addict who came in having lost everything. He got out a few days ago and gave me an emotional goodbye hug along with a really beautiful and heartfelt letter saying how I'd helped save his life. He signed it "former drug addict, reformed offender and loving husband and father to a wife and three beautiful kids." Wow. What makes this powerful is the shift in identity. Anyone who's been to Day One of the Sage Business School will have a direct experience of how powerful this is. I also outline it in my first London Real interview where I give the example of how much easier it is to quit smoking when you change your identity to a non-smoker. This is in contrast to what most people do, which is shift it to being a *smoker who's quit*. This puts the focus on a change in behaviour (quitting) but not a change in the identity that supports the behaviour, i.e. still a smoker. It's also why most 'smokers who quit' go back to smoking when the willpower they use to resist their identity runs out. Incidentally, I've had so many people write in, stating they hope Brian Rose puts the interview back online. I do too, as it has helped tens of thousands of people. Remember, it's his decision, but rather than blame him for being reactive or self-centred, as hundreds of even his closest followers are, it's worth instead to look at the patterns that govern why someone would rather be right for their own benefit than serve the greater good. At least that way we can seek to understand rather than blame or judge. If we go to the Map Of Consciousness, as outlined in Volume 1, we see this pattern show up predominantly between level 175 and 199, as it is inherently pride-centred and based on a lack of courage. Courage is the starting point for overturning the ego's need to prove a point which, for many of us, is the biggest hurdle in the journey towards emotional maturity. The real test for Brian will be to see if he has the Courage to put the interviews back up when I either defeat HP in the civil action or (more likely) they withdraw their allegations.

The second part of Oliver's sign-off reconnects him to a reason bigger than himself, and one that gives his life meaning and purpose, i.e. a loving husband and father to a wife and three beautiful kids. This echoes one of the main messages that came out of Viktor Frankl's book 'Mans Search for Meaning' where he saw those who had the highest will to live in Auschwitz, were those who had loved ones to go back to (or clung to the hope of seeing again). These people were far more likely to outlive those who were fitter and stronger physically but had no-one other than themselves to focus on. We also see this in the animal kingdom where, even though males are often the larger size, the strongest driver by far (even more than hunger or defending territory) is the female's commitment to protect her young.

Oliver's wife was inspired by his progress (I even talked to her briefly on the phone during one of his calls) and this gave him a bigger sense of purpose and belief in being a better and more loving husband and father. This was a big factor we worked on during the last few weeks of his sentence as the methadone withdrawal really swung its bat. I've not heard from him yet, although it's only been a week and mail here can typically take up to two weeks on its mysterious journey from arrival to cell. A journey that must be somewhat perilous on account that around 20% doesn't make it at all but, hey-ho, all par for the course. Obviously, I'll let you know if I hear from him and his progress. I also told him, if he ever came back here I would commit a crime just so I could also come back to kick his ass. (And, yes, before somebody pedantically reports me for conspiracy to commit crime, I was joking. Even if I hope Oliver didn't think so.) Ironically, if I was a criminal, I'd already be released on parole, but as a civil prisoner, there is no provision for parole, tag or home curfew, etc. So, if I'd actually committed a crime, I'd serve less prison time for the same sentence. Again, it's stranger than fiction.

So, where were we? Ah yes, the door that never opened, the transfer that never happened. I will admit, I was disappointed when nobody came to collect me and I sounded down on the phone to Thea that day. Being moved closer to her meant she could visit more often and this was a big part of why I really wanted to go. However, this does highlight one of the central lessons of this entire journey and one I wish we could teach everyone. Not just in prisons but in schools as well, and that is this: *Our environment and circumstances do not define us. They simply provide the opportunity for us to define ourselves!* It is a hard fact that unmet expectations are a major source of stress and disappointment for billions of people, along with trying to control what they cannot control and/or resist that which has already happened. This creates a negative attitude that quickly consolidates into an 'attractor-pattern', bringing more of the same as the heart and mind unify in their agreement on why life isn't fair. This attractor-pattern usually produces more misfortune, perpetuating the hamster wheel of negativity, together with a conviction that the world is somehow trying to spite us. All of which could be avoided if we simply switched our attention, at least emotionally and energetically, away from the environment and circumstances we are complaining about, and onto what we want to replace it with.

Within a few hours of realizing no one was coming and the transfer wasn't going to happen, I shook it off and asked a better question. Remember, *questions are the steering wheel of the mind.* A simple switch from asking 'what's wrong with me?' which presupposes you are flawed, to 'what am I good at?' which presupposes that you have skills or gifts, can be the crucial difference between draining or filling the tank of self-esteem. Questions direct our focus and call upon the brain to do what it loves best – find answers to any question you give it, which it will dutifully do. It also doesn't care about the nature of the question and whether the answer will likely upset you or cheer you up. So, if you ask yourself 'Why does my life suck?' the brain, like a faithful dog running after a stick you've thrown, will go off to find the answer and bring it back. Don't be surprised if it returns with something like 'because I'm just not good enough' or some iteration thereof. The point here is obvious. *Ask a lousy question, get a lousy answer.* Knowing this, the question I asked was 'OK, by staying in Pentonville, what opportunity does that give me to make an even bigger difference?' The steering wheel turned, the focus narrowed, and the brain ran after its stick.

The first thing it brought back was a statement. 'Don't reinvent the wheel', which led to another question: 'How can I capitalize on the momentum I've already created?' The answer to that was obvious. While I can, and often do, give all of my free time to working with or helping others, I'm still very limited by the basic fact there is still just one of me. However, the most feedback I've had, and still continue to get from all over the prison, is from people who have read *Mud or Stars?*. Even the Deputy Governor, Mr Gardiner, went out of his way to say he'd read it on the train and paid me a great compliment. Incidentally, I've built a good rapport with the Deputy Governor. He's a solid guy who seems to take a genuine interest in matters and is committed to helping run the prison as best he can. Though he, like many staff here, is often thwarted despite best intentions by the restrictive, bureaucratic and political nature of an ageing and ineffective system. He's been fighting in my corner on both the transfer and the X-ray for weeks but, as neither of these seem likely to materialise, it appears that even the prison's second-in-command is limited to being somewhat of a toothless tiger in this regard. Back to *Mud or Stars?* If you recall, it was Wing Governor Hipwell who wrote and expressed interest in the new prisoner booklet I designed and after setting the intent, I finally managed to meet her for the first time since I arrived. Her feedback was encouraging but also stated the main challenge which was that, while I am in here, there's little they can do. In other words, it's virtually impossible to help or impact the prison system from the inside. Just as it's equally as hard to help prisoners from the outside. However, once I'm released, she has stated that she'd be happy for me to work with her on getting the booklet put together and see if we can trial it for new prisoners. That was the news I'd been waiting for. Operation Chrysalis has regained a pulse!

In the meantime, I've also begun dialogue with various organizations with whom I can help leverage change, even before I'm out. Stay tuned.

Before we switch gears, I'd like to end this section by recapping and expanding on one of the main lessons in *Mud or Stars?* and look at why it's been so successful in having the impact on inmates that it has. The answer returns us to the concept of acceptance. By accepting 'what is' we can deal with it from a more empowering place. The problem many people have, and especially in here, is they 'accept' their circumstances somewhat begrudgingly, which is to say with a certain amount of resistance and reluctance. This 'pseudo-acceptance' sucks energy and creates fertile ground for disempowering, low frequency, low energy thoughts such as apathy, sadness and fear. Or low frequency, high energy thoughts such as stress, drama and anger. True acceptance is free of resistance. It's empowering, almost liberating, as it destroys the illusion that you can change what has happened and instead allows you to focus more intelligently on what you can do about it. Or, if nothing, then at least better come to terms with it. However, if used smartly, it can also set you up to win in advance and help us break through many of the false and self-imposed limits that keep us from our goals. I'll give you an example.

Running From A Ghost

A long time ago in a galaxy far away (well, twenty-five years ago in Leicester to be precise) a certain man, yours truly, had a dream of becoming a professional speaker. A lofty dream at the time and with one slight problem. I was an insecure, significance driven, fast-talking fidget head with virtually no speaking skills other than a desire to share information which I thought could help people. But, as daunting as that seemed, it wasn't my biggest challenge. A far bigger hurdle lay in the fact that I knew for at least the first ten times I spoke, I was going to suck. Really suck. That meant I knew audiences wouldn't like me, they would judge me, question everything about what value I could offer, and I would most likely melt into an embarrassing puddle on stage under the heat of their glare. Didn't sound like fun. Though, the fact is, every one of us faces similar fears at some point when confronted with stepping out (or being forced out) of our comfort zone. But what was I actually resisting? Essentially, a whole lot of uncomfortable emotions I knew I would have to face if I started down the path towards my dream. These included feeling judged, not good enough, embarrassed, unworthy, looking stupid and being unloved to name a few. An important point to realise here is that, while these were emotions I had to face and deal with, they were often not actually representative of what is going on in the heads of the audience. In short, they weren't even real. They were a ghost. However, even though these were my own projections of what I think others were thinking, it still formed my reality, meaning they were real for me. Whether they existed in the minds of others or not was irrelevant, and herein lies the tipping point that can allow you to walk through the golden door to your future, or have it slam shut before you get there. You see, once I knew I was going to have to face all of that in order to be a speaker (or fill in whatever your blank is along with the corresponding emotions), I had a simple decision to make. Either give up on my dream, because I can't face or include the emotions I decided are too painful (did you catch the words 'I decided' there? Nobody else has the power over you!) Or, use the power of acceptance and say 'OK, that's the price of admission and I accept it, so how fast can I get to speech number eleven where I know I'll be better?' The irony is that, once I'd done just a couple of talks, the fears lost most of their impact as the reality of them being nothing but my own mismanaged imagination revealed itself. It wasn't even a ghost. It was a little midget with two broomsticks holding up a sheet. Face your fears, the sheet is pulled away and you realise there was really nothing to be scared about. But turn and run, and the ghost will forever chase you.

The fact is, acceptance, as a central theme, can be found throughout the entire self-help and spirituality genre. From the Susan Jefferies classic, 'Feel the Fear and Do It Anyway', to the hugely successful twelve-step programme started by Bill Wilson and introduced through Alcoholics Anonymous. Simply put, *acceptance of the issue is the first and most critical step to transcending the issue.* This is why it calibrates at 350 on the Map Of Consciousness. A level that is very powerful. Whereas resistance requires force and therefore, by definition, calibrates below 200.

The obvious question that presents itself is 'What have you been resisting in *your* life because of your unwillingness to accept and embrace the inevitable emotions it will initially entail?' It brings to mind a quote from Robin Sharma who eloquently stated, 'the fears we refuse to face become our limits'. From this place you can hear my former message crystal clear: *Our environment and circumstances don't define us, they simply allow us the opportunity to define ourselves.* If this is the only message I can get across to someone in here out of all the work that I am doing, then that alone is worth it and can be a game-changer in and of itself.

Appeal

OK, I think it's time I gave you an update on my appeal that was heard last week, as you've been waiting a few pages for it. I won't bore you with the details other than to tell you that they cut a third off my sentence, meaning I have just (drum roll) nine weeks left of my field trip. I guess I better get busy! It did, however, shed some more light on the justice system, and the politics of how it works. In short, the three appeal court judges were balancing the fact that they have a duty to look at the law objectively, against the personal aspect of not wanting to go against or criticize a fellow judge. Having presented evidence which I felt would allow me to be released, various aspects were ignored or minimised (mainly, those that would have reflected poorly on the initial decision) while other aspects, which wouldn't have merited much impact on the sentence (and therefore not look as bad on the original judge), were given higher credit. The result was a compromise, resulting in the reduction of my sentence by a third. Under the circumstances, it was probably the best I could have hoped for, seeing the nature of how it played out and the political dynamics at work.

I also have the option to put in a purge application where I can seek to 'undo' the contempt, but there are two things against me here. The first is that I can't pay back the wages I paid to Carolyn, my former CEO, which incidentally, was considered the most serious breach of the freezing order and the main reason I'm here. Even though the order itself fully allowed the funds to be paid and no evidence was (or could) be presented to say otherwise. Crazy, I know. If she had simply confirmed that she was owed the funds, as per her contract, then it would have been a different result, but she was unwilling to get involved. Secondly, HP themselves are not likely to support a purge application as they are trying to go for summary judgement in the original civil action, which means it's decided upon written submissions, not trial. This is in order to take full advantage of my inability to respond or prepare a defence against it in here. I can't blame them. As I said in Volume 3, civil actions are little more than a chess game to win corporate points of self-interest and these guys, HP and Mishcon de Reya, are effective and ruthless players with deep pockets. It's not so much kick a man while he's down as stamp on his throat and put a nine-millimetre in his chest. The good news is that if I ever need a legal team with that focus, I'll be hiring them! Oh, come on, you have to smile. Either way, and regardless of what happens, my default psychology, as outlined from my very first letter, is that this is part of an amazing adventure and no matter where the river bends from here, I'll bounce back better, stronger and more experienced than ever to live the life I choose to create. Not only that, but it will make for some great stories for the grandkids one day. A journey I plan to start on as soon as I get my hands on Thea (wink) and that, my friends, leads us nicely into date night.

Date Night Prison Style

One of the challenges I have in a High-Security Cat B prison is the severely restricted access to phone calls. There are many factors that aggravate this. To begin with, there is only a small amount of time you are allowed out of the cell each day which, education aside, is between four and forty minutes. Also, the phones themselves are only switched on during a few small windows throughout day, many of which do not correspond to access times such as free-flow. In addition, one needs to factor in that there are around fifty-plus inmates per phone (half of which are broken and rarely repaired). This leads to an average wait time to make a call of up to half an hour and therefore takes up most of the allowed social time. The call length is also limited to less than five minutes, with no redial or second calls allowed. Finally, all numbers have to be security cleared first with pedantic rules. For example, in trying to prepare for my appeal, I applied to add the High Court to my authorised numbers list so that I could speak to my case manager. This was refused as I did not have the number on an official court letterhead to show them. I'm sure you're getting the picture. What this means is that I only get to speak to Thea four or five times a week. That's if she answers and if I give up most of my social time waiting in line. As a result, when we speak there is usually a lot of time-pressure where we try and 'cram in' a lot of things during the brief few minutes a week we get. This makes it hard to find time to connect to just 'us'. It's also the same with visits.

Now, for many people, this is a story that is not confined to prison. One of the biggest causes of relationships going stale is a decline in intimacy as other priorities (work, kids, money issues, home life, etc.) all take a piece out of the finite time and energy pie, leaving little time left over to enjoy the chemistry and magic that flourished so freely in the beginning. In other words, once you both take it for granted that your partner is your partner, and there's no red flag to suggest otherwise, it's easy to be distracted by everything else that comes up and screams at us from its own time-sensitive agenda. The decline here can be subtle, creeping up on you, like a tumour and not really being noticed until something is wrong, by which time the relationship is either flat, or worse, in crisis and now finally competes as a priority for attention. Thea and I noticed this on a visit last week. It was actually the first one where it's been just the two of us (not counting the other 100 people in the room). We had both set the intention of having a really connected visit. But halfway through, it turned into more of a stressful catch-up and Q+A session as we tried to make the most of the ninety minutes we had to deal with several weeks' worth of issues. At this point, we stopped and recognized the pattern. Which is when Thea came up with the idea of us having a date night inside, just as we often do on the outside. We decided to do it on Tuesday evenings around 7pm, as this is when I get the one extra social time a week for being enhanced. It's therefore scheduled and, thankfully, not as busy as only around a fifth of the wing qualify to be let out. On date night during our call, the <u>only</u> things we talk about are how much we love each other, what we are most excited about doing together when I'm out, our favourite *magic moments* together and more. We don't talk about prison life, work, problems, issues or anything else that's negative. Not only that, but we make it as real as we can. Before the call, I have a shower and put on my best clean clothes, Thea puts on makeup and perfume and we turn it into a feature. I have to say the first call was magical. It lit up my evening like a technicolour fountain of light sparkling in a monochrome world. It shifted all the stress of the outside world and made us feel closer than at any point during the last four months. And guys, if we can do that in five minutes over the phone through shifting focus and the right prep, it shows what is possible on the outside if your relationship gets out of balance. That is providing you don't wait until the tumour is inoperable before you make it a priority. After all, there are very few things in life, from challenges such as this, to deadlines at work or health problems, that cannot be faced from a much stronger place when you have love in your corner.

'Breaking News'

OK stop the press! I have some breaking news. I just returned from a surprise day out in London! No, I haven't found a secret tunnel, the breaking news is about my foot (excuse the pun). An officer knocked on my cell door and told me they were finally taking me to the local hospital for my X-ray! Well, score one for Deputy Gov. Gardiner! The trip, which I have just returned from, took three and a half hours (by which time they could have taken me to the other jail) and involved two officers escorting me in a cab. Even though I am a civil prisoner, I was double handcuffed to one officer at all times (even in the X-ray room) and, after getting to the hospital and waiting an hour, we got called in. This is after five-plus weeks of waiting and it was finally going to happen. This was the conversation:

Nurse: Please lie down (still handcuffed) so we can X-ray your ankle.

Me: My ankle is fine, it's the outside metatarsal bone near the toes that I felt break.

Nurse: Oh, well we can't X-ray those.

Me: Why not?

Nurse: Because the prison doctor has written down ankle on the form, so we can only X-ray your ankle.

Me: But I never saw a prison doctor, only a nurse who knew it was the bones at the front of the foot. My toes were black for over three weeks, but I've never had a problem or any pain in my ankle. We need to check the foot.

Nurse: Sorry, I can't X-ray your foot, only your ankle…

And the Pentonville Pantomime continues. Even the two officers, Mr Lawler and Miss Murray (who were great) were shaking their heads at the lunacy of it all. Oh well, at least it got me out of the house for a few hours. And the good news? Err, it turns out my ankle is fine!

Well, that wraps things up for this issue as I continue this incredible and extraordinary adventure. Even though there are only a few weeks left, I'm still fully committed to making whatever difference I can to as many people in here as I can. Of course, I'm also hoping to leave this place a little better than I found it. Now that Operation Chrysalis has regained traction, that hope has a decent shot at becoming a reality.

Wishing you all a wonderful week, stay amazing and I'll see you in Update 9!

Volume 9: When Unfair Is Fair Game
(Week 18)

In the ninth letter that Peter wrote, he delves deep into the hidden patterns that govern much of our behaviour, introduced via the breakthrough he has with his new cell-mate. There is also a fascinating and eye-opening look at the real agendas driving the legal process, and why you need to know them. In addition, there is a surprising finale to the transfer saga.

My dear and amazing family, students and friends

Welcome to the ninth issue of Inside Track. There is much to cover on both the update front and also the learning/insight front, as I share with you the big breakthrough my new cell-mate had and how it almost certainly affects all of us to some degree. On a fun note, I've been recruited into the *Prison Debate Team*, and we are set to do battle with a surprising adversary. It also reveals further insights into what really lurks behind the curtain of the Wizard of Justice. Insights you're going to want to know for many reasons. In addition, there are the usual off-piste ramblings I still hope to add value with or, if not, share anyway for my own distractive sanity.

Two and a Half Men – minus the half

Let's start with my new cell-mate, Patrick. Yes, Jin has served his time and been let out into the big blue yonder which created a rare opening on landing three. The 'three's is the level of the enhanced prisoners, but even if you reach the status of enhanced, as I now have, you only get the full privileges if you move to a cell on that particular landing. Of course, it doesn't make sense but remember the question you never want to ask here about anything is 'why?' This is kind of tough as it is an Indigo's driving question when faced with rules they don't agree with. Asking 'why' in here will drive you crazy because nobody can answer it from a perspective of logic or common sense. Welcome to prison. What this means is that 'enhanced' prisoners on the other floors literally battle, often violently, over spaces on the enhanced landing so they can actually get what they are entitled to in terms of the one extra gym and social session a week. It doesn't leave much room for choosing a new cell-mate. However, as a civil prisoner, I have discovered I have special rights and privileges that criminal prisoners do not have. (Note - none of this information has been volunteered or explained to me. Instead, I've had to search archives in the library to find out.) One benefit for civil prisoners is that I can refuse to share a cell with a convicted criminal. That may sound good but out of 1300 inmates in Pentonville, I have yet to meet another civil prisoner. Not only that, but I'm focused on helping people, so rooming on my own isn't an option I'd take. Therefore, having set the intention to find the right person to share a cell with, I let go and trusted the river.

It was shortly after that, and a few days before Jin left, that I met Patrick. A Nigerian born guy in his thirties who was awaiting sentence for having a domestic with his girlfriend. He'd just been transferred from another jail where he'd spent three months on remand. He'd kept his nose clean and was now enhanced. We met in the gym and he seemed a decent guy. He's a smart and educated man with a pleasant demeanour and, as it turns out, a strong interest in personal growth, spirituality and consciousness. In fact, our first chat made my *magic moments* list. This may surprise some of you as that profile doesn't fit the cultural stereotype of what the public considers a criminal. However, a useful observation here centres squarely on the fact that prison is not full of 'bad people'. There are a lot of good people who have just made bad errors in judgement. I think most of us can put our hands up to that at some point. Sure, there are people who definitely belong in jail as they are a danger to society and need to be kept away from the public so they can learn lessons. However, many people here are not in that category. There are also a significant number who serve no purpose and nor deserve to be in jail but have been dramatically let down by the fundamental flaws of the so-called criminal justice system. I touched on this in other updates and have more to share later. Though for now, let's just say that the amount of horror stories and absolute blatant, abject injustices I've discovered, are *way* beyond the bounds of what the public are even remotely aware of. I say that with zero exaggeration and it's another reason why I'm grateful to have seen it first-hand.

Back to Patrick, who happily accepted my invitation to fill the gap Jin had left. I can understand it may seem strange or rash that I'd choose someone who I'd just met and was in for what was a violence-based offence, but I felt that I had a good enough read on him to make the call. Besides, I was curious how someone who I'd pegged for being over level 200 on the Map Of Consciousness would get caught up in that kind of deal and end up here. I wanted to see if I could help the guy, but also hunt down what I could learn. Every day's a school day.

On our first evening together in the cell, I asked about him and his background but I had to be wary. If you remember the suicide intervention I did with Gary in Volume 7, you'll recall that most people use their 'story' as a way to justify their current behaviour or circumstance. Therefore, if you are looking to actively help someone, rather than just be an audience, it's important to subtly manage the flow of information. You need to elicit enough intel to uncover some valuable context and insight (so as to help spot their patterns) but not allow them to cross the threshold of getting stuck into their story, which will just result in them reinforcing it and making change even harder. It's a fine line, and part of the art and science of understanding these weird creatures called humans.

For Patrick, here are the relevant parts of his story: He was found guilty of domestic violence after a drunken argument in a hotel lobby at 2am with his girlfriend. This resulted in him grabbing her, causing a scuffle where they clashed heads and left her with a cut. Add shouts, mutual drama and verbal retaliation and you get the scene. A key point to mention here, is that she did not want to press any charges but, as the event was caught on the hotel CCTV, the police (who were called by the hotel) and the Crown Prosecution Service (CPS) felt they could obtain a conviction regardless. This is largely due to the way the system works and is one of the major root causes of why there are so many injustices. OK, I said I wasn't going to dwell on it but as we are breaking down patterns in this issue, here it is in a nutshell. Police forces and the CPS are always under pressure from the government. This is not to 'clean up crime' as such, but instead, they are evaluated, held accountable and ranked against targets that are linked to, and driven by, conviction rates and percentages. The effect of this results in a stronger focus on obtaining a conviction and therefore prioritising content over context. In other words, common sense does not prevail because common sense doesn't score on the statistical ranking tables. Neither does common sense result in promotions, better careers or bragging rights. Convictions do. Therefore, even though it was a relatively minor incident that could happen to almost anyone and that neither party wanted to involve the police, it was still dragged to court by the CPS. His girlfriend even testified in court that it was a storm in a teacup, out of character and that she didn't want to press charges or even have him punished. However, due to the CCTV evidence combined with the underlying objectives of the police and the CPS, Patrick was found guilty and could be looking at three years in jail.

Now, don't get me wrong, I am NOT making excuses for Patrick's behaviour or cutting him slack for his actions in any way. Knowing me as he now does, he'd be the first to confirm that. This is not about arguing who is right or wrong so please unhook from that game if you think I am playing it. What I AM interested in is the question, 'why would someone who seems a decent guy do this?' It was a question he'd been asking himself since that night. He also had a caution for something similar a few years ago, indicating that it was almost certainly related to an underlying pattern. It didn't take long to spot it, and the revelation floored him. I'll share a bit of his story and see if you can spot it too.

Patrick was born in Nigeria and, unfortunately, his mother died while giving birth to him. He grew up with his father constantly blaming him for 'killing' her and taking away his wife and soulmate. In fact, being chastised by his father is his earliest memory. He went to school and became highly educated, obtaining a degree in computer science, a second degree in human anatomy (following five years at medical school) and a Masters in Business. Not too shabby. He came to the UK, found a wonderful woman and got married. The family seemed to be complete when his wife became pregnant with twins. He was the happiest man on the planet. Unfortunately, the twins were born three and a half months premature in a London hospital and sadly, both died within hours. Naturally, both parents were devastated and his wife suffered severe postnatal depression. A while later, they separated and then divorced. The girl he was with on the night of the altercation was leaving the hotel after they'd had an argument and intended to drive home. They'd both been drinking. What happened next was virtually predictable.

Can you spot what is driving his behaviour? I'll give you a clue; it wasn't the result of Patrick being an aggressive asshole who fights with or gets physical with girls. (Note - that pattern is largely due to emotional immaturity as the ego expresses itself in tantrum under the pretext of being macho and using force to gets its way. This is in contrast to the higher levels of emotional maturity where reason, understanding and love are more obvious choices. All of which are somewhat foreign and indeed threatening to the ego.) Let me remind you that many, if not all, of these patterns are deeply rooted and largely subconscious, yet are responsible for much of the behaviour and actions we engage in under the illusionary guise of 'free will'. Or, worse, we justify poor behaviour by saying it's just 'who we are' or our 'inherent personality' which is nothing but ego-speak for "don't blame me, it's not my fault."

Any thoughts on what's driving Patrick yet?

Here's what jumped out at me. Many of my students, and those of Tony Robbins, are familiar with the primary fear all human beings have, which is the fear *we are not enough*. This links to the principal fear that we won't be loved. This fear is commonly set up when we are around two years old and discover that love appears to switch from being unconditional as a baby, to being behaviour-based as a toddler. [This is the context behind the 'terrible two's', which is nothing more than a two-year-old who's been the centre of the universe as a baby, now realising they are no longer in that role, but still want to be.] We begrudgingly come to terms with learning that, when we do as we are told, we are rewarded with a mix of love, recognition, validation, approval, etc. and when we misbehave we are punished and have these rewards taken away. In other words, we learn that love is conditional and must be earned by fitting the profile of what mom and dad want. Remember, it doesn't matter whether the parent is right or wrong or even loves the child unconditionally or not in their *own* mind. The only thing that matters is the *perception* of the child in relation to this. (i.e. Mummy telling me off or saying that I can't have something, equals a lack of love. Even though it is very likely that this does not have the same meaning in the mind of the parent.) With Patrick, not only did he not feel love from his Dad, but he was also made to feel guilty about causing the death of his mom. There were several behaviours that were formed from this and I don't have the time or space to go into too much detail, but I will highlight the two predominant ones that stand out.

Firstly, he clearly felt that he wasn't worthy of love and therefore, tried to see if he could find it by proving himself to the world academically. Two degrees and a Masters. If he had not had part of his lung removed due to a tumour a few years ago, he would have completed his PhD. (note - stress thrives in the absence of love. Stress causes many illnesses. Connection to a lung tumour in his twenties? Hmm...). One thing for sure is that his striving for educational excellence was not due to a passion for learning. Nor was it driven by his heart's desires calling out to a career that lit him up with joy. Instead, it was more of a desperate attempt to earn the right to be loved by proving to everyone (his Dad, friends, the world, etc.) that he was good enough. Education simply became a vehicle that offered a way he could win the game called 'I'm worthy of love'. This is a common mistake that many parents unwittingly make with their kids. They are berated for 'only' getting 80% rather than praised and encouraged to build on it. Of course, most parents mean well and their intention is for their kids to do well at school. The problem is, it sets up a similar trap to the one Patrick fell into, i.e. if I do well in school then mum and dad will love me more. The travesty here is that regardless of what the mind will try to convince you of, no amount of certificates or degrees on the wall can ever paper-over the cracks of an empty heart.

The second pattern was that if any girl seemed to offer Patrick what he felt was love, he'd reach out and grab it with both hands. (Beware, this is usually just connection which desperation will turn into the appearance of love). This would likely lead to many relationships with people who were not a good fit and that wouldn't last. This could either reinforce his belief that it was him who was at fault because he wasn't good enough or, in denial, blame all the people 'out there' for not being Mrs Right. This is why many people have the same relationship but with different partners. If you can't see your own blind spots, the logical conclusion is that the right person just isn't out there. A useful pointer here is that if everyone you meet is the wrong person, maybe it isn't them.

He is also likely to have an internal conflict in committing to one girl. This would be due to a combination of a) finding it difficult to turn down love & connection when presented with it and, b) even though he did not want to hurt other women, he unconsciously hedged his bets in case one source of love went away. Bearing in mind, he experienced this massively on the day he was born. Then, when he finally found a woman who seemed a perfect match, he married her. After the twins died, she (understandably) withdrew all love for herself. This was likely caused or exasperated by huge guilt-related issues, especially if she identified herself with or as her body. This identity link would cause her to blame herself for causing their deaths through messing up the birth timing, rather than acknowledging 'the body' just went into labour when it did for reasons beyond 'her' conscious intent or control. Patrick, despite his academic intelligence and good intentions, simply had not got the tools or resources available to help her through the trauma and, as she was *his* source of love, he therefore had nothing to offer when that source withdrew. Remember the analogy of certificates being futile in helping you love yourself? Even with the best will in the world, with the relationship running on that kind of emotional fault-line, it would have been virtually impossible for them to survive that scale of earthquake as a couple.

A while later, Patrick meets this other girl. The same patterns are running. One night, they have an argument and she storms off (defiant and hurt) with the intent to drive home (escape). He freaks out, grabs her and won't let go, causing her to struggle and resist (naturally), they clash heads, there's blood and the hotel calls the police. Let's not forget the effects of stress and alcohol which promotes automatic behaviour patterns and immobilises rational thought. In other words, he's more likely to act stupidly and from fear instead of love, so that when his words fail to keep her from leaving, he grabs hold and won't let go. The important point to note here is the reason for his behaviour, i.e. the CONTEXT. Is he acting out of anger or juvenile ego-based bullying? Not in a million. Is he a typical wife beater, responding with forced dominance because his pride got threatened and his ego jumped up to defend it? Not on your life. (Although, for people who do that, prison can be a suitable response to for them learn that society shouldn't and doesn't tolerate that kind of immature macho aggression. Especially against women.) Or did he act more out of desperation because her threatening to leave triggered the fear of a lack of love, which he'll do almost anything to avoid, including behaving irrationally. Add to that the fear that she may hurt herself driving drunk, or worse, which, concern for her safety aside, could result in the equivalent outcome of her not being around. You see, the court looks at this as assault first and (maybe) mitigating circumstances via context later down the line. Whereas, in this situation (and life), *context is always definitive*. Of course, the prosecution doesn't care about the context in this case, as it could affect their chances of chalking up another point on the conviction scoreboard. You get the idea.

When I shared my thoughts with Patrick, his jaw dropped. For the first time in his life, he could clearly see and understand the predominant patterns that were driving him. It also back-tested perfectly against virtually every relationship he'd ever had. It was an emotional and cathartic experience, and one that came with a visible sense of release, as a lifetime of underlying emptiness, together with the accumulating pain of dysfunctional relationships, revealed itself for what it really was: a flawed and unwinnable treasure hunt.

He finally realised that the fault wasn't linked to him not being worthy or good enough, but because he was simply playing the game with the wrong map. That's when his entire world shifted.

Why did I share all of this with you? Because it highlights an exceptionally common and underlying pattern that affects nearly every one of us in varying degrees. I'll say it once and then let you explore and reflect on the meaning for yourself:

Most of our habits and decision making are based on automatic behaviours, go-to's and hidden personality traits. These were developed unconsciously in an attempt to fill the gap, or avoid the

pain, caused by our perception of where we feel we did or did not get love as a child. Especially from the people we most wanted it from.

You may want to sit with that one for a while.

What does all this mean? Well, it doesn't take a genius to figure out that the world is full of people searching for love but who often end up settling for a much poorer quality of connection. This is underpinned by the undisputed first law of relationships, that states: *No one can ever love us more than we love ourselves.* Even if we happen to stumble across what we think is love, if we are not full of it ourselves *first*, then how can we possibly give it back in return, if not from our own overflow? Put simply, we can never give what we don't have. And if you're expecting to get it from someone else first, I'm sorry but that isn't love, it's dependency. Sure, a relationship based on that can be better than a cold bed, but only in the same way as a mouldy carrot is better than starving. The good news, my friends, is that access to the love banquet of life IS available and it offers many exquisite flavours to share and enjoy with each other. That's when one plus one becomes eleven.

The challenge for many of us is that the banquet only opens after we outgrow certain false beliefs and realise that the hunger we feel, can never be solved by someone else. Instead, when we realise the first person who has to nourish us with love is ourselves, we break free.

[Note – A higher level distinction for more advanced students is to recognise that self-love is an essential pre-requisite and a huge source of personal growth and power at all levels up to 540 on the Map Of Consciousness. In fact, without self-love there can be no self-esteem, which is required to cross the threshold of courage at 200. However, between 540 and 599 the concept of self-love is transcended and is eventually absorbed by, and into, the larger and all-encompassing field of Love itself, to which one then simply becomes an extension and radiating expression of. The ego, with its constant 'how do I get love', 'please give me love' neediness and strategies (which in reality frequently mistakes 'thoughts' of love for actual love), then becomes surplus to requirements and falls away at level 600 as duality dissolves.]

Up for Debate

Yes, as mentioned earlier, I've been selected for the Pentonville Debate Team. It's actually part of a prison initiative started by Malcolm X in the 1960's and has been running for decades in prisons all over the world. Our opponents are (wait for it) Cambridge University! Yep, in a couple of weeks' time, an elite team from Cambridge will take on Pentonville's best and brightest in a head-to-head. Last year, Pentonville beat Cambridge and this year they are keen for revenge. It promises fun. Each Tuesday for the last couple of weeks I've been taken to the library for 'training'. It's been fascinating in many respects and I'll share a few points of interest with you. The event is organised here by a team called 'Vocalise' who are made up predominantly of young lawyers and barristers who come in to do the training. There are eight of us in the class with the best four going forward into the competition.

On my first session, I was teamed up with a drug dealer and two convicted murderers who were both serving life. One guy, Jon, had done thirteen years and was due for a parole review in two more. He'd just come from Woodhill, an A-Cat facility in Milton Keynes and, surprise surprise, was complaining he wanted to go back, as Pentonville was, quote, "a hell hole". (I know - this is getting old.)

The session started with a brief history of Vocalise and the whole debate structure. It then became apparent why the young legal-beagles engage in this so keenly. In fact, it put so many things into perspective that it was uncanny. The bottom line is that debating has nothing to do with the content or subject of the debate. Instead, it has everything to do with winning your argument any way you can. Sound familiar? I know, I know, more old news. Anyway, each week we are given ridiculous and inconceivable topics to vehemently debate. Here are some from our last session: 'Why euthanasia should be compulsory at age fifty'. 'Why the whole world should be forced to go vegan'. Followed by; 'Why the whole world should only eat meat', 'Why all social media should be banned' and finally, 'The first thing we would enforce if we ruled the world and why'. It's a riot. Not literally as that would be bad, but it is a lot of fun. We are given twenty minutes with our team to prepare for the formal 'battle' and then the debate itself follows with specific guidelines, structure and protocol. First, we debate *for* the topic, and then we switch sides and debate against it. Are you getting the idea? It has *nothing* to do with personal beliefs, viewpoints, fairness, logic or the reality of what is deemed good, bad, right or wrong. It's all about winning by twisting the argument any way you can in order to make your case look good and the other side look bad. Solicitors mainly do this in writing. Barristers do it verbally in court. Remember guys, lawyers and barristers do not build careers around doing the right thing. That's the illusion the public still largely buy into, based on the false assumption that the legal system is driven by fairness. It's not. (For clarity here, I am talking mainly about the sector of law that is focused on litigation. There are plenty of lawyers doing great work in other sectors.)

I don't bang this drum for my benefit as the reality is obvious to me now, but we live in a world where many of you could be exposed to litigation at some point, especially in this climate of victim-reward mentality. It's therefore prudent, if not imperative, to at least have a heads-up, rather than blindly walking into court (civil, family, commercial or criminal) and thinking you can simply trust the process to do the right thing.

You may ask the question, 'How can a system whose very foundation is meant to be based on fairness, be fundamentally unfair?' It's the right question to ask, but it still doesn't change the answer. What I will say is that it isn't because of systemic corruption or some high-strung conspiracy theory. It's nothing that malicious. It just boils down to the fact that *what is right and fair is often ignored or subverted as it simply serves no purpose when the real agenda is winning*. And make no mistake.

Nobody walks into court with the agenda to lose. This is why lawyers and barristers are essentially professional debaters whose allegiance is not to justice but to whatever flag their clients want nailed to the mast. Hmm... maybe we should call them mast-debaters.

Humour aside - it doesn't make them good or bad people, they are just adapting to how the game is set up. Their role is to not to tell the truth, but to practice the art of verisimilitude, a wonderful word which means to create the 'appearance' of truth. This leaves the jury in the middle acting as umpires and the judges deciding the fate of the loser. Make sense? And please don't take my word for any of that. Especially as some may think my current situation makes be biased. I can assure you, I have zero attachment. Neither would I ever swap this amazing experience for anything else. I simply have a passion for discovering and passing on deeper levels of understanding in the hope of inviting people out of their daily sleepwalk. Besides, it's easy to validate. Just speak to anyone who is either in the legal profession or has experienced going through the system and they too will expose the Grand Wizard of Justice and reveal a very different picture to the stereotyped image sold to the public by the mass media. (To be fair, most journalists are largely oblivious themselves and are often too busy focused on their own agendas, which as we know, thrive largely on feeding the public partially selective content, contextually distorted facts, or even outright misinformation.)

This sentiment was beautifully echoed in one of the most revealing (and honest) things that came out the debate session from one of the Vocalise girls, Amore, who said, and I quote "I got into law hoping to make a difference, but I quit right after graduating as I realised the justice system was no longer about fairness but instead far more about manipulation." She added "I don't mind doing that in debate forums as it can be fun. I just could never bring myself to do it in court where people's lives are at stake." Wow. Credit given, girl. Sounds very Indigo to me. It's rare someone has the personal power to turn their back on years in law school because their heart is saying no. Instead, many lawyers are happy to toss chips around the legal table to score points for their own career-based self-interest, but with no real connection to what actually happens in jail. Personally, I think spending seven days in prison should be a mandatory and practical part of the Bar exam, if only to put into perspective the consequences and stakes of the profession. Of course, this will never happen due to what I said in Volume 3, and that is when it comes to the nature of the lessons we need to learn, most people will pick an easier exam to the one that would really challenge them. Even if they know it would lead to higher levels of growth.

Are you getting the picture? And, of course, this kind of thinking is not just confined to the legal industry. Another example comes from a close friend of mine, Hilary, who lives in Geneva and who followed her dream to work at the United Nations, hoping to make a difference. She quit in disgust after that delusion was shattered and replaced with the sobering realisation that the UN is far more about extraneous bureaucracy, political manipulation and national self-interests. The primary agendas seem to be about grabbing what you can while giving the least you can get away with in return, all while waving the flag of higher morals and the best interests for all, so they can justify a large budget which is continuously exposed as misspent.

This also was my experience when I spoke to a UN audience in Geneva last year at an energy symposium. In fact, the first words out of my mouth when it came time for me to take the floor, having watched the squabbles all morning, were that I think the UN should be renamed the United Nothing! It was quite the opening and not exactly out of the playbook of how to win friends and influence people. Though, by the end, I had (hopefully) demonstrated, or at least exposed, the futility of their playground posturing and how, if they were to fulfil their aims of driving sustainable energy agendas over finite sources, then cooperation and contribution with each other is a far better strategy than arguing the point over whether my wind farm is better than your solar plant. I did get the best ovation of the day, but I'm not holding my breath on anyone improving policy as a result. Or even getting a Christmas card. Effective long-term policy changes are infinitely more likely to happen as a result of a rise in consciousness than debate. Incidentally, the UN as an organisation calibrates between 185 and 195 which, as many of you now know, is just below the critical threshold of integrity at 200. (See Chapter 14 'Truth vs. Falsehood', David R. Hawkins M.D., Ph.D.)

This isn't surprising when you look closer. Just like any open system, it contains a mixture of people who all calibrate at different levels. The downside with modern politics is it has a strong disposition that fosters and supports egoic self-interest. It therefore attracts more people with agendas of personal aspiration, than a commitment to serve from a place of truth.

Being willing to be unpopular for what you believe to be the long-term greater good is rare and more the character of statesmen, rather than politicians. A good analogy every parent would understand would be telling their five-year-old that they can't have another ice cream because it's not good for their teeth and because dinner is nearly ready. The child then stamps their feet and screams hate for the parent. It would be ridiculous if the parent then books into counselling because they are traumatised that their child no longer loves them. And it would be irresponsible parenting to give in to their tantrums because it keeps them quiet. A wise parent realises their child's behaviour is simply a natural emotional reaction to a view of life grounded in instant gratification, synonymous with immaturity. They know they are doing the right thing and its very likely that their child will thank them when they are old enough to understand. Especially when they still have all of their teeth and are not overweight or diabetic. In politics, even those who start their career with the best intentions, soon realise they are playing a game where the child can vote in a new set of parents every four years and so adopt a survival strategy of learning to pander to the short-term popular view. One only has to measure the health of many countries (economically, socially, levels of fulfilment and actual health), let alone the ecological condition of the planet, to see the unfortunate effects of short-termism. While detailing a way to improve this is outside the scope of this update, to many people who follow the path of personal growth, along with the philosophies of people like myself, Dr Hawkins and many others, the solution is as easy as it is obvious.

The Surprising Conclusion to The Transfer Saga

So, back to prison matters - It was official. I was <u>not</u> being moved. I was called to the transfer office and told that, due to the partial success of my appeal and that I now had less than three months left to serve, no D-Cat facility would take me. I thought to myself, you know what, no big deal. After all, I'd done over four months here so what's another few weeks? It would be fine. I'm settled in, I'm helping tons of people, there's obviously more people I'm meant to work with. It's all good. So I let go of any attachment and embraced Pentonville as my sole home for the sentence. A few days later Thea came to see me and we had a great and really-connected visit (date night is working well!) My actual words to her were "not to worry as I'm fine staying here." The visit ended, though I was held in the visit hall for an hour as several inmates were found smuggling drugs back into the prison and most were strip-searched. I then get back to my cell, spend an hour working with Patrick on a syllabus we'd put together to help him (he's a great student!) and a letter gets pushed under my door. 'You are being transferred tomorrow at 7.30am to Sudbury'. Excuse me? Well, I didn't see that one coming! I even said to Patrick it's probably just another test from Life to see if I can handle being teased again and we both laughed. I really didn't think it would happen, and then...

I'm in Sudbury! Yep, holy cow, it actually happened. The funny thing is, I was the only prisoner transferred that day to anywhere (even though there are others waiting to be transferred). They allocated one large wagon and two officers for the three-hour trip north. Something which they said would never happen. I'm starting to think that they may have read my last update where I wasn't exactly complimentary on their commercial logic. Oh well, no complaints from me, and I'll still offer them a ticket to the next business school. Though to their credit, within a few days of arriving here, I received a really touching letter from the Governing Head of Residence at Pentonville, stating how much they and the prison appreciated all the positive work I had done while I was there. I wasn't expecting that either and it echoes what I said in the last issue, in respect that many of the staff are just trying to do their best in a system that often works against them. But reading that letter was another reminder of how grateful I am for the many great experiences this incredible and once in a lifetime opportunity has granted me.

So, what's it like here? (I hear you ask) In a word VERY DIFFERENT. OK, so that was two words, but still. After four and a half months to the day in one of the worst and most violent jails in the UK, this place is a massive contrast. I'll give you a few highlights as so much happened since I arrived, it would take another update. To begin with, there's no razor wire and I even have the key to my own cell. The first thing I noticed is that the prisoners walking around all say hello and hold the doors open for each other. There is also no violence which, in many respects, is not surprising. These are D-Category prisoners. Many of them who were initially violent would have tried for years to earn the right and privilege to be here. If they get involved in just one fight, that right can be taken away and you're back to Bang-up Boulevard. It's perfect leverage.

The layout and structure here at Sudbury is the same as an old army base. This is because it used to be one. Having served and spent time on dozens of bases for years, as a cadet, instructor and soldier, this is an easy deal for me. Plus, (wait for it) I get access to a keyboard and printer in the library! Oh, praise the Lord for small mercies and Christmas coming early. Even the food is good! Although to be fair, I'd become so used to slop with extra slop that Pedigree Chum dog food would have been an upgrade. But don't get too carried away, there are still no Michelin starred chefs, waitress-service or cell-delivered fresh juice. Even so, I'm certainly not complaining, although I am a little sad that I'll miss the debate with Cambridge.

Obviously, there's still no internet access, personal phones, ability to send email, etc. which, trust me, I am NOT missing. In fact, I mentioned to Thea over a month ago that the quality of my personal daily journaling and meditation was reaching levels I'd never experienced. What I *can* say is that over the last six weeks, my daily practice has channelled and delivered SO many high-level insights, distinctions, messages and metaphors that it's blown me away (like standing behind a 747 at full thrust – Mmm, must try that some day) There are many days that I just cannot write fast enough, and I'm in awe of the connection. My next four books are already mapped out and the content and quality of my planned events and programmes has shot up to a whole new level. I'm thrilled for what I want to share and how many people it may help. Although, the juxtaposition of being simultaneously excited and deeply grounded is an interesting feeling. I also won't say more than that for now, only to point out I'm convinced that much of the information I seem to be streaming started as a result of being 'unplugged' from the electronic 'Matrix' for the last four to five months. Think about it. The average five-year-old in the modern world is now unlikely to spend that length of time unplugged *during their lifetime*. The mental consequences of this are massive. Just a tiny peek behind that particular curtain will show you that there is a lot of good research linking personality disorders in kids to the amount of TV they are (or were) exposed to under the age of three.

However, mental health issues aside, when you understand the changes to the actual physical structure of your own brain that result from being constantly distracted and triggered by short-term interruptions which are the hallmark of modern life, you'd book into hotel Pentonville for a break yourself. OK, maybe not there but you get the point. Let's just say I won't be running to the iPhone store as my first priority on release. Though even if I don't call – please know I still love you all.

Well, that about wraps things up for this issue. I could go on but I think I've harped on at you long enough and now that I have access to a keyboard, I'm in danger of doubling the content, so I'll practice holding back. Having said that, I do have a feeling you'll like what I'm planning to share in Volume 10. For now, I'll leave you with a quick recap on a few key takeaways from this issue that may serve as a useful reminder.

- Many of our behaviours and decisions are made way before they get to the stage we call 'free will'.
- Free will is often just the expression of how our unconscious pre programmed patterns play out and are expressed under the illusion of personal choice.
- A lot of these patterns are driven by the limiting beliefs formed around our perception of where we did or did not get love as a child.
- The civil and criminal justice system is not driven by fairness but instead has evolved to be based largely on the agenda of winning your debate. This may be constrained by legal parameters, but certainly not ethical ones.
- My letting go completely of any attachment to moving, just happen to 'coincide' with it finally happening. This is a classic transition from 'by-me' to 'through-me' and shows even teachers need reminding of their own content. Therefore, never beat yourself up for forgetting things you feel you are supposed to know.

- As electronic distractions and mass communication encroach further into daily life (social media, push notifications, etc.), it becomes even more imperative to carve time out to be 'unplugged'. Prison is not mandatory for this. ☺

All I have to say now is a big thank you for taking the time to indulge in my sharing. My intention in taking you on this journey with me is always to serve but also to help you discover and learn things that can help you walk your own path in a more empowering and self-sufficient way. After all, regardless of age, I know our true potential is constantly emerging as we accept the golden invitation this incredible gift of life offers, which is to continually strive to be the best version of ourselves we can be. Pass it on.

All my love and a big hug,

Peter X

Volume 10: Starlight at The End of The Tunnel (Week 20)

Volume 10 reveals how Peter became a 'prisoner at large'. He explains why coincidences exist and how he managed to start shifting dozens of mindsets in his new jail within the first week, using 'Project Starlight'. We also find out how he helps a convicted murderer find meaning in his life by helping to prevent more murders.

My dear and amazing family, students and friends

Welcome to the tenth issue of Inside Track. I start with some big thanks as always for the many letters I've had from all over the world since my last update and the feedback on the previous issue. It seems that reading Patrick's story made many people spot some patterns in their own lives. It's amazing how much of what we do is automatic, unquestioned and unconscious. A state that I collectively sum up in the phrase, 'sleeping awake'. It seems from your letters that Volume 9 was a good wake-up call for those ready to leap out of the walking dream world and start looking to see or realise (real-eyes) more of their potential.

So, what do I have in store for you this time? It's probably no surprise that even though it's been just three weeks since I arrived in my new Jail, there is already a growing list of prisoners I'm helping. This includes Brad, a guy on my dorm who has served twenty-one years for murder and whose interaction with me on my first night offers lessons for us all. There is an update on the injured foot saga as I finally managed to get my X-ray some two months after the accident. Let's just say the result surprised me for a couple of reasons. In addition, I give an explanation as to why 'coincidences' happen to us the way they do. I will also let you know the outcome of 'Project Starlight' which

I just completed and, no, it does not involve midnight escape plans! *Plus*, there is a pretty incredible update to Operation Chrysalis, which falls squarely under the Masters Circle motto of 'constantly amazed, yet never surprised.' But to begin with, I'll share what happened on my first day and why my being here has caused such a stir.

Welcome to Sudbury! – Err, you're a what?

On arrival, I was assigned a cell on the induction wing. Think college dorm type set up. A long corridor with double rooms either side. The wing is run by prisoners and rarely sees an officer. Welcome to D-Cat. I walked into the two-bedroom cell and was greeted by Fidel. A big Jamaican guy in his late twenties whose first impression probably wouldn't have won favour with a potential girlfriend's parents. Here's the conversation.

Me: "Hey, my names Peter, good to meet you, looks like we are going to be cell mates."

Fidel: "No man. That ain't gonna happen, I told them I don't want no cell-mate – go find another room." I smiled, replied things were cool and headed off to speak to an officer. I went to the central office and had the following conversation.

"Hi Officer, my cell-mate has made it clear he doesn't want to share. What do you suggest?"

He replied "Tough, they all say that – go back and tell him you have no choice." At this point, I weighed up my options. I had no doubt I could turn Fidel around but did I really want to roll that dice on my first thirty minutes here? Also, having my own cell would be useful, especially as I'm no longer confined to lengthy periods of 'bang-up'. It could, therefore, act as a base and I could still help people throughout the day. This also took out the variables of sharing with someone who wanted to watch News, Soaps or other brain dissolving activities that poison their potential.

I looked at the officer and said as naturally as I could "Actually, as a civil prisoner, I am entitled to my own cell. Would it be possible to arrange that, please?"

For a moment you would have thought I'd just told him I was from another planet and was singing the galactic national anthem. No part of his brain was expecting that and, judging by the facial expression, neither was it processing it. He said, "Err… you're a what?"

"A civil prisoner." I reiterated.

Another blank stare, followed by, "What's one of those?"

"It means I am not a criminal and therefore have different rights, one of which is I can only room with another civil prisoner."

"Who says?"

"Prison Service Order 4600, Annex B, Paragraph 2, Point No.9" (I wasn't trying to be a smartass, but he did ask).

"Do you have a copy of that?"

"Yes, sir. Here it is." I said politely, as I handed him a printout I'd taken from the library in Pentonville.

At this point, his brain went back into a closed loop of uncertainty as he reached for the paperwork. After he read it he said, "Oh. Well, errm, it seems you are right. The only problem is we don't have any other civil prisoners. In fact, I've been here sixteen years and never heard of us having one." He scratched his head and mumbled, "Hmm, pop back in twenty minutes and I'll see what I can do."

I went back to Fidel and told him it was all good and I should be moved shortly. I also clocked a book that was open on his desk that was 'Maths for Dummies'. I pointed with my head and said – "How's the learning going? Anything I can help with?" He told me he was taking a test soon at the education wing but thought he'd be OK. However, while I was gone, he'd seen one of my books through the clear plastic garbage sacks we transport our stuff in from prison to prison. It was 'Transcending Levels Of Consciousness'. He pointed and asked, "What's that about?" I gave a rudimentary overview of the difference between the victim vs achiever mentality and why many people end up in prison by trying to make money doing the wrong things in achiever mode, but then drop into victim mode when they come to prison. By the time I left the room to go back to see officer Blank Stare, Fidel and I had become friends and he now always makes a point of speaking to me whenever he sees me.

I was then given the keys to a cell on 'P-Dorm', which stands for Privileged Dormitory. This is where the single cells are and they are called privileged because it usually takes months to earn the right to have one. It was here that I met Brad.

Life After Murder

Brad was convicted for murder and sentenced to life in prison after stabbing a guy in a fight when he was twenty-two. That was twenty-one years ago. For the first decade of his sentence, he was angry at everyone and was always looking for a fight. (Note - Anger calibrates at level 150). It was an excuse to show the system he wasn't going to conform, regardless of the amount of solitary confinement it came with. His resistance was largely fuelled by resentment, hate and having a point to prove. Prison gives you a lot of time to think about things and after ten years he finally recognised the futility of screaming at a system that was deaf to his anger. Instead, he wrote on each of the bricks of his cell his own personal obstacles and demons he faced; short-temper, hate, ego, drugs, alcohol, resentment. This was the wall he had to break through in order to win his inner freedom as he finally realised that *it was his own choices that determined his destiny, not luck or misfortune.* In short, he matured.

However, he still had the look of a man who was wondering how one stupid act, fuelled largely by alcohol and significance, could end the life of someone else and waste over two decades of his own here in prison. If you recall in Volumes 1 & 2, I mention the book 'Man's

Search For Meaning' which details the harrowing account of Viktor Frankl and his survival in German concentration camps. Poignantly, the book reveals his observations on who kept or lost the will to live and why. One of the most interesting aspects was the lack of correlation to any physical attributes such as size or strength. (Anything physical is based on force and is always temporary or transient). Instead, the 'x-factor' boiled down to having a big enough reason and a purpose that was bigger than you. (This is non-physical which is based on Power and not subject to the law of impermanence.) And while we are thankfully not gassing people in modern prisons, many prisoners leave with a sense of having wasted their life in jail as they struggle to find an empowering meaning in the time they feel they have 'lost'. This leads to resentment, grief, anguish, guilt and a whole host of low-level emotions which prevent them from reengaging in society in a meaningful way. It's the classic – 'Brooks Was Here' syndrome in Shawshank Redemption. In the two hours I spent with Brad on the first night, I was beyond convinced that he'd learnt his lessons. Twenty-one years will do that to most people. What he now needed was a way to give a more empowering meaning to his past and tie it in with a purpose that could inspire him, rather than cripple him. It wasn't hard to spot.

One of the unfortunate aspects of current society is the rapid increase in knife crime. Currently, the UK government statistics show over 5000 knife possession offences in England & Wales in the last three months alone. However, the most shocking part is that over 20% of those arrested for possession of knives are between the ages of ten and seventeen! Brad was from a town whose rise in knife attacks has risen sharply this year and the local police, newspaper and MP have been very vocal about trying to stop it. I asked Brad what he would say if he were sat in front of a bunch of teenagers who thought it was OK to walk around with a knife. His response was immediate and one of almost panicked concern. "Oh, God! I'd tell them the dangers.

How fast it can go from being cool or feeling big, to seeing someone lying on the floor in a pool of blood and you spending the best part of your life inside." He continued, "They need to understand what can go wrong and why the consequences can be disastrous for everyone." The sincerity was unmistakable. I spent the next hour with Brad outlining a plan on how he could set up talks in trouble spots, in tough neighbourhoods, schools and community centres. How kids in those areas rarely listen to the advice from the police or teachers or even parents, as they are too busy hooked into their own gangs or dealing with life on the street. It's a different world, a different language. But listening to someone who's come out of prison after spending twenty-one years inside, someone who grew up in a tough neighbourhood and thought all of the same thoughts they are likely thinking, carries quite a different message.

In Pentonville, we had a few people that came in to give talks. The 'social worker' types were only an excuse to get out of the cell. However, the two most memorable and impactful talks were by ex-prisoners. One was a former top London Gangster who'd served twenty-plus years. The other, an ex-mafia boss who had served longer and whose dad was currently the oldest serving Prisoner in the U.S., having just turned one hundred and *still* with ten years to go from his fifty-year sentence. Their stories were jaw dropping and right out of the movies, though they all carried the same message. The glam life of crime with its shortcuts and violence are not worth the price. Case closed. Game over. We didn't 'hear' their message, as you would with advice from the police or a probation officer. We 'felt' it as it echoed from the depths of their own experience.

Brad started to see the bigger picture. He even suggested organising knife amnesties while delivering the talks to young people, where he could persuade and encourage them to 'drop it in the box' and which could then be handed to the police. More importantly, he began to feel something he hadn't felt in a long, long time. Purpose. This allowed him to start seeing the last twenty years in a very different light. Not just wasted time but instead, in essence, it became his teachers' qualification. Being able to use that as a way to do good by helping *reduce* knife crime, and being recognised by society for that, rather than being viewed suspiciously as someone who may commit more of it, was a massive shift. It would also be the very thing that would help circumvent the *defensive probation* challenge I covered in Volume 6 and that he had also constantly faced. This is where, no matter how hard you try and tick the boxes, no probation officer has any incentive to let you out. Not because you don't qualify or are outside of the legal risk profile but primarily, because you may pose a threat to their own career if you reoffend, as they would ultimately be responsible for allowing you to be released.

Brad had been turned down several times and was coming up for his next parole hearing in a few months. However, he had already been cleared for the occasional home-leave as part of the prison's resettlement programme and these had gone without a hitch. I, therefore, encouraged him to use his next home-leave as a test bed for his talks. If he could show probation that he's proactively helping to reduce crime, not just abstain from it, then that would be a different ball game altogether and would leave them needing an excuse *not* to let him out. In fact, Brad could even become his local town's unofficial 'poster boy' for standing against knife crime. After all, who's better qualified than someone who knows the consequences first-hand? Of course, no amount of actions could ever bring back the poor soul who died, but if something good can come from it that prevents even a few more deaths, would that not be worth it? Is that not a way for Brad to repay society in a way that makes a positive difference rather than another million or so pounds to the taxpayer he's already cost? I mean, if we've already paid that for him to get his 'teacher training' then maybe, with the right parameters, we should think about letting him use it? Obviously, the ultimate decision is Brads. I have no control over what he does and neither should I. In the words of the great Morpheus, I can only show him the door, he still needs to have the courage to walk through it and for that I'm happy to offer guidance, direction and encouragement.

There's also an important distinction here that has relevance for most people. Especially those running around chasing and achieving goals and wondering why they're still unhappy. An answer can be found simply in understanding that many goals are driven by desire, which is essentially the energy of wanting something you don't have. (For people in jail, this could be focused on getting out.) However, desire is a two-edged sword. If you feel your desires are possible, then it can galvanise into determination and action. Although achieved goals are then replaced by the next desire as we mistake the source of happiness to be something outside of ourselves. Something to be 'got' rather than recognise it can only come from within. Conversely, if you feel your goals are out of reach then desire transforms into longing, which is akin to a chronic ache of emptiness. An example is someone who's lonely and longs to meet the right person but wonders why they never show up. They fail to realise that, by concentrating on what's missing, they vibrate in the world as 'empty'. Even if they do meet someone, like attracts like and who wants to meet another empty or lonely person? That would simply mean there are now two people who feel alone.

Purpose is different. Purpose is driven by *meaning*, not desire. It manifests through focused intent, not lack. It's the heart expressing itself in its fullness, yearning to play the game of life. Purpose is focused on context, whereas desire is focused on content. One lights you up, the other distracts you into an ego-fuelled tail chase. You get the idea. So did Brad.

Anyway, that was my first day.

Prisoner At Large

The next morning word had spread to most of the staff that there was a 'Civil Prisoner' on site and I felt like the new animal in the zoo. Officers literally came just to look and say "Oh, you're the civil prisoner." I could almost hear the internal follow-on, which said, "How strange." It turns out nobody has a clue what to do with me. One challenge is that this is a working prison, which means everyone has to be assigned to some sort of employment. Either inside the grounds, on things such as kitchens, making fence panels or gardening, etc. (the large gardens are immaculate and look as if they could be part of a country club.) Or, depending on risk factor and how long you have served, about a quarter of the six-hundred inmate population have earned the right to work outside in charity shops or in normal businesses and then return each evening. (There are many large companies, such as Boots or Marks & Spencer, who run partnerships with prisons for work allocation in order to help prepare people for resettlement back into the community.) But no matter what your story, the rule is - everyone must work. That is unless you are a civil prisoner. I have therefore chosen to exercise my right *not* to work. This means that, apart from standing outside my cell-door to be counted for 'Roll Check' a few times a day, I am free to roam the hundred plus acre site and pretty much do as I please. In fact, I have appointed myself the title of 'Prisoner at Large'. However, as I am sure you can imagine, as I am now effectively 'unleashed' from the confines of a B-Cat, I'm certainly not spending time with my thumb up my ass or my brain in neutral. Oh no. In actual fact, I'm far too busy to work. Apart from a growing list of people I'm helping, I've also written to the head of reducing-reoffending and also met with the drug rehab unit, all offering my services and showing them the evidence of what I was able to achieve in Pentonville. I also offered a series of talks to both inmates and staff here, the first of which I gave today.

From an official perspective, I've caused a lot of staff to scratch their heads. The problem is that the prison has only had half-a-dozen or so civil prisoners in the last twenty years and most officers have never met one or understand the rules surrounding them. As it turns out, neither does the system. In fact, it's not designed for it. For a start, all officers have agreed that I am technically the lowest risk prisoner. However, this can't be logged or made official because I don't have a probation officer, because I'm not a criminal and haven't committed a crime and as such, I don't qualify for probation. Not even the police know I am in prison because I was never arrested or charged. Therefore, I can't be risk-assessed. Therefore, I cannot be categorised. I'm an oddity, a misfit, and I keep getting passed around in a giant game of prison pinball as no one wants my file on their desk when the music stops. During the first few days, it was hilarious to watch. That was until I met one particular Senior Officer (SO) who, it appears, I was destined to meet.

What was that, some of you don't believe in destiny? You think things unfold more by chance than design? Don't worry, it's a common and prevalent misnomer perpetuated by an outdated model of science still grounded in the blanket Newtonian denial of anything non-physical that cannot be objectively measured or labelled. And while everyone is welcome to their own personal opinion, the darkness of ignorance can usually be extinguished by the light of higher knowledge and understanding. Therefore, before I share how I met this particular SO, whom I shall refer to as Officer P, permit me to share a quick insight into a subject many people struggle to wrap their head around.

Coincidence vs. Synchronicity Explained...

The term many materialists use is Coincidence which has its basis in randomness. The term used by non-materialists is Synchronicity, which suggests there is more to it than randomness and that a hidden order of some sorts exists outside of the linear realm accepted or measured by traditional science. This brings it into the domain of Meta-Physics and ties in branches of science such as Chaos Theory and good old Quantum Dynamics. Incidentally, the word Synchronicity was first coined by the renowned psychologist Carl Yung (Calibration 520), in an attempt to find meaning in apparent coincidences that appeared to be far outside the realms of 'randomness'. Ready to explore? Great, grab a life vest as we are going to use the ocean as the primary metaphor.

In the ocean, there are various ecosystems that all exist simultaneously depending on the depth one examines. For example, a coral ecosystem will contain certain fish and organisms that are all designed to work with each other. Factors include types of creatures, food, temperature, pressure, levels of sunlight and more. However, if we go deeper into the ocean and sink several hundred feet, many of those factors change. Go to the bottom of the ocean and again, it's a completely different world to the one up top. Bottom feeders never meet the top feeders. They swim along and meet other fish and creatures who are at their own level. They enjoy their own little world and go along quite happily but with a very different set of friends, food, predators, challenges, advantages and daily goals and agendas.

You see, when we apply a two-dimensional depth model to it, most people have no problem understanding this. Even though it's all the same ocean.

For us, being together in the same room is like the fish all being in the same ocean. However, all of those 'eco-systems' are still operating at various depths, *but on an energetic level*. This gets ignored because we are under the illusion we are all swimming at the same depth called 'surface of the Earth' and therefore get sucker-punched into applying the wrong criteria. We miss it because when we look at ourselves, we clearly don't live above or below each other, but we DO live at different depths, frequencies and levels of *consciousness*. Have you ever noticed that in a crowd of people (or a planet of seven billion) you just 'happen' to meet or get drawn to people who are on a similar 'level' to you? That even in a new environment (workplace, school, holiday resort) you often 'randomly' find or are 'drawn' to people who are your 'kind' of people? Spatially, there appears to be all kinds of fish in the same tank which is why energetically, you will quickly form cliques with those on a similar 'level' or avoid or draw boundaries against those who you don't 'resonate' with, i.e. are not on your 'level'. This depth game goes on 24/7 and many are oblivious to the nature of it and hence, ascribe the word 'coincidence' to what is actually a common and predictable phenomenon of how things that appear random, show up in your layer of the world. Finding your current partner, house, business opportunity, etc. is about as surprising as a hermit crab finding a seashell.

In other words, when it comes to how your life unfolds, you don't get what you wish for but, as in the previous example of the two lonely people, *you get what you resonate with*. Thinking thoughts of scarcity? Hmm, check your bank account and you'll probably find a perfect match. Think habitually about abundance? Money and/or opportunities to create it probably come easily to you. It's not complicated. It's just that most people have it wired backwards. They see the empty bank account and then react with vibrations of scarcity. Remember, outer world FOLLOWS inner world. Stop looking through the wrong end of the telescope.

It's the same principle behind how and why I met Patrick in Pentonville the week I was looking for a new cell-mate. Here was a guy who just 'happened' to have a strong interest in personal growth and consciousness. We just 'happened' to stand next to each other in a 'random' line up at the gym and immediately get onto a topic we both 'happened' to resonate with and one that was outside of the frequency of 99% of the prison population. Hmm. Again, this isn't difficult to understand once you have a context for it, which is why the ocean metaphor is useful. The exciting part is that once you start to get your head around it, you can start to 'back-test' it and see where it has shown up throughout your life in all areas from work to finance to relationships. This is always a far more reliable way of verifying something than blindly believing what somebody else (i.e. me) is telling you. Personal experience is always a more reliable barometer than third-party persuasion, which can often come with hidden agendas.

Indigo, Indigo, Wherefore art thou Indigo?

So, here I was swimming around my new jail where I found myself waiting at a door. I was looking for a Centre Manager who I'd been told to ask for. At this point Officer P fishtails out of a different room and, as he walks past, asks me what I want and who I am waiting for. When I mention the name, he says "Ah, I don't think he's in today but follow me and let's see if we can get you taken care of." Over the next ten minutes, we walk around and have a good chat. As we part company I turn to him and I say: "Have you ever heard of the term Indigo Children?" To which he replied he hadn't. I then invited him to look it up and we parted ways.

The next day he came and found me, looked straight at me and said "You! You have scared me!" I wasn't sure how to respond to that, but I smiled, and he continued. "I was up until 1am researching Indigos – I can't believe it. It makes total sense." He went on to say that all of his life he had felt different and now he understood why. He listed all the typical signs that I outlined in Volume 6 and had even taken one particular online test and scored 28 out of 30. He was, in essence, a classic Indigo. Of course, I already knew that which is why I threw it out there. That was two weeks ago. Since then, Officer P and I have become good friends and often spend time discussing life at high levels of awareness. As a result, he has single-handedly challenged the logic around civil prisoners that was causing the 'Prison Pinball with Pete' game mentioned earlier. He's taken me away from my assigned officer and put me on his roster. He has also persuaded the Governor *and* the Probation service that, as a civil prisoner, I should be allowed to circumvent the three months 'lie down' period that would have prevented me from having home leave. When Thea came to see me, he made a point of coming to the visit hall to tell her that, at fifty-five years old, things finally made sense and I'd given him a different perspective that has changed his view on life. It was quite moving.

He has even asked me to collaborate on a proposal to the Secretary of State for Justice, outlining our perspectives on the faults within the prison service and our suggestions on how to improve it. Thanks to the work I'd done in Pentonville, I handed him a draft within an hour.

On top of that, he has also arranged with the Governor and the probation service for me to have some nights at home. Incidentally, as far as I can tell and outside of emergencies, no prisoner *in the history of the system* has been granted a licence for multiple-night home leave within three weeks of arriving at a D-Cat. In short, both he and the Governor have been amazing and a rare example of reasonable and progressive thinking. Both are assets to a system in desperate need of more of it and a stark contrast to the 'can't do' attitude I experienced in Pentonville.

More on the home visit later.

Project Starlight

Now I was free to play and one of my first action items was to see if *Mud Or Stars?* would have a similar impact in this prison as it did in my last. I had a few copies sent in by the amazing Anita Langley and chose a cross-section of prisoners to share it with. This included those serving short sentences and those with longer ones such as Russ, a guy in my dorm who was sentenced in 1974 for murder and has now served forty-two years straight. The feedback was universally positive. Even Brad came to my cell right after reading it and said that if he'd learned those lessons when he first came to jail, it would have saved him ten years of heartache. He also gave some constructive suggestions along with permission to share our interaction above.

After the feedback was in, I retyped it onto one of the library computers and tweaked it based on the suggestions and observations I've received in the four months since I'd first written it. I then counted the number of dorms and rooms and printed the equivalent of one copy per room. That evening I went to work as the secret agent of change in the guise of an anonymous mailman.

Every copy got delivered and the next day people started talking. Not everybody read it, obviously, and not everyone who did would resonate. That wasn't the purpose of the mission. What mattered was that those who were ready for it, got it. And then came my biggest magic moment of the week. As I walked to the education block the following morning, someone shouted over 'Mud or Stars?' Now it was me shouting back 'Stars!', along with a big smile. And so the ripple continues.

Give Me A Break

After my first week settling in, I was sent to medical for a more in-depth check-up. Mental and physical. During the mental check-up I was asked standard questions about depression, addiction and self-harm. Then the session finished with me being asked if I felt I was OK or if I wanted to see anyone else with regards to a treatment plan while I was here. I commented that there was no one in particular but if any of the officers did want to see me I'd happily map-out a course of therapy that may help them. The nurse burst out laughing.

The physical was standard. Blood pressure at 110 over 70 with a resting heart rate at 62. Everything else was tip top. After four and a half months of bang-up and dog food, I was actually pretty happy with that. I then mentioned my foot and the X-ray saga from Pentonville. However, as it had now been two months and there was no more pain, she thought there may not be much point. Besides, Sudbury has a one kilometre perimeter path that many prisoners walk or run along and that morning I had built up to my first 'five-K'. She examined the foot and noticed it was still a little swollen and recommended me for X-ray just to see how it was. I went to see Officer P and asked if I'd be allowed to go to hospital on my own. After all, why waste prison resources when I'm a civil prisoner? He agreed and, like a star, managed to get me authorised for unaccompanied release the next day to hospital.

I then called Thea and asked how she felt about picking me up for the day. I'm not sure if she replied with a word or a loud squeak but she was there at 9am and we had our first day together since this adventure started. It was magical. However, the X-ray showed something I wasn't expecting. My foot was still clearly broken with a bad break across the fifth metatarsal. I thought 'what dummy would run five kilometres on a broken foot?' The only good news was that the hospital wanted me to come back the next day to the fracture clinic. Again, Officer P arranged the paperwork, Thea squeaked, and we were 2-for-2 on days out. It was worth every step hobbled in Pentonville.

Once back at the ranch, I took the results to the Healthcare unit. The prison nurse was mortified and said I should immediately put in for a claim against Pentonville for medical negligence. She said that with the paper trail of evidence showing my constantly unanswered requests for an X-ray, the misdiagnosis from the doctor I never saw there together with the lack of treatment and painkillers, it all amounted to a legal slam dunk. Add to this the higher likelihood of healing complications, compounded by the fact that I'd been running on it not knowing for sure if it was broken and just using lack of pain for guidance, and I would be looking at around £20,000 in compensation. I smiled, thanked her and left. I mean, how do you explain to someone who lives and breathes in an industry so tightly gripped by the compensation culture that I'm not interested? That I teach and stand for personal responsibility and owning my circumstances, not complaining about them. And yes, while £20,000 would be very useful in covering some of my crippling legal costs, from what I have seen of the state of the prison service, it needs it a lot more than I do. After all, I'm trying to help make a positive difference, not add to its financial problems and lack of resources. Speaking of which…

Operation Chrysalis – The Butterfly Beckons

As early as my first update, I have been committed to trying to add value to the prison system through what I called 'Operation Chrysalis – A Four-Step Approach To Tackling Britain's Prison Crisis.' This was in response to the woefully inadequate attempts at rehabilitation, which currently see *over 70% of prisoners reoffend within two years*. At the heart of my proposed initiative was a strong focus aimed at upgrading the thinking patterns and mindset of new and existing offenders. This is based on the glaringly obvious pathway that demonstrates all behaviour is preceded by thought. It is a neurological fact that without the thought we cannot have the behaviour. Thoughts are also habitual, which is nature's way of making us more efficient by taking our repeated actions and making them automatic. Nature's logic, I assume, is that if we keep doing something over and over, then it must be either important, necessary or beneficial. It's clearly been evaluated by the reasoning part of the brain (prefrontal cortex) and passed inspection, so why waste time taking up more thinking resources when we can hand the program to the back part of the brain where it happily runs without conscious thought? This is very useful, as it means we don't have to relearn how to walk every day but it also means many of our poor thinking habits result in habitually poor and often unquestioned behaviours. This is why simply educating people, especially in prison, accomplishes little more than knowledge transfer and does virtually nothing to shift the quality and type of thinking patterns which cause many of them to reoffend.

As outlined in previous issues, behaviour and the thoughts which precede it are more determined by the level of consciousness and emotional maturity a person is at. Therefore, an effective platform for long-term change *must* have its basis in *personal* growth and development and be aimed at upgrading a person's <u>mind</u>set. It should NOT be based solely on *knowledge* growth and development which is simply aimed at upgrading their <u>skill</u> set. The two are different and until the mainstream recognises this then modern education, and its premise of thinking that knowledge is the sole platform upon which the success or quality of life stands, will remain flawed. This is the same for the classroom as well as the prison education wing. Hence my passion to bring in a programme aimed at helping people upgrade their mindset.

One of my challenges has been the stark resistance to change from inside the system itself. This isn't surprising and is usually reflective of almost any ageing institution. The life-draining commitment to the status quo is based on a combination of being addicted to certainty, ego-based significance, denial of the need to change, turgid projection of authority and an unwillingness to take risks due to protective self-interest. I've therefore been looking to work with various charities and non-profits to get traction for Operation Chrysalis and with a view to solving the distribution side of the equation. One challenge is that many charities are not personal growth minded. Just like the prison service, they are more focused on managing symptoms than addressing the cause. This has been frustrating. And then I met Ben.

Ben is a great kid who is on my dorm, works outside during the day, and is in prison for a dangerous driving offence. Good guy. One stupid act of behaviour. Prison. It can be *that* quick and simple. I've been coaching Ben most evenings and one night he and I were talking outside the dorm and I mentioned I was looking to help bring personal development into the prison system as it's the most effective way of shifting the prospects of reoffending. Ben said, "Oh, that sounds like something we had at the last prison I was in before being transferred here." He went on to describe a programme he did that was set up by a magistrate who sounded like he shared the same values. He also had one of the workbooks and went to get it. I almost fell off my chair. It was called The Chrysalis Programme.

The Chrysalis Programme is the brainchild of David Apparicio, a Justice of the Peace who was tired of sentencing the same offenders for similar offences. Some of them soon after they had served the prison sentence he'd given them previously. Recognising first-hand that rehabilitation was ineffective, as the system clearly did not understand the principles of it, he set about to create something that would help. I also knew he was someone that I needed to talk to and for that, I needed to get out of prison a little earlier than planned. Everything is possible.

Home Sweet Home! Well, for 3 days

I mentioned earlier that I didn't fit into any kind of box the prison was geared up for. I used this fact to challenge the logic around Sudbury's three-month risk assessment phase, known as the lie-down period and during which time you are not allowed or eligible for any kind of home leave. In some D-Cat's it can be as little as twenty-eight days but the period itself is non-negotiable and all prisoners must abide by it.

I won't go into the exact details as to how I became the first person in the system to circumvent this, as it involves an equation I teach my advanced students and can't really be summed up in a paragraph. What I *will* say is that it combines the active meditation technique covered in Volume 4, with some pro-active Newtonian hustle. I was actually approved and scheduled for a five-day home leave by the Governor but unfortunately, he was away. The Deputy Governor (who I've never met) couldn't get his head around it and, as a compromise, reduced it to three days. Of course, I was still happy. Needless to say, I had a wonderful three days, the personal details of which I will not reveal other than to say there were many *magic moments* and some, especially with Thea, were slightly longer than moments. Naturally, seeing her and the dogs was a major highpoint and there were lots of walks, licks and cuddles. I even got to broadcast live to both the Elite Mentorship Forum and Masters Circle for an hour each. Although that only went a small part of the way to thanking them for their incredible support during this adventure and to say how incredibly proud I am of how they have all stepped up in my absence and grown to become the people they now are.

I also called David Apparicio at The Chrysalis Programme. We had a great conversation and connected exceptionally well. Needless to say, our ideas on enabling reintegration are very much in alignment. We then arranged a meeting for when I come out which, wait for it, is now less than two weeks!

The end of the journey is nigh

Yes my friends, as I write this I have less than two weeks to go before I leave the sunny shores of Sudbury and return back from my adventure. And what an adventure it has been! I'll sign off now as I plan to share a summary and reflection of the journey along with my thoughts on where, how and why the river unfolded as it did. Especially now that I have the privilege of looking back and seeing how the dots have joined in relation to how I thought they would, when looking forward nearly six months ago. Stay tuned for my next and final update and I'll see you on the other side.

All my love and respect,

Peter X

Volume 11: The Final Stretch (Week 22)

In the last chapter of this incredible journey, Peter takes an objective look back over the lessons he's learned and the shifts this experience has caused. He shares some deeper insights into understanding ourselves and the nature of what it means to be a better human. Finally, he takes a look at a new path for his future and seeks to hopefully show that no matter what happens in life, there is always a way to come out better, stronger and wiser.

My dear and amazing family, students and friends

Welcome to the final instalment of the Inside Track. In this concluding episode of my six-month journey, I share an update on some of the things that have happened since my last letter, as well as coming full circle on many of the key lessons, revelations and *magic moments* that have transpired along the way. As usual, there are some interesting self-reflections and some powerful lessons to share, as well as a strange sense of completion. Let's get started.

It's been a busy two weeks. As word spread that my release date was approaching, I started to notice more people reaching out for help and support.

One interesting interaction was with a guy named Carlos who is a Muslim with a large beard and curious yet peaceful eyes. He'd found me in the education block after I had gone there to print some more copies of *Mud or Stars?* for the day's new arrivals. He joined a queue of three people waiting to speak to me and sat patiently for almost an hour. When I was free, he came in, introduced himself and asked if I'd be able to help him. Carlos is in his thirties, serving an eight-year sentence for robbery. He'd also been in and out of prison for various crimes since he was fifteen. He's currently thirty-two.

Like many who follow that path, he was tired. He now had a new wife and son but just didn't know how to change.

After reading him as well as I could, I felt he was sincere, so as usual, I stress-tested with a couple of questions. The first was, "Why, out of all the times you've been inside, do you want to change now?" His reply was exactly what I wanted to hear. He looked me straight in the eye and said "To be honest, I've grown up. I realise how much of a dick I've been and it really is time to change. I'm done with this. I wish I could give you a big or important reason, but the truth is it's just not who I want to be anymore." I could relate to this as, although I'd never been a career criminal, I had certainly walked the 'I am a dick' path, mainly in my twenties and had struggled to let go for a while after. What stood out with Carlos that was different to many other prisoners was that there was no defensiveness or ego. Just raw honesty and openness. This is a big plus as it saves me time deconstructing and eliminating the various layers of excuses and protection that many of us have around our habits and patterns of behaviour. These mental layers, which are often unconscious but strongly defended, range from ignorance to denial. I know mine certainly did and I'm sure some still do, yet without understanding them we may go to our grave being powerless. This is why I try and take so much time in these updates to talk through these hidden aspects of behaviour with you. I want to offer a higher level of self-awareness, as that is always the first step. Eliminating them is next and that is why I design my programmes the way I do. After all, a small transformation will *always* beat a large amount of information.

You may ask why we have so many destructive patterns operating below our own radar? The answer is critical to understand and also helps us define where we are on the path of our own growth. In short, they act primarily as a circuit breaker. Kicking us into attack or defend mode on whatever we feel is right, whilst at the same time hijacking our ability to hold an objective view of whether or not we may actually be wrong. They are usually what keep us from being open to a different viewpoint or even saying sorry. It's also why I often state that the first belief you should question is the one you are most certain about. That lesson comes from a large part of my life where I was more committed to being right than being happy. An honours graduate of the school on how to be a dick.

Going deeper, the role of the circuit breaker is to protect us from facing the primary fear we all have, which is the fear we are not enough. Not good enough, not rich enough, not certain enough, smart enough, good-looking enough, tall enough, short enough. It doesn't matter. If you peel back the onion far enough the primary fear is always there, even if it's patched over with confidence. It's also one of the reasons why having confidence is never enough and why those who appear confident on the outside are often the most insecure on the inside. Don't get me wrong, confidence can be useful as a gateway to build self-esteem but when taken for what it is, it's simply the flip-side to shyness on the coin of insecurity. What many people fail to realise is that it's still the same coin.

For example, shyness is nothing more than you denying your gift through fear of being judged. The subtext to shyness is 'please don't discover me'. Confidence is the overcompensation of this as you put on the seemingly indestructible armour of certainty that seeks to show the world you've got what it takes. That you can do it. However, truly owning something at your core gives off a different energy to confidence. Instead of showing up with a cape, there is just a calm powerful sense of equanimity. A total absence of doubt where confidence is not required and neither is there any fear of judgement. Stated plainly, there is nothing to defend, nothing to attack and nothing to prove. You simply know.

Carlos knew. And he owned that fact with his heart on his sleeve. This meant he qualified for my second question. "And why are you coming to me, not your offending supervisor?"

He replied that he'd had a couple of conversations with people and been told I was the person to talk to. After so many years in and out of jail, he'd learned not to rely on the system for the kind of help he wanted. This is because officers are mainly trained to monitor or control behaviour, not help change it. Unfortunately, many also seem more interested in how quick they can deal with your query and get you out of their office via the path of least resistance and paperwork. Carlos knew the drill, which is why he didn't trust the system to help him change. He wanted a mentor, someone who could guide him on a better path. Someone not afraid to call him on his bullshit. I think it's fair to say that I liked Carlos from our first conversation and over the last two weeks we've had several sessions together. He's been a sponge for information, asking many great questions, and we've put a strategy together to help him qualify for his earliest release date, including a plan to get him into college while still in prison.

With only a few days to go before my own release date, my challenge was there were simply too many people like Carlos who wanted my time, and only one of me. It got to a point where it would take me over an hour to walk around the perimeter fence as almost every billet I passed someone would come out to try and engage or catch-up with me. I needed to better leverage my time and decided to see if I could arrange an official talk that I could invite all of the inmates to. This required three levels of authorisation. The chapel, which would be the perfect venue. The head of resettlement, which was the department in charge of reducing reoffending, and a senior governor who would need to sign off for overall responsibility. Through a combination of rapport, social proof and enrolment, I had all approvals within twenty-four hours. I then went to work on designing a poster promoting the event (see Appendix E) and plastered the prison with them. Word soon got around and on Sunday I was blessed to have a full house show up. Not the easiest crowd to try and win over but I've certainly had worse.

One of the main shifts in thinking I was trying to effect centred on the stigma many people carry with them after leaving prison. I'm talking about the label of 'ex-offender'. Or what's known in the US as a convicted felon. For some, carrying this identity, together with their thoughts around how society, and especially potential employers, would then judge them, sets them up to fail even before they leave. If they believe they can't get a job because nobody will employ an ex-con, or that they'll be the last choice, etc., then the attitude they show up to an interview with is just as likely to cause them to be rejected than the fact they were in prison.

Many of us do similar things to ourselves. Not just when it comes to job interviews but in virtually all aspects of our lives. We think we are not good enough compared to the person who we perceive is smarter than us, better looking or appears to have their act together more than we do. It's called a negative comparison frame and the problem is with a mismanaged imagination, we can overlay it onto virtually anyone or anything. We then inadvertently create the circumstance in the outer world that perfectly matches our expectations and fail to see the connection on how we set it up. The classic self-fulfilling prophesy.

I'll give you a simple example. You see someone who you think is more talented than you in the waiting room of an audition. You get nervous and imagine them giving better answers to the questions you will both be asked. Your nervousness comes across in the interview, causing you to fumble your own answers and, surprise, they get the role instead of you.

What's worse, our mind then points at the scene and says, "See, I told you so!" in an attempt to at least make us right about something and soothe the disappointment. The final nail in the self-esteem coffin happens when we give justification for why it wasn't our fault, thereby reinforcing our role as victim. Even if there is no one else to blame, the mind will happily sell you on being a victim of 'circumstance'. Anything to avoid taking responsibility for the fact that it was largely our own thinking that created the unwanted outcome.

A Heavy Problem

Not to put too fine a point on it, this is the same pattern that keeps a lot of people who are overweight and single, well, overweight and single. The problem is not that they can't find the secret to losing weight. Everyone on the planet knows how to lose weight. It's that if they lose weight and then still get rejected, it triggers the fear they are not good enough. Instead, the circuit breaker kicks in and creates a weight problem which allows the ego to tell the story that they *are* good enough, but it's just the fact they have a weight problem which is why people reject them. Of course, it still hurts being single, alone and overweight so it's rarely a deliberate choice, but at least it's less painful than being blown off without the excuse of having that. It's a sad trap because in this example, the problem isn't the weight or their eating habits. *It's their fear of being rejected.* Solve that and there's no need to unconsciously protect themselves with the excuse that it's just their weight problem. But rather than address this, they focus their time, energy and money on consciously trying to lose weight, while being massively encouraged (programmed) by a multi-billion-dollar industry that is happy to agree with them. Then, when they start looking good enough to be accepted, *and therefore also rejected,* for who they are, many start to self-sabotage and put the weight back on. This is then blamed on either things that are out of their control (hormones, metabolism, thyroid, etc.) which means it's not their fault. Or things like lack of willpower or being stupid, which leads to beating themselves up and ironically reinforcing the very belief they were trying to avoid, i.e. not being good enough.

The fact is, our beliefs and fears control so much of what we do, even though a vast majority of them operate outside of our awareness. And, as with the 'I told you so' example above, poor beliefs affect much more than just our attitude. At the non-physical level, they actually influence probability and make circumstances more or less likely (see

Volume 4). In other words, they powerfully shape and create our reality. At the physical level, this is demonstrated robustly in the medical field by the placebo effect. It proves our beliefs around our illness or the treatment we get for it can massively affect the outcome of our health and even make big changes at the molecular and cellular level. It's not exactly a secret.

To Err Is Human

Back to the talk in the chapel. A lot of the guys I would be addressing were coming in with massively limiting beliefs around employers and future job prospects. If there was some way during the talk I could show them that being an ex-offender could actually be an advantage, that would be a big turnaround. I stared from the back of the room at the largely sceptical crowd, said the silent prayer I always say before I speak (which helps focus me on adding value, rather than trying to get approval) and stepped up to the front.

Firstly, I shared a bit of my own story. The fact that I'd messed up too and that some poor decisions and ego at various levels had landed me in jail and now I was faced with losing everything. My business had already gone, my reputation had taken a massive blow, I was drowning in legal fees and could easily lose everything, including my home. From a personal perspective, each time over the last six months I'd seen a light at the end of the tunnel, it turned out to be a train coming this way. More than that, I'd let a lot of people down who trusted me and as much as I wanted to help, I'd been unable to do anything about it for six months. Even some of my most popular work online, such as the London Real Interviews, had been taken down in a knee-jerk reaction to what was largely misinformation. This hurt because it had helped so many people. I also had no clue what I was walking out to, other than to apologise to any and all who had been affected, answer any questions honestly that people had and try to reflect on what I could learn from this so I could move forward on a better path. That's all we can ever do. I wanted to show the room that even a bad experience can be a good experience if it allows us to learn lessons we wouldn't have learned otherwise. I explained it was the same for them and especially when it came to things like a job interview. That as long as they were upfront and honest about their past, most people realise we all make mistakes. After all, every single one of us is a liar, a cheat, a good person, an angry person, a kind person, a fuck-up and a rock. At some point, we are all of those things. It's called being human. Fortunately, a lot of employers understand that. They realise, through the reflection of their own lives, that generally everyone deserves a second chance. There will also be those who will flat-out judge you out of their own projections. Just like in life. The nature of the offence would obviously have some bearing. For example, it may be harder to get a driving job if you were inside for reckless driving. Though generally, providing the guys were upfront and willing to own their mistakes, then they have as good a shot as any.

More importantly, they were able to see that who they had become as a result of their experience inside, actually gave them many qualities that could be very valuable to an employer when presented in the right way. For a start, their ability to handle uncertainty was enormously higher than people who have not gone through an experience as unsettling as prison. Some people would balk if their employer said they had to go to a different office location for a week, or may panic at a shortened deadline, or get flustered because a delivery didn't turn up or an order didn't happen. Or they may go to pieces at the threat of redundancy. Compared to handling the trials and tribulations of prison, that is about as unsettling as ordering coffee. Add in their ability to fall into and follow a structure, to understand and appreciate instruction from senior management (i.e. officers). The ability to mix and survive in a massively diverse and multi-faceted social environment, and more. They got the idea. In short, they got to see that prison had not made them flawed future employees but *upgraded* ones. You could literally taste the difference in attitude. After the talk, I spent the rest of the day around the grounds following up, drilling down and answering questions to a hungry crowd who seemed like they'd had their first taste of inspiration and possibility-thinking in years.

That night, a sixty-six year-old Jamaican guy named Frank knocked on my door. He'd been at the talk and explained that he'd had an idea for creating a range of Caribbean jerk chicken products he wanted to sell. He'd even gone as far as having the prison kitchen follow his recipe and make samples and had put a business plan together for opening a small deli when he was released. However, he'd given up on the idea months ago as there was not much support and he could never get past his limiting beliefs, such as thinking he needed money to start or that people would judge him for having been inside. After having those beliefs blown away in the first twenty minutes of the talk that day, it had reignited his enthusiasm and he sat explaining his idea with passion. I helped him rework his plan and vision into something highly doable and he left the cell at close to midnight, almost skipping down the hall. I collapsed on the bed and quickly fell asleep in one of my favourite end of day states. Exhausted but fulfilled. A day well-lived.

The next afternoon, a senior officer pulled me aside and said he'd spoken to several people that day about the talk and the feedback was split in two. Some were raving about it and others were complaining. I told him that was great, as any feedback that could help me make it better is always welcomed. He said that the only people complaining were the ones who missed it and were upset they didn't get out of bed in time. We both laughed. He then said that based on what he had heard and his own experience, the session had probably done more to rehabilitate prisoners than the whole education block had done in the previous month. It was *magic moment* number 196 and further cemented my commitment to bringing this kind of mental change and support to those who need it most.

Navigating The River

It also brings me to one of the biggest lessons of this whole journey and ties in with one of the most common questions I am currently asked by people on the outside, especially as the end draws near. Namely, how have I managed to survive the way I have in what has to be one of the most challenging, negative and dangerous environments I've ever faced? I'm guessing if you have read this far the answer is obvious and it applies equally to all of us in day-to-day life. It has to do with identity and focus. Looking back at what I wrote six months ago when I first arrived, I stated openly that I saw myself as a 'secret agent of positive change'. I never for one second saw myself as a prisoner and certainly not a victim of circumstance. Not because I'm better or smarter than anyone else. Hopefully that Clark Kent type of illusion has been completely shattered and rightly so. I simply recognised, as you can, that much of life happens outside of our immediate control and we have to learn to sail with the river, not resist or complain about the current or the winding path it takes. I shifted my identity to that of a sailor. A captain on the boat of courage and hope in a fast flowing and dangerous river. Sure, I may have been able to make different decisions that could have prevented me from being sent here. That's hindsight and if we all had it, it would cheat us out of many of the lessons we need to learn.

Remember, unless you are under the illusion that you are meant to live on planet perfect (and in which case put down whatever you are smoking), realise your mistakes are your best nourishment for growth. I've certainly made my fair share, as I am sure many of us have. It's probably why Life gave me a tough river to sail as my latest graduation exam. As I said in Volume 3, we all have them, and we either step-up and pass or we miss the mark this time and re-sit the exam in some other form. But either way, at no point do we get to go back and change what has already happened.

Then there is the second part. Our focus. It took me a long while and many years in the slow learning club to realise that nearly all of our stress and fear can be attributed to being too focused on ourselves. Much of that stress goes away when we switch our attention to what we can give instead of take. That's why, from the moment I walked down the steps in court, I tried to shift my entire focus away from my own personal dramas and onto doing whatever it took to add as much value to as many people in the system as I could. Granted, at that point I had no idea how bad, floored and dysfunctional the system I entered was, but it doesn't change the lesson or the opportunity that came with it. That's what growing up is all about and it has nothing to do with age. Though beware, as there is one honey-trap our ego can fall for. Trying to manipulate the system by 'giving so we can get'. That doesn't work, and it violates the spirit of authentic contribution. It's the same difference between unconditional love and 'rules-based' love. You cannot say you love someone one minute, i.e. as long as they behave the way you want, and then argue with them the next.

Another part of the trap is giving from empty in the forlorn hope that you will get back or fill up with what is missing. That kind of emotional horse-trading can never be sustainable. Instead, seeking to contribute from a place of genuine intent to serve is different. It shows up as a by-product of who you are, not a strategy to win points or score favour. Unconditionally giving also fosters one of the most beautiful of all human character traits. Humility. It was, after all, a lack of humility in court that caused my ego to land me in here. And it was the lessons of letting go of some of that which have probably been the most powerful. Being given the opportunity to serve from behind bars as an inmate, rather than on the big stage in front of the lights and cameras, has taught me a lot about the power of surrendering ego and choosing love instead of fear in challenging circumstances. Together with being grateful for what you have, not what you've lost. I'm also massively thankful that Life chose this particular classroom for me to deepen that lesson, instead of, for example, the loss of a loved one or a terminal illness diagnosis.

It also begs the question that, if this is such a massive lesson, why do many of us miss it for so long? The answer has to do with the illusion of separateness. When we feel disconnected from what spirituality would call our 'Source' and the intrinsic life-force that permeates all of us, then it's easier to make self-serving decisions based on fear instead of love. As our consciousness and spiritual maturity rise, we begin to realise that, even though we appear separate physically, we are in fact all connected at a deeper level. This is easy to understand when we look at our own blood cells. At first glance they appear separate and individual. They have their own agenda, come in different colours and each have different times of birth and death. But at a higher level of understanding, you and I both know they are not really separate but instead part of a bigger and more encompassing universe known as our body.

When we begin to raise our understanding and realise we are all blood cells in the universal body of consciousness, it becomes easier to broaden our focus and decision making to include more than just ourselves or our own needs. The feedback from Life isn't subtle. We always feel better putting a smile on someone else's face than we do our own.

Want To help people? Help Yourself First

Having shared with you one of the fundamental insights into transcending hardship, I'd be remiss if I didn't mention some other distinctions that may help when it comes to helping others and especially if it's in a professional capacity such as a life-coach or mentor, etc. Apart from the honey trap mentioned earlier, there is another pitfall to avoid. This is where it's easy to become addicted to the feelings we get when helping others and forget about helping ourselves. Giving from our overflow is always the most powerful place to give from. If we forget this or get side-tracked trying to balance a limited resource such as time against an ever-growing demand, things can quickly deteriorate. This can show up as easily as mild stress through to full-scale burn-out, as our own boat sinks in the ocean of other people's problems under the false belief that it is our duty to solve them. Some of you I am sure know what I'm talking about. It's the classic martyr pattern, though this is one time the captain does not want to go down with the ship. I touched on this in Volume 2 and it's something I'm familiar with as it was a pattern my mother ran for years. For those who have listened to my *Straight Talk Volume 3* on advanced human behaviour, I share the story. (See www.InsideTrackBonuses.com)

A critical tip for those looking to help others and one that can save you a great deal of time, frustration and heartache is to be selective with who you choose to help. It may sound simple but, from the perspective of the coach or therapist, the temptation to take on clients, or even help a stranger, can come from one of those hidden patterns we talked about earlier. The usual suspects include the following: *Unwillingness to turn your back on someone in need. Financial scarcity/neediness (if it's a potential client situation). Self-validation through being good enough to solve someone else's problem.* Or commonly, *eagerness to prove your answers are right by forcing your solution onto someone you think needs 'fixing'.*

When operating from any of the above, it's also easy to attract someone who has less commitment to actually transforming and more interest in using you as a permanent crutch or excuse as to why they can't. That's why it's important to have boundaries around client selection as well as have your own issues handled first. Of course, I'm happy to give everyone a chance, especially in here but it's still important to 'stress-test' someone's commitment like I did with Carlos.

Another example is Danny. An inmate I have been coaching on weight loss. Before I agreed to help, I insisted he bring me a minimum of ten reasons why he absolutely must lose weight. He did and so

I agreed. I sat with him and worked through some of his patterns, helped him remove some blocks and gave him a strategy to follow taken from Tim Ferris's four-hour body called the Slow Carb 1 Diet. Exceptionally effective for weight loss and good news for those who still like to eat donuts, pizza and ice cream. No, I'm not making it up. I handled the ordering for him on his canteen, set him up and he's getting great results.

The Training Of A Trainer

As this is near the end of the Inside Track, there is something I'd like to address. Throughout these eleven updates, I have tried my best to not only share the journey with you but also break down some of the what's, why's, how's and wherefores, so you can have a better understanding for yourself. To not just feed you a fish but teach you how to fish. This is so you can take the lessons and apply them to your own life in ways you can help yourself and others. As many of you know, I am keen to state I am no smarter or gifted than any one of you reading this. Don't buy into the illusion that just because I know how to work my way through some of the hidden mazes of human behaviour, that it makes me any more or less special than anyone else. This just happens to be one of the very few areas that I have more experience in than others and seems to be where my path has led me in terms of focus. We all have our 'thing' and this seems to be mine. At least for now. But it's not inherent. At the time of writing, I've been immersed in, and part of, the personal development world for nearly thirty years and been blessed to have had some incredible mentors and on whose shoulders I am honoured to peek from.

Much of my early lessons came from my mentor, George Zalucki and to whom I owe an enormous amount. Following that, a lot of my experience came from my role as a trainer for Robbins Research International, which is Tony Robbins's seminar company. I say this with as much humility as honesty but it is probably one of the hardest and most exclusive roles in the personal development industry. It takes years and with no guarantee of ever getting there and I was very privileged when, in 2002, I became Tony's youngest serving trainer. It was a demanding role and we were constantly in service. At some events, it would be common to finish so late we'd see the sunrise. We worked back-to-back twenty plus hour days, conducting all types of interventions with what seemed to be an inexhaustible number of clients. Issues ranged from lack of self-worth to chronic overachievement. From multi-millionaires who were depressed, to homeless suicidal drug addicts. Over the fifteen years I did this, I was lucky to have some more incredible mentors. Too many to mention here but I would be remiss without mentioning the amazing Vicki St George.

Vicki was a Master Trainer who helped coordinate the Trainer program. To us, she was the boss and her skill sets and experience were legendary, matched only by the size of her heart. She also held us to the highest possible standard. There was simply no room for slacking when the future of others, their potential and even lives, were at stake. There were many times over the years we'd be tested to our own limits, such as being thrown out of aeroplanes or made to swim in pitch black shark-infested waters miles out to sea. At one event in Hawaii, two days before the participants arrived, they even left the trainers overnight on the edge of an active volcano to see how they'd cope and manage their state. (Remember, theory doesn't cover the price of admission to the higher levels of awareness.) It was some of the most challenging but rewarding times of my life. However, through all of that, our primary rule was to always take care of ourselves *first*. After all, we cannot give what we don't have. This is what I mean when I talk about giving from our overflow. Many don't. A lot of people, including coaches, get addicted to the deeply satisfying feelings of helping others. These become a comforting - even rewarding - distraction that prevents them from working on their own issues. If you ever find a coach, consultant or trainer who makes themselves out to be perfect or flawless then my advice is to turn around. A good coach, just like a good actor or athlete, is likely to be constantly working on improving themselves and also be open about what they are working on. They also surround themselves with the best people they can find and look up to. This is something an ego struggles with as it likes being top dog. Though, at the end of the day, you don't become better at chess by playing people you can beat, and a high quality peer group or support team is usually the difference between success and failure.

The Real Secret Agents of Change

Speaking of support, there is one final area where I also owe a massive debt of thanks. To read in the press the growing reports on how unforgiving the state of the UK prisons are, together with the drugs, violence, despair and squalid conditions is one thing. To live in it is another and I don't think I could have ever gotten through it or given anywhere near what I have if it wasn't for the help and encouragement I have received from so many of you. Not just letters and emails (now totalling hundreds) or even the visits which were such an oasis in a desert parched of love, but also energetically from *so* many who kept me in their thoughts and prayers. That has been a huge part of easing the pain of the journey and handling some of the roughest parts of the river. The words 'thank you' don't even begin to cover it. I am incredibly grateful and it is no exaggeration to say that feeling your strength and love allowed me to make the difference in here that I have. It has also given me more conviction to want to help others in ways that can make a lasting change. To pursue knowledge that will help people and then explain it in ways that give context and meaning to the challenges in our lives.

Tuning into where I go from here, I feel drawn to sharing the best of what I've learned in a book on how to deal with adversity. This is because I see so many people struggle with their own self-imposed prison-terms. Allowing life to hand down lengthy and indeterminate sentences of unhappiness or stress because they don't have the tools to construct a powerful defence. This book will be a tribute to the very people who have helped me overcome the adversity of my time here. In short, it will be a tribute to you: the *real* secret agents of change.

Escaping Groundhog Day

And on that note, my dear and amazing friends, this brings my updates to you from this side of the fence to a close. It has been a HUGE pleasure taking you on this journey with me. And as I head off to pack my kit and say a final farewell to the people here, I'll share one last reflection.

Many have asked the key question of how do I think the whole experience has changed me? For insight into this, I return to Nelson Mandela. When he was eventually released from prison he was repeatedly asked the same question but never gave an answer. When pressed a few years later by his auto-biographer, he finally responded with just two words: "I matured." Personally, I don't feel that is the right comparison as I've served less than one fiftieth of the time he did, but the word I would use is 'grounded'.

I decided on this word based on my feelings about being released. I thought it would be different but, being honest, it seems, well, normal. Like the end of one part of a movie which has naturally run its course before transitioning into the next scene, act or part of the script. Sure, there's joyous anticipation at being reunited with those I care about, but there's no kind of 'OMG' energy around it. It's simply time.

I got curious about this as it's in contrast with some of the 'can't wait for my release date' energy I had during parts of the journey. Always keen and open to introspective learning, I meditated on it this morning and got an interesting hit. After setting my intent, it took a couple of minutes to lower my brainwaves into Theta, a state largely recognised as a doorway to higher levels of intuition and inspiration, at which point I was instantly and surprisingly taken to the film *Groundhog Day*. While this is a true classic that has endured for years, when I looked at it through the mirror of self-reflection, the message became so clear I burst out laughing. So much for my Theta state.

For those not familiar with the movie, the character, played by Bill Murray, finds himself trapped in a temporal time loop where every day he wakes up to relive the exact same day. Without giving away too much of a spoiler, the only way out of this loop is for him to live the perfect day. However, this is not the perfect day most of us focus on and which we measure by how well it goes for us based on what we can get or get done. Rather, it's the perfect day based on us contributing and expressing the best of our potential to Life and the bigger picture around us. In order to do this, he essentially has to grow up emotionally. To be far more focused on other people than himself and add tons of value to the community around him. This then 'allows' the woman he so desperately wants, to begin falling in love with him as a natural result of who he has become. Up to this point, he had been struggling in vain to 'get' her to fall in love with him by trying to impress her. The classic 'power vs force' demonstrated via 'contribution vs significance'. Love was clearly the pass mark on the graduation exam he'd been forced to sit and, once reached, became the key to him leaving the time loop (classroom).

In a similar vein, I look back at the classroom I've been in for the last six months. Part of which definitely felt like *'Groundhog Day'*. Recognising the role my courtroom ego had played in me being here. Seeing the lessons I needed to learn in terms of humility and surrendering the addictive need to be right. Focusing more on what I could give than what I could get. The difference I could make to many others in here rather than the difference I wanted to create for myself out there. Coming to understand some of the most fallen members of society and, in doing so, have more compassion than judgement. To realise I too had been guilty of judging others by standing behind labels of my own moral superiority rather than recognise the old adage of "There, for the grace of God, go I." And, ultimately, learning to love the wisdom in the nature of the exam and the supreme intelligence behind how it was set up. These last few days and interactions around the prison felt to be the most complete, perfect and harmonious of my whole journey. Hence why it now feels natural to be allowed to leave.

Is this the end? Of course not. There is no end. There is only the beginning of the next part of our adventure. Just as when one understands that death is not the opposite of life, it is simply the opposite of birth, we have no fear in leaving this classroom and no doubt head for another. In the fractal nature of life, I believe Earth School is similar to high school. If we don't do well, we get downgraded to a life where we are given the same lessons. Re sit the exam. If we get enough answers right, we get the chance to go to college. Did I pass the exam? That's between me and the examiner and only time will tell.

Personally, if I died today I would die peacefully, even joyfully, at the small positive ripples created over the last six months and the legacy that now continues. Not in my name (thankfully), but in the hearts, minds and actions of many of the people I've been blessed to try and hold up a mirror for. Allowing them to glimpse the brightness of their own greatness as it shines through the clouds of fear, doubt and limiting beliefs. In my experience, once people are exposed to the light of their own potential, it acts as a guide, helping those who have the courage to do so walk the path of their own truth. For this alone, the journey has been more than worth it.

Peter Sage. July 20th 2017

Epilogue

Peter was unconditionally released on the 21st July after serving six months. A few weeks later he went on to win the Koestler Award he was nominated for by the staff at Pentonville. In the weeks that followed, he kept his promise and produced the New Prisoner Welcome Booklet that he designed within the first fourteen days of his sentence. After working with various prisons and charities, including the Chrysalis Programme, the booklet is now being used across the globe, helping thousands of new prisoners every month.

In February of 2018, he re-held his postponed Sage Business School, honouring all of his previous obligations. In attendance were several prisoners who were awarded scholarships to attend. One was Patrick, his former cellmate, who was released after the Judge read the letter that Peter outlined for him to send. He has remained a model citizen and asked Peter to become the Godfather to his latest son, which he accepted. After publishing the Inside Track, Peter is now working on his next book which is focused on helping people from all walks of life handle any kind of adversity in an empowering way.

The initial civil action by Hewlett Packard that led to the contempt never did make it to court.

Appendix A:

Mud or Stars? A Prisoners' Story

This fictional piece of work was written by Peter within two weeks of his arrival and was designed to help prisoners with their mindset. It made, and continues to have, a huge impact, earning Peter a Koester award nomination from the staff, which he went on to be awarded.

Read, enjoy and pass on…

I couldn't believe it. I was still in shock. One minute I'm a free man walking into court and the next, I'm an inmate on my way to prison. Life sucks. I kept thinking of my family and friends. Obviously, I was hoping for a 'not guilty' but even when the jury found against me, I was shocked to get three years. Man, now what? It was though my whole life had just fallen apart. I felt a rush of emotions; from denial, to regret, then anger and uncertainty, as the fear of the unknown and the reality of being inside hit me. This was my first ever time in prison. Little did I know that what happened next would have a big impact, not just on my sentence, but on the rest of my life.

I arrived at the Jail and was given clothes, bedding and a medical. I answered the various questions, still feeling numb and disorientated, and went into a waiting room with a dozen or so other prisoners waiting for a cell. There were only two places to sit. One next to a huge guy with a shaved head and a beard, who appeared to be in his late twenties, and one next to an older guy who looked around fifty and fairly unfazed. As I thought about where to go, someone came in and sat next to the guy with the shaved head, so I sat next to the older guy. I avoided eye contact but I could feel him look at me. Eventually he spoke. "Hi."

I replied, more with a mumble than a greeting. I was still numb and starting to feel sick.

"First time inside?" he asked.

I nodded.

He said "Yeah, I can tell. My name is Dell."

I found out that Dell was on his third year of an eight-year sentence. He didn't say what for. It was also his third time inside. As we chatted, I started to tell him about my case - how I felt it was unfair for a first offence and that the jury hadn't been told some key facts and why I was sure that I shouldn't really be here. Before I could get into more details, he cut me off with an open palm and some wise words. "Listen mate," he began. "You seem like a decent bloke so let me give you some advice." I wasn't sure what he was going to say but I thought any advice right now on how to deal with this nightmare would be welcome.

His first comment caught me off guard. "Let me tell you straight. No one gives a crap about your story. We all have one. Everyone you meet in here will tell you why they don't belong. I've heard it all. The truth is, 80% of people don't care about your problems and the other 20% are glad you have them. But the worst part is thinking like that will eat you away inside."

Before I could think about what he'd just said, he added: "Can I ask you a question?"

I nodded.

"Can you go back and change anything that has already happened?"

I thought about it. It hurt, but he was right. I could waste my whole life, or at least my sentence, complaining about what had happened but none of that would ever change a single thing. In fact, it would just make me more miserable.

"So what should I do, just lay down and do nothing?" I was still feeling anger at the system and wanted to at least show I wasn't going to take it lying down. Dell sighed.

"No mate, I'm not saying that. What I'm saying is that the biggest mistake I see people make is the one you're making now. They spend hours, days, sometimes longer, wasting energy thinking 'if only it happened this way' or 'if only I'd done that instead'. What's done is done. You can't change the fact you spilt the milk, you can only decide how to deal with the mess. And wasting time thinking 'coulda-woulda-shoulda' is a guaranteed way to stay miserable or full of piss and vinegar. And neither of those will do you any good in here." He paused. "Now, if there's a way to do something *about* what's happened, that's a different story. Whether it's an appeal or a way to change circumstances going forward, or just learning from your mistakes, that's something you can look at. But the best place to look at it from is with a clear head and you'll never get a clear head until you first accept what's already happened."

Smart guy. He was right again. I was massively resisting my situation even though in this moment I couldn't change a thing about it. I gave it a try. I started to drop the inner resistance to where I was. It wasn't easy at first but when I got to grips with accepting my situation instead of fighting it, I instantly became calmer. Maybe there was something to what this guy was saying after all. I decided to ask a question of my own.

"Dell, what's the best way to cope with being in here?"

He paused. A serious look fell on his face. And then he smiled, as if he was actually happy to use his experience to help. Something I'd learn the power of later.

He looked as if he was remembering a time long ago and then, in almost a distant voice, he answered, "When I came in here the first time, I was just like you. Full of reasons why I shouldn't be here. Angry at everything. The judge, the system, my lawyer, the people I hung around with. Even myself. I remember feeling righteous one minute and then scared and depressed the next. I didn't want to talk to anyone either unless they wanted to hear why I was right about everyone else being wrong. It was only a short sentence, a few months, but it seemed to drag on for years. Man, it was tough."

"That sounds like a nightmare." I commented.

"It was, but do you know what? The main reason it was so bad, wasn't down to the system or even being in here. Give or take, the environment's pretty constant for everyone. What made the difference was all down to how I used, or rather misused, my mind."

I looked confused and he obviously picked up on my reaction because he began to elaborate. *"There's an old saying. 'Two men sat behind prison bars, one saw mud, the other saw stars.'* The condition is the same for both, but they chose to see it differently."

I countered, "Isn't that just positive thinking?"

"Positive thinking is one thing. Being smart and making better choices on how to think, so you can get through your sentence, is another." Again, he made sense but I wanted to know specifics and pressed him for an example. "OK," he started. "Let's play a game. Let's just say I was able to offer you a deal to shave some time off your sentence, and all you had to do was write a list – would you do it?"

"Sure, just tell me what to write." I replied.

"Could you write a list of ten things that suck about your life?"

This was too easy and I had a lot more than ten.

"OK, but what if we play the same game but this time you have to write a list of ten things you could be happy about in your life?"

"What, now?" I laughed. I really wasn't in the mood to play games and certainly not think about what was right in my life, especially after the events of today, but Dell pushed.

"Yeah, right now. You asked for some advice on dealing with life inside and I'm giving it to you. So, let me ask you again. If it really was for a sentence reduction, could you write a list of ten things in your life you could be happy about or grateful for, if you thought hard enough?"

I drew a blank and he prompted me.

"What about the fact that you didn't get a longer sentence?"

Good point. All this time I'd been focusing on why I hadn't got a shorter sentence. It never occurred to me to be grateful for the fact it wasn't longer. Hmm, one saw mud, the other saw stars. I was starting to understand and came up with a few more reasons. For a start, I was reasonably healthy. Not in the best shape of my life but I could only imagine what it would be like to be inside and be really ill. Or have a leg or an arm in plaster or, worse, be in a wheelchair. I suddenly had a lot of respect for people in that situation but at the same time felt grateful it wasn't me. Plus I had friends and family on the outside. Not a lot, but at least they could send a message or visit. Suddenly, I didn't feel as bad, but what Dell said next really woke me up and made me think.

"My point is this. You can win both of those games. The question is, *which one do you want to play?*"

His point was as simple as it was powerful. You can always focus on what's wrong. But at the same time you can also focus on what is right. I couldn't see why this simple choice had not been as obvious as it was now. He added "And you think it's only a game? Let me show you what happens when you play it from both sides. Let's say you come in here and focus on all the reasons why you can be miserable. Oh, you'll find them. But then what? You walk around pissed off at the world, ready to react to prove your point that you're a victim of circumstance. Next thing you're either on medication for depression or you have privileges taken away, or even have your release date pushed back because you pushed back against another inmate. Or worse, an officer."

I butted in "But aren't all officers like that?"

"Listen to me," he spoke firmly. "I've been in this game a long time; the officers are like a mirror. Smile at them and they're more likely to smile back. Get angry and upset and they'll do the same. Just like you or I would. Besides, everyone knows the system ain't perfect. Show me one that is. Many of the staff and officers are just doing the best they can but some stuff is bound to fall through the cracks. When you're smart enough to see it for what it is, that the system is old rather than vindictive, you learn not to take it personally. Like toothache. It doesn't try to upset you on purpose. The big problem is you can't smile if you are playing the game of 'what's wrong with my life'. Plus, walking around with a chip on your shoulder trying to prove to the world you're right is a waste of time. Especially when, as I said before, nobody really gives a crap."

"You're saying that by just changing my mindset I can change my experience? It can't be that simple." I almost scoffed. I struggled to believe it could be *that* easy.

"Oh, can't it? Well, let's play it from the other side. You walk around searching for reasons to be grateful, and trust me, there are many. Take for example the soldier who had his leg blown off in Afghanistan but convinced the army to let him continue with a prosthetic leg. He was asked 'But aren't you now handicapped?' and replied saying it was the enemy who was now handicapped as he had a bulletproof leg."

I thought wow, what a powerful way to look at things.

Dell carried on. "Do you know how many homeless people would love the bed you are getting tonight? Or how many refugees in Syria that would give anything to be fed three times a day? Or the people just around the corner in the local hospital that would swap places with you in a heartbeat, just to get their health back or another few months of their life?"

He'd made his point, and I couldn't deny he made a lot of sense.

He then added, "Once you accept where you're at and try to have a good attitude, you can make more intelligent choices. The first one I'd make is deciding to set yourself up to win."

Again, I asked for an example. "There's an induction book in your cell, read it. It gives you the ins and outs on the basics of how things in here work. How to get visits, buy canteen, get burn (tobacco) and more. Next, I suggest getting a job or education ASAP. It gets you out the cell a lot more and makes the time go quicker. Focus on a goal. It could be anything. I suggest getting to the level of enhanced, as it makes things easier and it's a piece of piss if you keep your nose clean. Or choose a health goal, to get clean, fit or quit smoking. Or learn a new skill, *anything* that gets you looking forward, not back. You can't change where you've been but you can change where you're going. It may sound strange but in here, boredom is optional."

I was making mental notes as fast as I could. This was good stuff. In a few words, he'd managed to completely shift my viewpoint of the situation. His next point was also bang on. "Next, be careful who you hang with. Even on the outside but especially in here. It's a fact that if you hang around with ten drug users, you'll usually become the eleventh. If you hang around with ten people who are thinking of how they can make their life better rather than blame everyone else, you'll usually become the eleventh. It's called the law of conformity."

I knew he was right as there had been many studies that showed exactly that.

He continued. "Also, understand there's a difference between liberty and freedom. Liberty relates to movement and it's really the only thing they've restricted. But freedom is a state of mind and no one can take that away but you. The problem is that those who see mud, not stars, are prisoners of their own thinking whether they are in jail or not."

"But why don't more people think this way?" I asked. His reply was insightful and hit me like a brick.

"Because by blaming others we get to feel like the innocent victim and feel justified about being hard done by. It may feel better temporarily but here's the problem. It also means you give up all personal responsibility and then wonder why life continues to throw shit all over you. It also means you're more likely to be back in here at some point. Screw that. You can't change being in here mate, but you *can* change who you are when you come out. In fact, the difference between looking at what you've learned instead of looking at what you've lost, can be the difference between a life you can be proud of versus a life on the street. It's taken me three visits inside to learn that."

Damn, I thought if ever there was a time I needed to hear that, it was now.

He then asked, "Do you have a partner?" I replied with a nod.

"Tomorrow, when they let you out of your cell for social time, ask an Insider to help you get their number added to your call list and then you'll be able to speak to them."

I said I was thankful for that but then he added something I hadn't even considered. "Go easy on the phone mate, don't just dump all your problems on them. Many people in here forget, but it can be just as tough for our loved ones on the outside. In fact, in many ways our spouses kind of serve the sentence with us."

I stopped and thought hard. I'd been so busy focusing on my own issues, I'd not even thought of it in that way.

Before we could continue, a door opened and my name was called. I stood up to leave and was told my cell was in A-wing, where I was being taken. It was also on the top floor, something they call 'the fives'. I turned to Dell and said, "See, things are looking up already, looks like I get the Penthouse!"

We both laughed and he said, "That's the Spirit."

I went to my cell and found the induction book he spoke about sitting on the shelf. But before I read it, I started writing down notes about all the things I could remember that he'd said. Once finished, I had a list of six key points:

1. Nobody cares about my story – 80% of people aren't interested in my problems and the other 20% are glad I have them.
2. I always get to choose what I focus on. Mud or Stars. At the end of the day, what's wrong is always available but so is what's right. Bulletproof leg. Awesome.
3. Resisting what I can't change is stupid. Accept the fact the milk is spilt and then figure out how to deal with it. Look forward not back.
4. Life acts as a mirror. If I'm pissed off at the world, don't be surprised if it gets pissed off at me.

5. Prison may restrict my liberty, but it can never take my freedom. After all, no one can ever do anything to me emotionally without my permission.
6. Set myself up to win. Learn the ropes, get busy, set a goal. Boredom is optional.

Within a couple of weeks I'd settled into a routine, had a good job and had even quit smoking. A few weeks later I made the enhanced level and life got better still. Not only that, but I was also helping other inmates make some simple shifts in their thinking using the six points above and many had seen similar results. That was probably the most rewarding part. It's called paying it forward.

I saw Dell a few more times after that as we sometimes passed in the hallways during what they called 'Free-flow'. He always smiled and said the same thing – "Mud or Stars?" I'd always smile back and shout "Stars Bro!"

I often wonder what would have happened if I had not sat next to him and listened to his sage advice. I'm not sure if he ever understood the massive impact his words had on me that first night but it was something at the top of my list of things to be grateful for. I remember Steve Jobs, the founder of Apple, once said something to the effect that, 'as the river of life unfolds we can never join the dots going forward, only looking back'. It wasn't until I came out that I realised what he meant and how much the whole prison episode had shifted me in a positive way. Of course, given the choice, I wouldn't have decided to go in, but I now know that complaining about what's happened is a waste of time. However, joining the dots, I know that who I chose to become whilst being inside is something no one can ever take away. It was then I finally realised the biggest lesson of all; my environment never defines me. It simply gives me the opportunity to define myself. It also made me a better man, husband and father and to this day I share those six points with my own kids. As a result, they're also making better choices in their lives. Choices that will not only keep them on the outside but maybe, one day, allow them to pay it forward to someone else who's in need too.

The End.

Appendix B:

Letters from Staff & Prisoners

HM Prison & Probation Service

Governor Adrian Turner
HMP & YOI Sudbury
Ashbourne
Derbyshire
DE6 5HW

Telephone 01283 584202
Fax 01283 584001

15 June 2017

To whom it may concern,

My name is Adrian Turner and I am the Governor at HMP / YOI Sudbury. I am writing to attest Mr Peter Sage's (A5648DX) application to purge his contempt in accordance with the Civil Procedure Rules 81.31.

Mr Sage recently arrived at HMP / YOI Sudbury after spending four and a half months at HMP Pentonville

I have spoken to staff at HMP Pentonville in order to help make an assessment of character. Following this I am satisfied that Mr Sage held himself to be a model prisoner in many respects. His attitude toward staff and prisoners was exemplary. In addition and on his own initiative he sought to selflessly add tremendous value. Examples include:

- Being nominated for a National Prison Award for his work aimed at counselling and mentoring numerous prisoners in a positive way.
- Writing several articles for the prison magazine teaching and inspiring prisoners to become better people as a result of prison.
- Ordering and donating books to the library at his own expense which he felt could help with rehabilitation.
- Re-contextualising the experience of prison for violent prisoners in a way that helped reduce enmity towards staff.
- Suggested and arranged gym rowing competitions that successfully channelled prisoner aggression into healthy exercise and camaraderie.
- Organised and conducted motivational talks in the chapel aimed at reducing violence and fostering better relationships between wings.

In summary I am happy to attest this application and feel Mr Sage's remorse and intent to purge is genuine and sincere.

Yours sincerely

A Turner
Governor

'Unlocking Potential'
HMP & YOI Sudbury

To whom it may concern,

I came to prison just over 3 months ago. My life a complete disaster. 15 years a Heroin and Crack addict. To say I had lost everything is an understatement. I was broken extremely lost, angry (at myself) and truly at rock bottom. I remember when I first met Peter - in the Library, - literally a Godsend. He has mentored me, been there for me and coached me through some extremely dark and troubling times. He has been a living inspiration and a shining light to me. I am extremely fond of Peter and regard him as a close friend. He has helped me become the person I am today. Accountable and realiable. I am stronger wiser and in touch with my Wife and, 3 children, that I lost to my addiction. Part of my recovery has been supported and helped by such a kind and loving person - Peter. People recognise me now for me - Oliver a proud Husband and Father to 3 children. I have seen Peter help countless people with his words of encouragement and wise words - and never ask anything in return. It is no exageration to say that he has helped me save my life, - and changed many others. He is an Angel and Godsend

Oliver Wright - ex drug-addict - reformed offender and proud Husband and father to 3 beautifull children -

Kind Regards

OLIVER WRIGHT.

20/07/2017

HER MAJESTY'S PRISON SUDBURY
ASHBOURNE
DERBYSHIRE

To Whom It May Concern:

My name is David Powell and I am a Senior Officer at HMP Sudbury.

I have known Mr. Peter Sage for approximately six weeks and I have to say it has been a very eye opening experience,

On arrival in this establishment Mr. Sage instantly caused a stir by the fact he was not a criminal prisoner but a civil one. This is exceptionally rare and many of the HMP staff were unfamiliar with the processes that applied to non-criminals.

As a civil prisoner Peter did not have to work. However, he did volunteer to assist around the prison as he had an agenda to add value and help the inmates. He also gave some inspirational talks to prisoners who were willing to attend and learn new concepts of life and alternative ways to live the rest of their lives i.e. break and escape the ongoing cycle of crime, court, prison, release, crime etc.

Peter also wrote a piece called MUD OR STARS? The prisoners who read it then told other prisoners and they told other prisoners until at least 60-70% of the entire prison population had read it and started talking about it. In fact, it became so effective and had such an impact that instead of the usual grunt in the mornings, you would hear them shouting to each other "mud or stars?".

Peter's last act was to write a poem for the prisoners called "Why am I here?" Again, an inspirational piece which resonates with all people in the establishment whether old, young, black, white, Asian, male or female. It poses and attempts to answer the questions "why am I here?", "what is my purpose?" etc. It does this by helping to shift and change the meaning of why they are in prison in a positive way by showing that God/Life has a bigger plan. This has been very useful for many. Having seen the difference he has made in such a short time, I believe Peter was sent to show us that there is a better way. To get off that hamster wheel and live a better life.

Whilst Peter has been here doing his talks and having heard prisoners talking about him, firstly as a person and secondly as a mentor, it is obvious to me that he has changed a lot of people's outlook on life while in prison, showing them a better way. I have been in the prison service for nearly twenty-three years and can quite honestly say the prison service simply fails to make a lasting difference when it comes to rehabilitating prisoners. In fact, in many cases we actually make them better criminals. In my experience, prisoners will only change once they have had their 'light bulb moment' and that is what Peter has done. For many in here he switched the power on. If there was some way Peter could devise and propose something for HMP Service to use, then I am sure it would make a massive and long-term difference in our ability to help rehabilitate offenders.

It has been an utter pleasure working with Peter, this may sound strange but I wish he was here longer. However I wish him and his future wife, Thea, all the very best and am grateful for the difference he has made.

D A Powell

Senior Officer, Her Majesty's Prison Sudbury.

When writing to Members of Parliament please give your previous home
address in order to avoid delays in your case being taken up by the M.P.

In replying to this letter, please write on the envelope:

Number _A716_ ▮▮▮ .Name ... ▮▮▮ _± Dear_ ....

Wing .... _1ST MAY 2017_ ....

Dear Sir/Madam

My Name is ~~Dear~~ ▮▮▮ . I have
spent 11 years in prison and at
times ive felt down and institution-
alized. I met Peter in the Gym
where he was organising a Rowing
competition for inmates. He has
helped me in my Rehabilitation
by reminding me of my value
and self worth. I have also
witnessed him disarm a potentially
dangerous situation between two
inmates and turn it around into
a positive situation. Whenever I
need a shoulder to lean on, peter
always has time for a chat.
My experience in prison has been
enriched because of him. I wish
him all the best in the future
and a great pleasure to have met
him.   Your Sincerely ± Dear

This is Moynul. I am serving three months in Pentonville prison. I met Peter Sage two months ago. But I have been following his work online for last two and half years. It was a great experience metting him in person. I feel verry lucky. Peter has helped millions of people all around the world trough his work, hence he recieved so many emails from his students which I have seen myself in his cell. I have conversation with peter pretty much every day. And I end up learning so much from those conversation. His advice on love changed my relationship compleatly. Thanks Peter! Peter is the go to person for many immates hore because of his knowledge and valuable advice. We get 45 min social time and 45 min exercise but peter spend all of his time helping people. Recently he injured his leg but still climbing landing to landing giving people books, notes, jarnal. Personally I have read 12 books from him. He is a awesome human being. I have so much respect and love for him. All the best peter! Moynul

My name is Kayvan ████ and I have been an inmate in Pentonville for 20 months. I act as an offical Insider which is, a term used for someone who is trained to help others.

I noticed Peter Sage when he 1st came to D-wing. He had a very different attiude to any other new person I'd seen. He was Pleasant, polite and always Very positive and cheerfull, I also noteiced he had a strong focus on helping others, especially those struggling with the enviroment which in here can become a very rough. over the last few months, peter has become a very popular figure on the wing, earning the trust and respect of virtually everyone. He has done this by dedicating himself to supporting and helping others. He has become an unoffical mentor to many and I have Personally seen peter make a Big difference to dozens of inmates.

to my knowledge he's never asked for anything in return which on prison is very reare. Since being here he has never become negative or waned in his dedication to be a role model. It's been a pleasure to get to know Peter and I know and I know for a fact Pentonville is a better place because of him.

Kind regars

F. ███████

Mr Delroy Wa ▮
HMP Pentonville
Caledonian Rd,
London, N7 8TT.
01 - 05 - 2017

Dear Sirs.

This letter is To certify That I have known Mr Peter Sage, he has been an inspiration to me, the impack he had on me is priceless my outlook on life has changed immensely in a more positive way. I am now looking forward To a new positive life. Mr Sage is a help in times of need a true gentleman.

yours faithfully

Mr Delroy Wa. ▮

I first met peter in education. We started talking because he wrote a story for the prison paper which i found very intresting. I told him I wanted to start a business and he gave me advice about what to exspect. I told him iv olny sold drugs as a business. He gave me confidence and understanding how to use the same principle in to something legitimate. peter even gave advise to the whole class including the teacher every one in the class was keen to learn from him he even taught us how to speed read. I have not yet met another person like peter in the prison system he gave me books to read such as The obstacle is the way he has made such an impact in my sentence I even told my mum about him. He is genuinly a good fella and inspiring he is the only person here to help open my eyes to a new way of thinking.

matthew c█████
M█████

29th APRIL 2017
H.M.P PENTONVILLEE
CALEDONIAN RD.
N7 8TT

RE: TO WHOM IT MAY CONCERN

MY NAME IS TEMI F. ██████ A, AND I HAVE KNOWN
PETER SAGE FOR FIVE WEEKS DURING MY STAY AT HER
MAJESTIES PLEASURE. I WAS INTRODUCED TO HIM
BY A FELLOW PRISONER DUE TO OUR COMMON PASTIME OF
WRITING.
SINCE I'VE KNOWN TIM HE HAS DISPLAYED A SELFLESS
DEMEANOR BY ADVISING MANY PRISONERS WHEN THEY NEED
SOMEONE TO TALK TO. HIM HAS BEEN A BEACON OF HOPE
IN A PLACE FULL OF NEGETIVITY & REGRET.
MANY PRISONERS HAVE LEARNED IMMENSELY FROM MR. SAGE
WEATHER IT BE ANGER MANAGEMENT, STRESS COPING SKILLS,
ETC COPLED WITH THAT (FACT) HE REGULARLY READS THE HOMILY
SCRIPTURES AT WEEKLY MASS.
I PERSONALLY HAVE BENEFITED FROM MEETING MR. SAGE IN
SUCH A SHORT TIME FOR HE SHIFTED MY WAY OF THINKING &
MADE ME REALISE MY INNER POTENTIAL.
I HOPE THE BENCH WILL HAVE CLEMENCY ON MR. SAGE
IN THIS SITUATION AS HE IS MUCH MORE OF AN ASSET
IN THE FREE WORLD AS HES PAST EXEMPLIFIED.

YOURS TRULY
TEMI F ██████ A
██████ 29.04.2017

Tyrone Ma███████R

Peter Sage has opened my eyes to alot of things in my life so far. In 5 weeks he's taught me more I think that I took away from school. He has made me realize the mistakes I've made during my life a█████ ████ which could of been avoided. He has actually made me look at myself instead of blaming others. He made me realize I've took my Pride too far. I'm a proud person always have been, but there's ways to channel my pride. I've taken things from him which I will definetly use with my children to make me hopefully a better Father. He's pointed out ways to make my Fatherhood postive and not negative which I as a Father never noticed, I really appreccte his information he has given me. He is a remarkable man that I've never met before, I truely thank him for the information he's given me.

Thank you.

, 07930 815████████

T████████

APPENDIX C

MAP OF CONSCIOUSNESS

LEVEL NAME	CALIBRATED FREQUENCY	ASSOCIATED EMOTIONAL STATE	RESULTING PROCESS	VIEW ON LIFE	VIEW ON GOD
ENLIGHTENMENT	700-1000	INEFFABLE	PURE CONSCIOUSNESS	IS	SELF
PEACE (LEVEL OF SPONTANEOUS HEALING)	600	BLISS	ILLUMINATION	PERFECT	ALL-BEING
UNCONDITIONAL LOVE [JOY]	540	SERENITY	TRANSFIGURATION	COMPLETE	ONE
LOVE	500	REVERENCE	REVELATION	BENIGN	LOVING
REASON	400	UNDERSTANDING	ABSTRACTION	MEANINGFUL	WISE
ACCEPTANCE	350	FORGIVENESS	TRANSCENDENCE	HARMONIOUS	MERCIFUL
WILLINGNESS	310	OPTIMISM	INTENTION	HOPEFUL	INSPIRING
NEUTRALITY	250	TRUST	RELEASE	SATISFACTORY	ENABLING
COURAGE	200	AFFIRMATION	EMPOWERMENT	FEASIBLE	PERMITTING

POWER / STRONG

LEVELS AT OR ABOVE 200 HAVE TRUTH, INTEGRITY AND SUPPORT LIFE — CREATIVE

LEVELS BELOW 200 ARE FALSE, LACK INTEGRITY, DO NOT SUPPORT LIFE — DESTRUCTIVE

LEVEL NAME	CALIBRATED FREQUENCY	ASSOCIATED EMOTIONAL STATE	RESULTING PROCESS	VIEW ON LIFE	VIEW ON GOD
PRIDE	175	SCORN	INFLATION	DEMANDING	INDIFFERENT
ANGER	150	HATE	AGGRESSION	ANTAGONISTIC	VENGEFUL
DESIRE	125	CRAVING	ENSLAVEMENT	DISAPPOINTING	DENYING
FEAR	100	ANXIETY	WITHDRAWL	FRIGHTENING	PUNITIVE
GRIEF	75	REGRET	DESPONDENCE	TRAGIC	DISDAINFUL
APATHY	50	DESPAIR	ABDICATION	HOPELESS	CONDEMNING
GUILT	30	BLAME	DESTRUCTION	EVIL	VINDICTIVE
SHAME	20	HUMILIATION	ELIMINATION	MISERABLE	DESPISING

FORCE / WEAK

POWER IS SELF-SUSTAINING, PERMANENT, STATIONARY AND INVINCIBLE.

FORCE IS TEMPORARY, CONSUMES ENERGY AND MOVES FROM LOCATION TO LOCATION.

ENERGY FIELD INCREASES LOGARITHMICALLY: 1 = (1) 2 = (10) 3 = (100) 4 = (1000) 5 = (10,000) 6 = (100,000) ...ETC

ALL LEVELS BELOW 500 ARE "OBJECTIVE" (CONTENT BIASED) AND ALL LEVELS ABOVE 500 ARE "SUBJECTIVE" (CONTEXT BIASED)

Credit: Dr. David R. Hawkins

Appendix D:
Overview Of Operation Chrysalis

A four-step approach to help tackle Britain's Prison Crisis.

OBJECTIVES (based against current figures)

- Reduce violence from new inmates by 10-15%
- Increase number of new inmates who qualify for 'enhanced' level by 10-15%
- Reduce the number of new inmates who get downgraded to 'basic' level by 10-15%
- Reduce the number of new inmates who go onto anti-depressants by 10-15%
- Reduce the number of new inmates who re-offend within two years by 10-15%

POTENTIAL RESULTS

When you take into account the current overcapacity of many prisons, and the average cost to the UK tax payer estimated at £40,000 per year per prisoner, the cumulative effect of achieving just the low end of the objectives would save places such as Pentonville, between £5 million to £10 million per year. If this money was then invested into more aspects of intelligent rehabilitation, rather than continue with the statistically failed concept of a deterrent, a lot of lives could be changed.

THE FOUR PHASES OF OPERATION CHRYSALIS INCLUDE:

Phase 1   New Prisoner Welcome Booklet
Phase 2   Updated Induction PowerPoint
Phase 3   Education Module focused on Personal Growth

Phase 4   Edutainment Channel on in cell TV's

Here I will offer a deeper look at the New Prisoner Welcome Booklet, as well as briefly outline the other four phases:

New Prisoner Welcome Booklet

BACKGROUND:

Very little is provided to new prisoners in the UK prison system that is either a) consistent, or b) strategically designed to address and support their mental and emotional state in a way that reduces violence, depression and non-compliance. Therefore, part of the goal of Operation Chrysalis, was to create a powerful tool that would be cheap to produce, easy to implement and have a high take-up and engagement rate by new prisoners. Something they would keep and read, not be inclined to lose and keep as a reference. It would seek to have an unthreatening name, not be overwhelming and speak to them about where they are at. In addition, thought must be given to the layout and cadence in order to support them going through it in an engaged fashion. Ultimately, it should aim to lay a strong foundation for mitigating some of the traumatic effects of first time incarceration, whilst supporting key fundamental aspects of the prison system.

In response to the above need, *The New Prisoner Welcome Booklet* was created.

The booklet consists of nine parts:

Part 1   Cover

Part 2   Introduction

Part 3   List of Famous People who went to prison and what happened next

The following is a breakdown of each section, together with the aims and objectives:

Part 1: Cover

Aims & Objectives: This is the first impression and wants to be friendly and inviting. The world 'welcome' should be incorporated and prominent. Suggestions are a bright blue background (open sky) with a signpost split between front and back, offering various resources they will likely be searching for or grateful to find (such as help, support, guidance, etc.)

Part 2: Introduction:

Aims & Objectives: This would aim to build rapport quickly by identifying with them where they are at. It would include compelling reasons as to why they should read the booklet as well as laying out the pre-frames, promises and expectations. It should also invite them to read and re-read often. The introduction should be limited to a maximum one page, supported by a graphic and signed 'An Insider'. This then sets up the frame for them to relate to the wing-insiders as sources of advice.

Part 3: Famous People Who Went to Jail and What Happened Next:

Aims & Objectives: One of the biggest outcomes of this section is hope. Many first-time prisoners will think that their future is now a lot bleaker. Sharing with them examples of famous people who have been where they are, or worse, and went on to live or create successful lives, gives a powerful reference for negating this belief. I'd also put this section before the main story because:

1. It's easier and shorter to read.
2. It gets them into the habit of reading the booklet and getting something out of it, which may lead to a higher uptake of people moving onto the story, which is where some of the 'heavier artillery' is aimed at supporting their thinking.

It would contain a small piece on each famous person with a picture, why they were sentenced, for how long and what happened to their lives afterwards. The section would finish with a soft invitation for them to use the opportunity to also change their lives for the better.

Part 4: The Story (Mud or Stars?)

Aims & Objectives: To produce a fictional story that helps new prisoners' better deal with the emotional adjustment to prison. To enrol and engage readers via a third-party storytelling (not imposition), into discovering empowering awareness's that can help them make better decisions on how to think and cope mentally inside. To set up a better psychological foundation on which to adapt to prison life.

Part 5: Helpful Tips For Life On The Inside

Aims & Objectives: To offer some useful and practical tips they would not normally know and that can make life inside easier. To include messages from other prisoners so as to create a theme of social proof, local authority and solidarity. This also demonstrates a high level of usefulness to the booklet, reinforcing the value and lowering the temptation to either discount it or throw it away.

Part 6: Resources After Release

Aims & Objectives: To list a series of employers who have specific policies of employing ex-offenders so as to prevent and pre-empt potential thoughts of them thinking they are unemployable, which could add to the psychological pain and potential path of depression.

Part 7: Useful Info / Contacts / Reference:

Aims & Objectives: To provide a place where they can find relevant and useful information on support that is pertinent, though generic, to the nature of their situation. To include organisations they can contact for advice in areas such as legal, financial and mental support.

Part 8: Inspirational Quotes:

Aims & Objectives: To offer some form of positive resources in the form of specifically chosen quotes, designed to improve their state of mind and direction of thinking.

Part 9: Personal Notes Section

Aims & Objectives: To provide space for prisoners to make their own notes, jot down ideas and offer a further useful and practical aspect to the booklet.

Format & Logistics

- Suggested size: A5
- Suggested or approximate number of pages – no more than 28
- Finish: full colour
- Approximate cost per unit in volume: < 20 pence.

A BRIEF LOOK AT THE OTHER PHASES OF OPERATION CHRYSALIS

PHASE 2

An updated PowerPoint presentation for the official induction. This would be designed in a way that has better flow than the current design, which contains a lot of information and is presented in a way that is not conducive to memory.

PHASE 3

An education module taught as an option. Ideally, this could have privileges or payments linked to completion as an incentive. The ideal format would consist of a 'Life Skills' or personal growth course, running over two weeks and would cover things such as understanding others, job interviews and how to get them and win them, and choosing their next steps and goals. It would also reinforce certain aspects of personal growth as well as some of the key messages in *Mud or Stars?*

PHASE 4

A proposed education/edutainment channel on the in-cell TV's which would stream existing content from places such as TED.com / London Real / Joe Rogan / Tim Ferris, etc. In short, quality and engaging footage designed to feed their mind, especially during several days of the week where the average cell time is between 20-23 ½ hours a day. It's literally a low hanging fruit no-brainer and I am sure there would be many sources who would happily support or affiliate, in order to have their content shown on the channel and royalty free. This could be in return for either a strong CSR aspect (Corporate Social Responsibility), which carries a lot of 'brownie points', or just because it would be the right thing to do to help.

Appendix E:

Referenced Articles & Links

Pentonville Murder Article:
http://www.bbc.co.uk/news/uk-england-london-37708697

Suicide Article In Prison Press
https://insidetime.org/suicide-rate-10-times-higher-in-prison/

IPP Article In Prison Press
https://insidetime.org/hes-given-up/

Panorama Undercover Prison Report
http://www.bbc.co.uk/news/uk-38931580

Link to Post Prison Interview
https://www.youtube.com/watch?v=5scAwCAmgFw&t=3406s

The sign Peter wrote and put above his cell door:

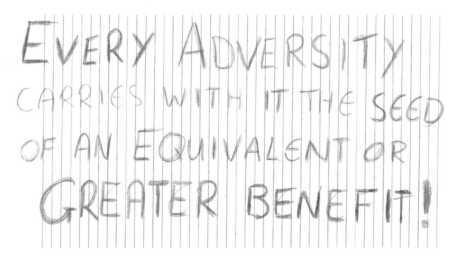

EVERY ADVERSITY CARRIES WITH IT THE SEED OF AN EQUIVALENT OR GREATER BENEFIT!

The Poster Created For The Final Talk in Sudbury

INSPIRATIONAL TALK
THIS SUNDAY !
with Peter Sage

THE CHAPEL, <u>JULY 16</u>th 10.30am – 11.30am ALL WELCOME

Invest one hour of your time to learn the following:

- **How to thrive not just survive on the outside**
- **How to start any business with no money**
- **Better understand money so you can make more of it without breaking the law**
- **How to turn being an ex-offender to your advantage**
- **Develop an empowering mindset to become stronger & deal with stress & negativity**
- **Plus more, including Q&A**

Who should attend?
Anyone who has or ever wanted to start a business. Anyone struggling with being in prison. Anyone interested in creating a better life after release and not coming back.

Brief background:
Peter has been a professional speaker & successful entrepreneur for 20+ years. He's spoken on 5 continents, at the United Nations, numerous TED talks and shared the stage with President Clinton, Sir Richard Branson and many others. His sentence finishes next Friday and he wants to give as much value to his fellow prisoners as he can before he leaves.

X-Ray From The Hospital After Two Months of Waiting

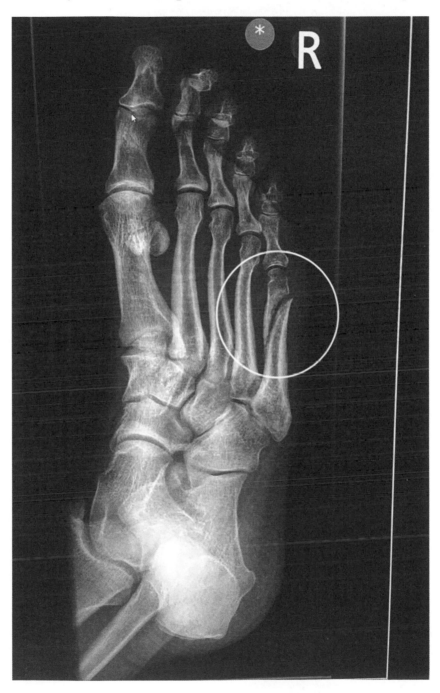

Summary Of the Latest Inspectors Report For Pentonville:
(the first three paragraphs say it all)

Report on an announced inspection of

HMP Pentonville

by HM Chief Inspector of Prisons

9–13 January 2017

Introduction

HMP Pentonville remains a large, overcrowded Victorian local prison serving courts in North London, holding over 1,200 adult and young adult men. The population is complex and demanding. Just over half are sentenced, often to long periods in custody, for serious violent or drug-related offences. Gang behaviour is pervasive and brings significant challenges for stability and good order. Around a quarter of the population are foreign nationals, and at the time of the inspection 40 of these were time-served detainees, held under administrative powers. In our survey, 84% of men said they had arrived at the prison with problems of some kind, and around a quarter said these included feeling depressed or suicidal; 28% said they had mental health problems.

During the inspection, our health inspector discovered that one in five men was taking anti-psychotic drugs, which has significant implications for all staff dealing with their care and management. In addition, in 2016, 111 patients had been transferred or listed for transfer to a secure mental health unit - this is the largest number of psychiatric transfers the inspectorate has ever come across. Half of these men had waited longer than the transfer target of two weeks, and one had waited 169 days, which was totally unacceptable.

At our previous two inspections, we became increasingly concerned about the poor outcomes for prisoners at Pentonville, and when we last visited in February 2015 we gave our bottom score for three out of four healthy prison tests. As a consequence, this inspection was announced, which we hoped would give prison leaders and staff the opportunity to address some of our main concerns before we re-visited.

What we found at this inspection was, in some ways, encouraging, with significant efforts made to address our previous criticisms. However, we continued to have significant concerns about poor outcomes, particularly for the safety of the prison. Levels of violence remained too high and some of it was serious, including a homicide in late 2016. There had been five self-inflicted deaths since our last inspection, and frailties in the case management and care for men vulnerable to suicide and self-harm were evident. Governance, reporting and quality assurance of security, adjudications and use of force needed attention to provide reassurance that poor behaviour was being identified, well managed and dealt with fairly. In contrast, there had been some proactive measures to address levels of disorder, and there were signs that this was having a positive impact. Additional investment, some of which followed two escapes in 2016, was supporting these early signs of improvement Work to limit the supply of drugs, and support for men with substance misuse problems, was well developed. Nevertheless, significant work was still needed to address our concerns about safety.

Given the challenges presented by being an inherently overcrowded, run-down Victorian local prison, Pentonville had made real efforts to improve the cleanliness of the environment and the ability of men to live decent lives. Much still needed to be done, but good progress had been made. It was obvious that there had been serious underinvestment in the infrastructure of the prison - illustrated by the continuing poor state of many cell windows, and the shabbiness and scarcity of cell fixtures and fittings. Staff-prisoner relationships had improved, although management needed to maintain focus on this to ensure staff continued to develop and improve how they dealt with the men in their care. While there was some good work with the large number of foreign nationals, the prison did not fully understand the needs of this group, and what they could do to support them better.

There had been a clear focus on improving the regime. It was now more predictable, and the number of activity places had increased significantly. Prison and learning and skills leaders now needed to work together to capitalise fully on the benefits of these improvements.

Resettlement work had improved and we now rated this as reasonably good overall. It was an achievement that, in a period of significant challenges to the prison, managers had maintained their focus on delivering resettlement support to the prisoners. Work to support the men held at

Pentonville with accommodation problems and in maintaining contact with their children, families and friends was particularly noteworthy.

It is clear that Pentonville remains an immensely challenging prison, and that outcomes for prisoners remain, in many respects, not good enough. However, we were encouraged to see at this inspection a tangible sense of purpose and optimism among the governor and his senior management team, which were having a galvanising effect on the staff group as a whole. Leaders had a plan for where they wanted to take the prison, and had introduced a number of helpful initiatives with more planned. Nevertheless, the complexities of the prison mean that its leadership will continue to need significant external support from HM Prison and Probation Service (HMPPS) if Pentonville is to deliver acceptable and consistent outcomes for prisoners.

Peter Clarke CVO OBE QPM   March 2017
HM Chief Inspector of Prisons

Appendix F:

Glossary

Active Meditation
A process of reaching 'point consciousness' [see passive meditation below] and then using intention to influence the probabilistic nature of reality. *(For further details see Volume 4.)*

Attractor Pattern / Morphic Field
A term used in non-linear dynamics to describe hidden, invisible and organizing fields of influence. It also establishes parameters that limit levels of understanding and awareness.

Civil Prisoner
In English law, a civil prisoner is a person who has been imprisoned for an offence that is not a crime.

Consciousness
The means by which we experience the act of living.

Content
Items, events, statements or facts that are objective and observable.

Context
The circumstances that form the setting and terms by which content can be fully explained and understood. *(For further details see Volume 6.)*

Emotional Maturity
Concept given to evolving past egocentric, selfish or childlike behaviour. Not necessarily correlated to age.

Egregore
A non-physical entity that feeds and grows on the energy of others, often via conflict and negativity. *(For further details see Volume 2.)*

Elite Mentorship Forum (EMF)
A six-month personal coaching programme designed by the author to positively and permanently transform people, raising both their skills and their level of consciousness.

Graduation Event
A term given to a strong challenge in life that is designed to test our ability to cope experientially, not just intellectually, and in doing so demonstrate we can handle a certain level of growth.

HMP Pentonville
A 200-year-old B-Category prison in North London where Peter spent the first four and a half months of his sentence.

HMP Sudbury
An open D-Category prison in Derbyshire where he spent the last six weeks of his six-month sentence.

Indigo Children
Term coined in the 1970's by Nancy Anne Tappe describing children who had the colour indigo as a predominant part of their bio-electrical field. This correlated with marked and inherently different characteristics than other children. *(For further details see Volume 6.)*

IPP
Imprisoned for Public Protection. A grossly flawed and inhumane sentence of indeterminate length introduced by David Blunkett in 2005. It allowed prisoners to be kept for up to ninety-nine years

with a minimum tariff. It was declared unlawful and abolished in 2012 though, at the time of writing, thousands remain trapped by the sentence. Many serving over five-times their tariff. *(For further details see Volume 6.)*

London Real
A popular YouTube and online podcast channel with the tagline 'People Worth Watching'. www.LondonReal.tv

Magic Moments
Events that are often unexpected but create amazing feelings and lasting positive memories.

Masters Circle (MC)
A highly exclusive peer group and coaching programme, designed and led by the author, that includes quarterly trips to spectacular destinations and a focus on high-level personal growth, fun and creating magic moments.

Map Of Consciousness
A scale that maps out and identifies various 'levels' of conscious awareness, together with corresponding characteristics. First developed by Dr. David R. Hawkins Ph.D. and outlined in the worldwide best-selling book Power versus Force. *(For further details see Appendix C.)*

Materialism
See Newtonian Physics.

Mud or Stars?
Inspirational short story created by the author that helps new prisoners better deal with the emotional adjustment to prison. Designed to enrol readers, via third party, to discovering empowering awareness's that can

help them make better decisions on how to think and cope mentally, and to set up a better psychological foundation on which to adapt to prison life.

Newtonian Physics
Branch of physics that govern the rules of the physical world of matter and three-dimensional reality. Largely credited to Sir Isaac Newton.

OMU
Offender Management Unit. The department within the prison responsible for logistically managing offenders and coordinating transfers.

Operation Chrysalis / Chrysalis Programme
'Operation Chrysalis' is the authors self-designed initiative aimed at improving the prison service. (*For further details see Appendix D.*) The 'Chrysalis Programme' is a separate and established initiative set up by David Apparicio, Justice of the Peace (Magistrate), and who's values and ideas overlap with that of the author. A collaboration between the two has now been established. *(For further details see www. chrysalisprogramme.com.)*

Passive Meditation
A state of returning to 'point consciousness' where the information coming through the physical and mental channels is reduced, no longer processed, or transcended. *(For further details see Volume 3.)*

Quantum Physics
Branch of physics that deals with energy and sub atomic particles that fall outside of the paradigm, understanding and explanations of Newtonian Physics.

Sage Business School
A powerful three-day workshop experience created and led by the author and designed for entrepreneurs and those looking to become one.

Spice
Synthetic and dangerous drug widely available in prisons.

Thea
The author's fiancée.

Tony Robbins
Globally recognised leader in the field of personal growth. A highly successful US based author, coach and businessman. Chairman of Robins Research International – the organisation in which the author worked as an Official Trainer for fifteen years.

Torus
Mathematical term often used to describe a powerful and self-sustaining energy field. This is found abundantly in nature, including around the human body.

Transcend
To go beyond, outgrow or supersede a certain range or limitation. Can apply to behaviour and beliefs when used within the context of emotional maturity.

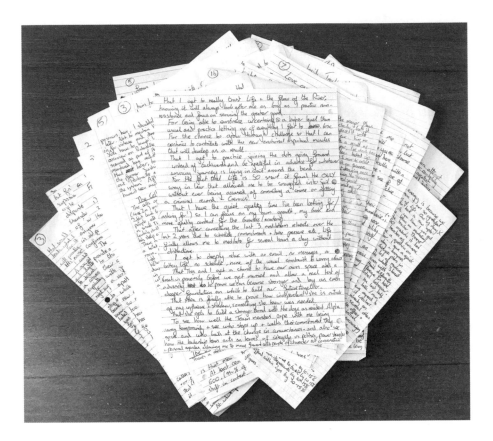

A selection of the Inside Track letters in their original form.

Appendix G

Index

About The Author

Peter Sage is a well-known international serial entrepreneur, best-selling author and expert in human behaviour. He is a highly sought-after speaker and coach and has spoken on five continents, sharing the stage with the likes of Sir Richard Branson and President Bill Clinton.

Due to his depth of experience, teaching style and unique way of looking at life, Peter's seminars and programmes have frequently been ranked amongst the most impactful in the world.

In 2013 he was awarded the distinguished Brand Laureate Award from the Asian Pacific Brands Foundation for extraordinary individuals. Previous winners include; Nelson Mandela, Steve Jobs, Keanu Reeves and Nobel Peace Prize winner Muhammad Yunus. In 2015 he was named one of the greatest leaders and entrepreneurs by Inspiring Leadership Now alongside Sir Richard Branson, Elon Musk and Mark Zuckerberg.

Peter is an accomplished athlete having completed several marathons and the formidable Marathon des Sables - widely recognised as one of the toughest footraces in the world. He also competed at British Championship level indoor rowing, is a qualified open water diver, an experienced skydiver, national champion marksman and a long-standing member of the infamous Dangerous Sports Club. In addition, he has been patron of two registered charities and has personally raised over $1m dollars for good causes all over the world.

He is a global citizen and currently lives in the Canary Islands with his two dogs.

MORE FROM PETER

If you enjoyed the Inside Track, you will love Peter's other programs. See below and choose the one that resonates the most.

Free Master Class For Becoming Limitless
A gift to readers of the Inside Track, this free one-hour training has been called the most impactful of its kind, anywhere. Using the latest discoveries in human behaviour and neuroscience Peter takes you on an empowering and jaw-dropping ride showing you the formula to achieve ultimate self-mastery. Watch now at PeterSage.com/selfmastery

5-Day Upgrade Your Peer Group Challenge
This completely free 5-Day online challenge is packed with incredible insights and knowledge. You will quickly learn why upgrading your peer group is the fastest and smartest way to effect positive change along with the exact formula for how to do it. Start now at TakePetersChallenge.com

Elite Mentorship Forum (EMF)
The EMF has been praised as the single greatest personal transformation program ever created. It was the students of EMF that Peter wrote the private letters to which you now hold in your hand. This definitive 26 week step by step program is designed to destroy limitations, unleash your true potential, eliminate self-sabotage and procrastination whilst raising your consciousness and allowing you to show up unapologetically authentic so you can live your life at a much higher level of fulfilment, passion and purpose. For more details visit PeterSage.com/EMF

More details about the services Peter offers, including hiring him as a speaker or coach can be found on his website at PeterSage.com

Contact Details:
Email: happytohelp@petersage.com